INSIDE RATIONAL–EMOTIVE THERAPY
A Critical Appraisal of the Theory and Therapy of Albert Ellis

This is a volume in
PERSONALITY, PSYCHOPATHOLOGY, AND PSYCHOTHERAPY
A Series of Monographs, Texts, and Treatises

Under the Editorship of David T. Lykken and Philip C. Kendall

INSIDE RATIONAL–EMOTIVE THERAPY

A Critical Appraisal of the Theory and Therapy of Albert Ellis

Edited by

Michael E. Bernard
Department of Education
University of Melbourne
Victoria, Australia

Raymond DiGiuseppe
Department of Psychology
St. John's University
Jamaica, New York
and
Institute for Rational–Emotive Therapy
New York, New York

ACADEMIC PRESS, INC.
Harcourt Brace Jovanovich, Publishers
San Diego   New York   Berkeley   Boston
London   Sydney   Tokyo   Toronto

ACADEMIC PRESS, INC.
San Diego, California 92101

United Kingdom Edition published by
ACADEMIC PRESS LIMITED
24-28 Oval Road, London NW1 7DX

Library of Congress Cataloging-in-Publication Data

Inside rational-emotive therapy : a critical appraisal of the theory
  and therapy of Albert Ellis / edited by Michael Bernard, Raymond
  DiGiuseppe.
       p.   cm. — (Personality, psychopathology, and psychotherapy)
    Includes index.
    ISBN   0-12-092875-2   (alk. paper)
    1. Rational-emotive psychotherapy.   2. Ellis, Albert.   I. Ellis,
  Albert.   II. Bernard, Michael Edwin, Date.   III. DiGiuseppe,
  Raymond.   IV. Series.
    [DNLM: 1. Psychotherapy.   WM 420 I59]
  RC489.R3I57   1989
  616.89′14—dc19
  DNLM/DLC
  for Library of Congress   88-10494
                                                                    CIP

PRINTED IN THE UNITED STATES OF AMERICA
89 90 91 92   9 8 7 6 5 4 3 2 1

Contents

But $5/8/90$ 30.45

8 Assessment in Rational–Emotive Therapy: Empirical Access to the ABCD Model
Timothy W. Smith

9 Outcome Studies of Rational–Emotive Therapy
David A. F. Haaga and Gerald C. Davison

10 Comments on My Critics
Albert Ellis

Contributors

Numbers in parentheses indicate the pages on which the authors' contributions begin.

Darlys J. Alford (69), Department of Psychology, University of California at Santa Barbara, Santa Barbara, California 93106

Michael E. Bernard (1), Faculty of Education, University of Melbourne, Victoria, Australia

Gerald C. Davison (155), Department of Psychology, University of Southern California, Los Angeles, California 90024

Raymond DiGiuseppe (1), Department of Psychology, St. John's University, Jamaica, New York 11439, and Institute for Rational–Emotive Therapy, New York, New York 10021

Albert Ellis (199), Institute for Rational–Emotive Therapy, New York, New York 10021

Sol L. Garfield (113), Department of Psychology, Washington University, St. Louis, Missouri 63130

David A. F. Haaga (155), Department of Psychology, University of Southern California, Los Angeles, California 90089

Arnold A. Lazarus (95), Graduate School of Applied and Professional Psychology, Rutgers the State University of New Jersey, Piscataway, New Jersey 08855

Richard S. Lazarus (47), Department of Psychology, University of California at Berkeley, Berkeley, California 94720

William J. Lyddon (69), Department of Education, University of California at Santa Barbara, Santa Barbara, California 93106

Michael J. Mahoney (69), Department of Education, University of California at Santa Barbara, Santa Barbara, California 93106

Louis A. Sass (9), Graduate School of Applied and Professional Psychology, Rutgers, the State University of New Jersey, Piscataway, New Jersey 08854

Timothy W. Smith (135), Department of Psychology, University of Utah, Salt Lake City, Utah 84112

Robert L. Woolfolk (9), Graduate School of Applied and Professional Psychology, Rutgers, the State University of New Jersey, Piscataway, New Jersey 08855

Daniel J. Ziegler (27), Department of Psychology, Villanova University, Villanova, Pennsylvania 19085

Preface

While rational–emotive therapy (RET) has grown enormously over the past 25 years, there is still room for improvement. An attempt to refine or expand rational–emotive theory will first require a critical analysis of the theory's heuristic value, logical consistency, comprehensibility, and empirical support. It was our belief that such criticism of RET would best come from those less committed to it. Therefore, we have chosen contributors who are not devotees of RET but who are well respected in their area of psychology to critically analyze the portion of rational–emotive theory or therapy that is in their respective area of expertise. In the final chapter, Dr. Ellis comments on the criticism. We believe the resulting dialogue has clarified many elements of Ellis's thinking, uncovered areas of RET theory that require further development, and suggested areas for empirical investigation. It is our hope that this book will result in the reader's rethinking of rational–emotive theory and therapy and that such rethinking will result in a more refined, precise, and empirically testable theory and in a more effective therapy. All of the proceeds of this book will be donated to the Institute for Rational–Emotive Therapy to help attain this goal.

Michael E. Bernard
Raymond DiGiuseppe

Rational–Emotive Therapy Today

Michael E. Bernard
Raymond DiGiuseppe

INTRODUCTION

Rational–emotive therapy (RET) has evolved since the mid-1950s largely through the effort of Albert Ellis (1957a, 1957b, 1957c, 1958a, 1962, 1973, 1985a, 1985b, 1985c, 1985d) and his collaborators (Ellis & Abrahms, 1978; Ellis & Becker, 1982; Ellis & Bernard, 1983a, 1985a; Ellis & Grieger, 1977; Ellis & Harper, 1961, 1975; Ellis & Whiteley, 1979). The early 1980s saw the publication of a number of important texts on RET by scholars who have had extensive training by and exposure to the work of Ellis at the Institute for Rational-Emotive Therapy in New York (Bernard & Joyce, 1984; Grieger & Boyd, 1980; Hauck, 1980; Walen, DiGiuseppe, & Wessler, 1980; R. A. Wessler & Wessler, 1980).

As any good psychological theory of maladjustment and psychotherapy, RET has been reformulated over the years, taking into account new insights and discoveries of Ellis and his associates into emotional disturbance, methods for facilitating cognitive, emotional, and behavioral change, and research studies. Indeed, ever since Ellis rejected psychoanalysis in the early 1950s as being unscientific and inefficient, he has striven to make RET as effective and economic as possible.

I experimented with other techniques which were non-Freudian and
kept the ones that seemed to work best and which happened to be
more philosophic than psychodynamic. They seemed to work. Had
they not worked then even though I might have liked them, I wouldn't
have kept them. You could say I have a gene for efficiency. You only
have one life and it has a limited time. Time is of the essence; therefore
I try not to do inefficient things. . . . But my belief is that the goal of
psychotherapy is not only to help people but to help them as quickly,
effectively, intelligently and adequately as possible. (Ellis, quoted in
Bernard, 1986, p. 15)

Our purpose in writing this chapter is to briefly bring the reader up
to date on the current status of RET theory and practice. We do this for
two reasons. Many of the readers of the book may have been exposed
to RET years ago and may desire a contemporary and general statement
of how RET has developed to over the years in order to fully appreciate
the specialized arguments contained in the chapters which follow. In addition, current students of counseling and psychotherapy as well as neophyte
RET practitioners can also use our overview of RET in this chapter as an
advance organizer for the material which follows.

HISTORY OF RET

The beginning of RET can be traced to Ellis's personal life in the 1920s
and 1930s when he began to cope with his own problems, including
shyness about meeting females and public-speaking anxiety. Over these
and subsequent years Ellis spent a great deal of time reading books and
articles by leading philosophers (Epictetus, Marcus Aurelius, Baruch
Spinoza, John Dewey, Bertrand Russell, A. J. Ayer, Hans Reichenbach,
Karl Popper) and psychologists (Alfred Adler, E. Coué, A. Herzberg,
W. Johnson, Karen Horney) as he became increasingly interested in the
philosophy of happiness.

Ellis's first university degree was a Bachelor in Business Administra-
tion from the City University of New York. He went on to earn a master's
degree in clinical psychology from Columbia University in 1943 and a doc-
torate of philosophy from the same university in 1947. During the 1940s,
Ellis was trained in classical psychoanalysis and psychoanalytically
oriented psychotherapy by a training analyst of the Karen Horney Institute
and commenced work in sex, love, and marriage and family problems.

In the early 1950s Ellis became increasingly disenchanted with
psychoanalysis. From his own practices, he began to see that he could

help people get better sooner by being more active and direct in his methods and by offering interpretations of people's problems in terms of the way they conceptualized and evaluated their world rather than in terms of intrapsychic conflicts, unconscious motives, and other early childhood influences characteristic of the psychoanalytic theory of maladjustment. It was at this time that Ellis vainly tried to reformulate psychoanalysis in scientific terms but gradually abandoned his attempts (Ellis, 1950). Ellis formally introduced his "radical" ideas to professional psychology in 1956 when he presented 12 basic irrational beliefs underlying psychological problems and emotional disturbance.

Today, Ellis rejects Freud's theory concerning the role of early childhood experience in later adjustment and is equally rejecting of the need to spend a substantial amount of time in therapy analyzing these experiences. According to Ellis (1962), people act for better or worse because of their current conscious and preconscious thinking and attitudes about themselves, others, and the world and not because of feelings concerning their parents. Ellis (Ellis & Harper, 1975) actively disputes the belief promulgated by psychoanalytic theorists that "it is the past and all its bad experiences which continually ruin the present and which can never really be overcome." Instead, he continues to forcefully argue that "people can overcome the effects of past experience by reassessing their perceptions of the past and re-evaluating their interpretations of its influence."

RET was called rational therapy (e.g., Ellis, 1957c) until the early 1960s because Ellis wanted to emphasize its philosophic and cognitive aspects. At first, it profoundly shook the therapeutic community. Not only did Ellis reject notions of the unconscious and the importance of analyzing early childhood experiences, but RET was also, unlike classical psychoanalysis and Rogerian client-centered therapy, highly confronting. Rather than relying only on genuineness, unconditional positive regard, empathy, and indirect and inactive methods of change, RET practitioners were ready to point out and help correct the unscientific and irrational assumptions, ideas, and beliefs which were seen to be at the core of the problem.

Ellis was practically alone in practicing and promulgating rational–emotive therapy from 1955 to 1963. But thereafter, largely as a result of his strong advocacy of cognitive–behavior therapy and because of the work of therapists whom he had trained in RET, his form of therapy began to take hold among professionals and to be adopted or modified by a number of outstanding practitioners and researchers. While many leading cognitive–behavior therapists have directly followed in the pioneering pathways marked by Ellis, a few, such as Aaron T. Beck (1967, 1976a, 1976b) and Albert Bandura (1977b), have independently arrived at principles and practices that significantly overlap with RET.

Today, RET has become one of the world's most popular forms of counseling and psychotherapy (Heesacker, Heppner, & Rogers, 1982; D. Smith, 1982) as well as marriage and family therapy (Sprenkle, Keeney, & Sulton, 1982). The popularity of RET with the general public is in part due to Ellis's literary accomplishments. He has written or edited 50 books and monographs that have sold over 6,000,000 copies. Ellis's well-known self-help book, *A New Guide to Rational Living*, first published in 1961 with Robert Harper and rewritten in 1975, has sold well over 1,000,000 copies. Indeed, stemming from Ellis's works, a variety of current general self-help books, including *Your Erroneous Zones* (Dyer, 1977) and *Feeling Good* (Burns, 1980), show how rational–emotive principles can help solve emotional problems.

Ellis's significant professional reputation stems from his professional and scientific achievements in the field of psychology. In 1985, Ellis was honored by the American Psychological Association with its major award for Distinguished Professional Contributions to Knowledge. Over the years he has received numerous special awards including the American Humanist of the Year Award (1971), the Award for Distinguished Contributions to Research in Sex by the Society for the Scientific Study of Sex (1971), the Distinguished Practitioners Award of the American Psychological Association's division of psychotherapy (1973), and the Distinguished Award of the American Association of Sex Educators, Counsellors, and Therapists (1975). Ellis's scientific standing can be seen in the more than 500 articles he has published in psychological, psychiatric, and sociological journals.

Perhaps more important than all these accomplishments has been the flexibility of RET theory and practice to take into account the newest insights about the relationship of cognition, emotion, and behavior in human disturbance and how to best go about bringing about change.

BRIEF OUTLINE OF RET THEORY

RET has as one of its basic propositions that people have basic goals, desires, and purposes in life which at a general level can be described as happiness, long life, and self-actualization, and can be seen more specifically in people's desires for success, approval, and comfort. Once these goals are chosen, and RET sees them as matters of choice rather than absolute givens, then RET hypothesizes that the "best" way to help people to achieve these goals is to help them think rationally (scientifically, clearly, flexibly), to feel appropriately, and to act more functionally (efficiently, undefeatingly).

According to RET, when people get blocked from achieving their goals, by some activating event A, they have a choice as to how they will feel and act at point C, emotional and behavioral consequences. If they strongly prefer to achieve their goals and are thwarted by themselves, other people, or outside events, they often feel the appropriately negative feelings of extreme sorrow, regret, frustration, and annoyance. RET sees these feelings as appropriate because, rather than causing people to feel totally relaxed and do nothing or to be so upset that they act in a self-defeating manner, these feelings help motivate people to work determinately to bring about a change in the practical problem represented by the activating event which is blocking their goals.

The core of neurotic behavior can be found in people's irrational tendencies to take their strong preferences for success, approval, and comfort and convert them into absolute necessities: shoulds, oughts, demands, or musts. For example, when the goal of success at work is blocked by a failure to achieve a certain standard, people initially think at B, their belief, "I strongly wish to achieve my goals, how very disappointing that I didn't. Now what can I do next time to do better?" However, people who experience extreme upset (depression, self-pity, despair, low self-esteem) at C because of failure at A will at B take their rational preference for success and make it into an irrational and absolute demand, "Because I very much want to succeed, I must succeed." According to Ellis the "tyranny of the shoulds" is at the core of most emotional misery and ensuing goal-defeating behavior.

Ellis (Ellis & Bernard, 1985b) has concluded that the irrational beliefs people tend to hold can be categorized under three major ones, each with many derivatives: (1) "I must do well and win approval, or else I rate as a rotten person." (2) "Others must treat me considerately and kindly in precisely the way I want them to treat me; if they don't, society and the universe should severely blame, damn, and punish them for their inconsiderateness." (3) "Conditions under which I live must be arranged so that I get practically all that I want comfortably, quickly, and easily, and get virtually nothing that I don't want."

While absolutistic thinking is central to emotional disturbance, RET postulates four other common forms of irrational thinking which derive from these irrational beliefs and which also contribute to psychological disturbance: (1) *awfulizing* ("It is awful, terrible, and horrible that I am not doing as I must"); (2) *I-can't-stand-it-itis* ("I can't stand, can't bear, the things which are happening to me that must not happen"); (3) *worthlessness* ("I am a worthless person if I don't do as well and win as much approval as I must"); (4) *allness* or unrealistic overgeneralization ("Because I failed at this important task, I'll always fail and never succeed").

While Ellis acknowledges the role of environment in frequently encouraging the acquistion of irrational beliefs, he strongly maintains that all human beings have a biological tendency toward irrational thinking and, in particular, for taking their preferences for values, goals, and desires and making them into absolute shoulds, needs, commands, and demands. Not been emphasized in some of his contemporary writings but an important assumption underlying personality development, motivation, and change is that people have innate tendencies toward *self-actualization*. This natural self-development tendency which brings with it satisfaction and happiness for the individual is often thwarted or inhibited by opposing irrational tendencies. Self-actualization and irrationality are seen as opposing biological tendencies which operate together throughout the life-span.

RET helps people to overcome their own emotional upsets by employing a variety of disputational methods for changing their thinking, feeling, and actions. Disputational methods involve helping people to discover the unrealistic, antiempirical, and irrational aspects of their thinking and to change their irrational beliefs to more rational ones. Teaching *emotional responsibility* and the *scientific method* for disputing demandingness, awfulizing, I-can't-stand-it-itis, worthlessness, and all-or-none thinking is essential to helping people bring about change.

In tackling the main emotional problems such as anger, anxiety, and depression which people create because of their disposition to disturb themselves over some failure, rejection, unfairness, or frustration, RET pays special attention to people's dispositions to secondarily disturb themselves about their disturbances. RET assumes people often get depressed about their depression, angry about their anger, and anxious about their anxiety and will work at changing these secondary symptoms before dealing with the primary disturbances.

The main cognitive disputational technique in RET is philosophical disputation and involves detecting illogical, unrealistic, and irrational beliefs, debating irrational beliefs, showing why they are irrational, and reformulating irrational beliefs into rational ones.

Cognitive disputation of irrational beliefs may also be effected in a number of other ways. They can be replaced by rational beliefs or rational self-statements; they can be influenced by semantic methods which seek to clarify the objective meaning of events (Korzybski, 1933); they can be combated by using referenting methods which have people focus on the advantages of giving up self-defeating habits and the disadvantages which these habits create; they can be put out of mind through cognitive distraction and by thought-stopping methods.

RET recognizes that antiempirical assumptions and inferences (conclusions, predictions), e.g., ''no one likes me,'' which people make about reality contribute to emotional disturbance and as such are targeted for change using empirical disputational and other scientific methods. However, RET considers irrational evaluations of these assumptions, e.g., ''I need people's approval,'' as the primary cause of disturbance and are the primary focus of RET intervention. Methods which bring about generalized changes in people's belief systems are referred to as *general* or *elegant* RET methods; the generalized changes themselves which are maintained over time are referred to in RET as *elegant* or *general solutions* (Ellis, 1980d). Methods which bring about changes in assumptions and interferences are referred to in RET as *inelegant* because they bring about more limited and situationally specific changes.

RET practice also involves the use of emotive and behavioral methods to help people dispute their irrational beliefs. Main emotive methods include rational–emotive imagery (Maultsby & Ellis, 1974), shame-attacking exercises (Ellis, 1969b), role playing (Ellis & Abrahms, 1978), unconditional acceptance of people (Ellis, 1973), and other use of forceful self-statements and self-dialogues (Ellis, 1979c). Behaviorally, RET uses a variety of methods including reinforcement, penalizing, assertiveness, activity homework assignments, implosive assignments, and skill training (Ellis & Bernard, 1985b).

While on a superficial level, RET appears easy to understand and apply, such appearances are deceptive. The theory of RET as applied to understanding specific disorders and, in particular, the relationship of irrationality to specific emotional and personality disorders continues to offer insights and new challenges. One of the main challenges is in mapping out the complex interrelatedness among different irrationalities in order to explain the unique qualities of specific disorders. RET scholars have been endeavoring recently to advance RET from being an effective form of therapy based on clinical intuition toward becoming more scientific and accountable. RET scientists are engaged in the process of making RET assessment methods more formal, standardized, and objective. Those aspects of the therapeutic relationship and active aspects of treatment responsible for bringing about increased rationality and improved mental health are being operationalized and empirically examined. This move towards science and accountability is seen most clearly in the dramatic increase in RET outcome studies. The chapters that follow demonstrate the dynamic and heuristic value of RET in generating new insights into understanding, assessing, and treating human problems. The chapters also reveal that RET as a philosophy, theory, and therapy is an open system allowing both for self-modification from within as well as accepting new insights from without.

Philosophical Foundations of Rational–Emotive Therapy

Robert L. Woolfolk
Louis A. Sass

INTRODUCTION

A chapter on the philosophical foundations of Albert Ellis's rational–emotive therapy is, in some sense, a more straightforward task than would be a similar undertaking addressing other forms of psychotherapy. There are several reasons for this. Ellis has always taken great pains to be explicit about his fundamental assumptions. Therefore, much that is tacit in other therapeutic approaches is duly acknowledged in Ellis's work and consequently requires little unearthing. Unlike most psychotherapy innovators, whose scientific or cryptomedical pretensions prevented them from recognizing the affinities between theories of psychotherapy and other methods for the regulation of *Weltanschauungen*, Ellis has always recognized that psychotherapy is, at its most fundamental level, intertwined with questions of ethics and epistemology. And, of course, Ellis's intellectual activities are hardly limited to communication with mental health professionals. In his championing of atheism, his debates with the Objectivists, and his advocacy of the sexual revolution, he has performed on a larger stage. Social critic and practical philosopher, Ellis has followed in the footsteps of his most important teacher, Epictetus, seeking to delineate a conception of life that is both true and pragmatic. In this undertaking he has exhibited greater ambition and vision than virtually all of his contemporaries. But projects of great intellectual scope invariably have their shortcomings, and the following analysis of the writings of Albert Ellis reveals some problems and potential limitations. The dissection of Ellis's intellectual corpus, however, is done with an appreciation for the difficulty of his undertaking and the clarity with which he has understood the philosophical issues that underlie the practice of psychotherapy.

First we examine the tenets and philosophical underpinnings of RET. Ellis's philosophy is characterized by epistemological positivism and moral situationism and by relativism, humanism, and atheism. It is a quintessentially contemporary view, one that fully grasps, articulates, and embodies the cultural and ideological changes wrought by the modern scientific transformation of social forms and intellectual practices.

POSITIVISM

The underlying philosophy of RET is a version of positivism which, broadly defined, refers to that philosophical tradition that views science as exemplary for all forms of intellectual activity. Positivism and a related perspective, scientism, tend to exhalt science and mathematics and their methods, while devaluing and raising epistemological doubts about less-exact approaches and belief systems whose practices are at variance with those of the sciences. One of the earliest exponents of positivism was David Hume, who suggested that only abstract reasoning (logic and mathematics) or direct observation yielded valid knowledge. The philosophers known as the "logical positivists" took the Humean categories and made them criterial and normative. The predicate "true" could only be applied to tautologies such as "All bachelors are unmarried males," or "2 + 2 = 4," or to statements that could be verified by observation, e.g., "There are two hundred words on this page." All other statements were thought to be meaningless, i.e., not expressive of propositions that could be assigned a truth value. Emotivist theories of ethics and aesthetics (Ayer, 1936; Stevenson, 1944) derived from this position. Emotivist theories hold that the statement "John is good," is equivalent to "I like John," or "I approve of John." On this view, to link such predicates as *good, bad, right,* or *wrong,* with a subject, simply indicates the speaker's feelings about or attitude toward the subject. Logical positivists thought that statements about right and wrong, good and evil could not be supported or defended. Ethical judgments were placed in the class of metaphysics, wherein reside all nonscientific expressions. Under this formulation, an individual's belief that an act is wrong can admit of no justification beyond one's personal preference or that of his or her social group. Positivistic philosophies tend to result in moral relativism. One's view of what is good is just that: one's view. Everybody has an opinion, and these may conflict with each other without there being any global issue that requires resolution. Ethics becomes an axiological horserace.

Ellis's adherence to positivism is manifest throughout his writings. He states that RET

> is closely tied to scientific empiricism, objectivity, and controlled experimentation. . . . [RET] relies on induction from empirical evidence and on logical deduction from fact-based hypotheses (as every rational method of discourse essentially does), it ties its man-centered, hedonistic goals to the best available logico-empirical methods of achieving those goals. (1973, p. 12)

It should be emphasized that although Ellis's position belongs to the generic category of positivism, his philosophy of science is more akin to the hypotheticodeductive model found in Hempel (1966) and elaborated by Kuhn (1970) and Lakatos (1970) than it is to a Baconian atheoretical inductivism. A greater emphasis on overarching theory has always distinguished Ellis's work from that of the behavior therapists, even those who are cognitively inclined. DiGiuseppe (1986), revealing the tendency of RET to model its methods on those of the "successful sciences," has described the analogy between RET's underlying hypotheticodeductive philosophy of science and its conceptualization of clinical problems and their treatment:

> The philosophers and historians of science offer cognitive psycho-therapists a theoretical framework upon which to base their own understanding and shaping of their client's thought processes. In their endeavor to explain the origins and evolution of scientific thought, they have construed a model of hypothesis generation, data collection, confirmation or disconfirmation—the generation that lends itself to generalization of all human thought. If we accept that humans proceed to explain the universe by generating theories about life's events as they occur, we will be helped to understand and change the dysfunctional ideas which cause emotional disturbance. (DiGiuseppe, 1986, p. 638)

The underlying assumptions of early RET seemed to overlap greatly with logical positivism (see Ayer, 1936) and its emphasis on empirical content of propositions leading to their ultimate verifiability through objective observation. As recently as 1973, Ellis wrote that demonstrating that irrational beliefs are 'unverifiable'' and ''unempirically based'' was the cornerstone of effective therapeutic disputation. DiGiuseppe (1986), however, has suggested a broadening of the criteria used to challenge the irrational beliefs of the client, and, a fortiori, a broadening of the implicit concept of rationality itself: ''Disputing, then, is not just empirical verification or logical challenging, but a complicated process whereby the logical consistency, heuristic value, and empirical evidence is used to evaluate the theory and the alternatives'' (p. 638).

In any case, it is clear that Ellis's ethics is situational and relative, with morals unquestionably subordinate to science: ''A moral code would better be constructed on the basis of as much empirical evidence about human beings and their functioning as it is possible for the morals-makers to obtain'' (Ellis, 1969a, p. 3).

Ellis here is advocating a kind of *naturalism*. Naturalism is that view in ethics which states that moral and empirical views should be linked, such that ethical principles will be in harmony with the needs, desires, and capacities of the human being, as determined by the investigations of the empirical sciences. Ethical naturalism tends to be a pragmatic position that seeks to align human morality so that it is accord with ''human nature'' and to limit what is expected of human beings to what they are likely to be able to achieve without fighting against their proclivities. The satisfaction of natural needs is often the equivalent of drive reduction or pleasure, so naturalistic ethics often tends to endorse hedonistic outcomes and to espouse human comfort. Ellis, however, does not commit the ''naturalistic fallacy'' (Moore, 1948) of believing that ethics is totally derivable from empirical science. He correctly recognizes the differences between empirical propositions and value judgments and understands that ''morality still has to be related to some underlying value system that is not completely determined by empirical findings'' (Ellis, 1969a, p. 7).

For Ellis, moral codes are human creations that vary across cultures and historical periods and hence cannot be substantiated or validated beyond their situational utility: ''There probably cannot ever be any absolutely correct or proper rules of morality since people and conditions change over the years and what is ''right'' today may be ''wrong'' tomorrow. Sane ethics are relativistic and situational'' (1969a, p. 3).

The rational–emotive therapist seeks not only to embody the ideals of science but also to train clients to utilize scientific method in their daily lives. According to Walen, *et al.* (1980),

> RET advocates a scientific thinking in arriving at conclusions. For every belief expressed by a client, the appropriate RET question is, ''What is

the evidence that what you believe is true?" In RET, we seek to make good scientists of our clients so that they can acquire correct information, use evidence logically, and construct sound self-helping beliefs. . . . We want our clients to know that a thing is true. . . because they know how to obtain accurate evidence and think with logic. From such evidence, we hope that they will construct a more realistic picture (or theory) of themselves and of the world in which they live. (p. 6)

HUMANISM

Ellis consistently has claimed that RET is based on a humanistic life philosophy. Sometimes this point is misunderstood by psychologists who identify humanism with the work of psychologists like Maslow, Perls, and Rogers. Humanistic psychology, or the "third force," was proposed as an alternative to both behaviorism and psychoanalysis, the dominant psychological schools of the 1940s and 1950s. As such it opposed the scientific determinism of both behaviorism and psychoanalysis. Behaviorism self-consciously sought to emulate its vision of the methods of the natural sciences with its rigorous advocacy of operationalism and empirical testing of claims. Similarly, psychoanalysis, since Freud's first writings, has always aspired to scientific status, despite the fact that controlled experimentation did not become part of psychoanalytic culture. Humanistic psychology, on the other hand, attempted to provide an alternative to psychology as science. It engaged in an extensive critique of both the methodologies and the scientific pretensions of other systems. Humanistic psychologists also opposed what they believed to be the excessive rationality and intellectualization promoted by both behavioral and psychoanalytic psychotherapy. Given the affinity between RET and cognitive–behavior therapy and the opposition of behavior therapy and the humanistic psychotherapies, can Ellis justifiably claim that RET is a humanistic approach? He can, indeed, for RET is clearly founded on principles of humanism, though of a different kind from that of the third force.

The confusion here results from the fact that there are two forms of humanism that serve as foundations for contemporary systems of psychotherapy. One of these, which we term *romantic humanism*, underlies the work of Maslow, Rogers, and Perls and derives from the romantic movement of the nineteenth century which arose in opposition to the Enlightenment's glorification of reason and science. Romantic humanism attempts to promote aesthetic and emotional sensitivity and the active cultivation of the passions. Romantic humanism is Dionysian. It values extremism, intensity of experience, spontaneity, creativity, emotionality, and passion. In contrast, the form of humanism to which RET subscribes is what we refer to as *classical humanism*. Classical humanism predates romantic humanism, having been in existence since the time of Erasmus. Rather than being opposed to the values of the Enlightenment, classical humanism is a distillation of those values. This version of humanism accepts the superiority of science to all other systems of thought and views *scientific objectivity* as desirable in most other human activities. Classical humanism commits itself to the primacy of reason as a guide to conduct and opposes all arbitrary and irrational authority. Classical humanism is Apollonian. It emphasizes reason, balance, restraint, and order. Despite the obvious differences, the two forms of humanism have in common an active dedication to the enhancement of human freedom and happiness. Both also view man as "the measure of all things" and tend to be antagonistic to religion or secular creeds that subordinate human needs to principles that putatively transcend them.

Ellis refers to one of his philosophical underpinnings as *ethical humanism*. It is clear from his writings that he is, under this rubric, advocating a form of classical humanism in which scientific thinking is put forth as a model for human evaluation and in which skepticism is considered superior to credulity.

> Ethical humanism, however, goes hand in hand with the scientific method. For its fundamental postulates are that, until someone definitely proves otherwise, there is nothing beyond human existence; and that for a human being to substantiate, or scientifically validate, any hypothesis, this hypothesis must be backed by some form of data which are, in some final analysis, observable and reproducible. Any hypothesis which cannot be backed by evidence which ordinary humans can observe and replicate is deemed to be a theological, supernatural, or magical hypothesis, and is not considered in the field of general or psychological science. (Ellis, 1973, pp. 2–3)

For Ellis, humanism entails abandoning a belief in the supernatural:

> Man is man; he will (in all likelihood) never be more than man. When and if he fully accepts that reality, together with the reality that there is no supernatural "force" in the universe that gives a damn about him or ever will, he will then be truly humanistic. (Ellis, 1973, p. 16)

Woolfolk and Richardson (1984) argue that behavior therapy also embodies the classical form of humanism espoused by RET. The affinities between RET and behavior therapy seem to have much to do with this overlap in classical humanistic sensibility. Both endorse rationality, advocate scientific method as a guideline in human conduct, and endorse empirical self-scrutiny and the objective evaluation of procedures.

GOD AND RELIGION

Psychotherapy, being the secular entity that it is, has been relatively antagonistic to religion. Even Jung, who could have been correctly described as possessing religious impulses and a genuine religious sensibility, did much to undermine traditional religion by subjectivizing it (Rieff, 1966). Jung took what was external and objective and in some sense preserved it by rendering it subjective or reducing it to psychological states. In Ellis, we see his typical forthright and perspicacious intellect grasping an inescapable fact. If one accepts his view that the ultimate aim of life is psychological well-being, then it follows that if individuals possess some allegiance to putative powers outside themselves and if those powers dictate conduct that is inimical to psychological well-being, then those powers or the belief in them must be opposed. He has beheld with clarity what other theorists have glimpsed only dimly and has been willing to bite the intellectual bullet: If religion stands in the way of happiness, then religion must go. Of course, a number of systems of therapy are tacitly antagonistic to any absolute and inflexible ethics that produces tyrannical "shoulds." But Ellis has raised the issue to a level of explicitness that clarifies whatever nebulousness had obscured the relation between traditional belief systems and the contemporary secular therapeutic ethos. And Ellis also has demonstrated the intellectual courage to act upon these insights by opposing many aspects of religious systems in his writings.

Ellis is an atheist. There seem to be two bases for his atheism. One is his scientific–materialistic epistemology, discussed earlier. If we identify the real and true with only that which can be observed empirically, then any belief system that requires faith in the incorporeal is placed on very flimsy underpinnings. The other is his humanist ideology in which human happiness and well-being serve as the ultimate justification for any normative system. According to Ellis, it is on this criterion that religion, especially that which breeds fanatical and dogmatic religiosity, typically falls short:

> Religiosity is, on almost every conceivable count, opposed to the normal goals of mental health. Instead, it encourages masochism, other-directedness, social withdrawal, intolerance, refusal to accept ambiguity and uncertainty, unscientific thinking, needless inhibition, lack of self-acceptance, and reluctance to acknowledge and deal adequately with reality. (Ellis, 1983, p. 8)

Ellis does not criticize all religious belief and all individual believers indiscriminately. He recognizes that, in some instances, religion may foster activity consistent with the secular humanism esposed by RET:

For some people some of the time religious notions, even when they are devoutly and rigidly held, have some benefits. Of course they do. Devout adherence to a theistic òr secular form of religion can at times motivate people to help others who are needy, to give up unhealthy addictions (e.g., to cigarettes or to alcohol), to follow valuable disciplines (e.g., dieting or exercising), to go for psychotherapy, to strive for world peace, to follow longrange instead of shortrange hedonism, and to work for many other kinds of valuable goals. (Ellis, 1983, p. 8)

For the most part, however, Ellis contends that human beings would be better off without religion and as believers in the secular creed of RET. His argument against religion turns on this point:

If religiosity is so inimical to mental health and happiness, what are the chances of unbelief, skepticism, and thoroughgoing atheism helping humans in this important aspect of their lives? I would say excellent. My own view—based on more than forty years of research and clinical work in the field of psychology and psychotherapy but still admittedly prejudiced by my personal predilections and feelings—is that if people were thoroughly unbelieving of any dogmas, if they were highly skeptical of all hypotheses and theories that they formulated, if they believed in no kinds of gods, devils, or other supernatural beings, and if they subscribed to no forms of absolutistic thinking, they would be minimally emotionally disturbed and maximally healthy. Stated a little differently: if you, I, and everyone else in the world were thoroughly scientific, and if we consistently used the scientific method in our own lives and our relationships with others, we would rarely upset ourselves about anything—and I mean *anything*! (Ellis, 1983, p. 9)

For Ellis, as for most modern thinkers, the belief in God or in any transcendental entity cannot be established on the basis of pure reason alone. Nor can it be established on scientific empirical grounds. Of course, Ellis takes this position one step farther and suggests that religion is usually a pathogenic influence, although (as indicated above) he is not doctrinaire on this issue. Perhaps of all contributors to the theory of psychotherapy, he has been most willing to formulate a clear position on the compatibility of religious belief and psychological well-being.

FREEDOM AND DETERMINISM

Perhaps no problem in the history of philosophy has proved more intractable than that of freedom and determinism. The question, stated succinctly, is "Is there a distinction between actions and events?" Much of the progress of modern science can be seen as a move away from animistic, magical, mythological thinking in which inanimate objects are viewed as agents with powers of choice. Science alternatively explains events as a function of causal regularities that are describable in terms of the invariant actions of physical and biological mechanisms. Few thinkers dispute the utility of determinism as a metatheory in the natural sciences. (The indeterminism of the subatomic world is a noteworthy exception to this.) The real difficulty arises when the attempt is made to subsume human conduct within a deterministic perspective. To use Sartre's famous example, let us say that a man is in the throes of a moral dilemma whose horns are "Do I join the Resistance?" or "Do I remain at home to care for my aged mother?" If determinism be true then is there a dilemma at all? Does the man really have a choice in the matter, or is his deliberation simply part of some invariant causal sequence that precludes the influence of an autonomous will? If his actions are determined in the same way as the motions of the earth and sun, then does it make any sense for him to take credit for his activities or to be held accountable for them? Why should he feel pride or shame in what he does? Many ingenious answers have been proposed to the various questions that arise around this topic. Ellis's own answer has been to adopt a kind of compromise between a position that advocates total freedom and one that sees all human actions as totally determined by past events:

> RET holds that man's behavior, although to some degree determined and limited by his biological nature and his history, is considerably less determined than the orthodox Freudians or behaviorists seem to think that it is. It shows people how they can extend their choices of action and significantly change their personalities by (1) understanding precisely how they needlessly constrict themselves; (2) uprooting and modifying their rigidicizing philosophies of life; and (3) actively working against their self-defeating habituations until they break through their gratuitously restricting shell. (Ellis, 1973, p. 10)

In so doing, Ellis allows a considerable role for client responsibility in his system:

> Rational–emotive therapy places man squarely in the center of the universe and of his own emotional fate and gives him almost full responsibility for choosing to make or not make himself seriously disturbed. Although it weights biological and early environmental factors quite importantly in the chain of events that lead to human disorganization and disorder, it insists that nonetheless the individual himself can, and usually does, significantly intervene between his environmental input and his emotionalized output, and therefore he has an enormous

amount of potential control over what he feels and what he does. Moreover, when he unwittingly and foolishly *makes himself* disturbed by devoutly believing in irrational and unvalidatable assumptions about himself and others, he can almost always *make himself* undisturbed again, and can often do so—if he utilizes rational–emotive procedures—within a few minutes. (Ellis, 1973, p.3)

Philosophically, Ellis is placing himself among those who believe that neither freedom nor determinism can give a complete account of human behavior, and that it is necessary to recognize the restrictions on human choice imposed by both biology and history as well as to emphasize human possibilities for choice and self-determination. Within experimental clinical psychology, perhaps the most commonly encountered statement of this position is Bandura's reciprocal determinism thesis which has come to be widely accepted as part of cognitive–behavior therapy's metatheory:

Because people's conceptions, their behavior, and their environments are reciprocal determinants of each other, individuals are neither powerless objects controlled by environmental forces nor entirely free agents who can do whatever they choose. (Bandura, 1978, p. 357)

It may be of interest to note that the substance of Ellis's position on this question was worked out years before discussions of freedom had become fashionable in behavior therapy circles. He thus, in some sense, anticipated such doctrines as reciprocal determinism and the concern on the part of empirically grounded clinicians to offer some account of human capacities for autonomy in their theories.

EVALUATION OF RET's PHILOSOPHICAL UNDERPINNINGS

RET as an Aspect of Modernity

In order to frame a critique and evaluation of RET, we must provide some context for our discussion of terms pivotal to that critique: *modernity* and *modern consciousness*. *Modernity* denotes the totality of social and physical transformations that occur during the course of industrialization and urbanization. The shift from traditional society to modern social forms is characterized by a shift in world view as well. *Modern consciousness* refers to the world view or the common elements in a family of world views held by the populations of modern scientific–technological societies.

Premoderns believed themselves to be members of a meaningful social order that was integral to a larger cosmological scheme. Codes of conduct, notions of beauty, as well as science were thought to be part of some external objective reality. Much of life concerned itself with the discharge of social responsibility and the performance of acts that maintained social solidarity. These were worlds in which one's personal existential security was given, and to some degree fixed. The individual as a modern psychological entity, an ego capable of isolation and alienation from the social whole, was not a prevalent type. Much of life was immutable. Options were rare and rarely significant. But people were at home within the family, the society, and the cosmos.

Modern consciousness is characterized by secularism, technicism, scientific rationality, amorality, and individuation. One of the basic features of modernity is the shrinking role of the sacred in the practical affairs of individuals. Virtually all other people existing at all other times in history seem to have believed themselves to stand in some meaningful relation to some divine force or plan that regulated the cosmos. Now, it is quite obvious to anyone who watches cable television that religion still occupies much media attention and commands many followers in contemporary American society. Some would have it that we are experiencing a recrudescence of religion, but these observers know little of social history and are not cognizant of how it used to be. Religious consciousness, at one time, permeated all phases of life. But the secularization of contemporary consciousness has little to do with church attendance or the continued belief in a supreme being, both of which are widespread. Secularization has not meant the end of religion but rather "a weakening of the plausibility of religious perceptions of reality among large numbers of people, especially as the world view of secularity has come to be 'established' by the intellectual elites and in the educational institutions of modern societies" (Berger, 1977, p. 79).

The enormous successes of science and technology have many legacies, not the least significant of which is the implicit assumption that the only viable epistemology must be materialistic and empirical. On this view, the real is that which can be studied through science; all else acquires a second-class epistemological status. Morality, the arts, the gods, and all phenomena outside the realm of science lose their status as constituents of objective reality and become reduced to subjective elements in the inner lives of individuals. As Heller has put it, "Religion and art lost their unquestioned birthrights in the homeland of human reality, and turned into strange messengers from the higher unreality, admitted now and then as edifying or entertaining songsters at the positivist banquet" (1959, p. 213).

Premodern consciousness granted individuals a sense of hope and belief in the ultimate meaningfulness of life. With the advent of modernity, this conviction is weakened for many. One of the meaning structures provided by tradition is what Max Weber called *theodicy*. A theodicy is an explanation that confers meaning on experiences of suffering and evil. While modern society has weakened the viability of religious theodicies, it has not, of course, eliminated the occasions that call for them—those inevitable sorrows and misfortunes that continue to befall us: "Modernity has accomplished many far-reaching transformations, but it has not fundamentally changed the finitude, fragility, and mortality of the human condition. What it has accomplished is to seriously weaken those definitions of reality that previously made the human condition easier to bear" (Berger, Berger, & Kellner, 1973, p. 185). One of the chief functions that psychotherapy seems to perform is to supply secular theodicies to individuals for whom other kinds of explanations have lost their potency. The advice and counsel of the therapist as well as the vast psychological literature on the dynamics of human conduct help us to structure and understand our experiences of suffering and sorrow, to make the pain of life comprehensible within a coherent system of explanation.

Individuation, or the increasing separation of the individual from social collectives, is a chief characteristic of modernization. The industrialization of the West has brought about unparalleled increases in individual liberties and possibilities. But the liberation of the individual from economic and social fetters has not been purchased without the impoverishment of many institutions that once gave emotional sustenance to the individual. The family, the community, the church, are tottering from the blows administered by the forces of modernization. The bright side of this phenomenon is an increase in the range of options, in the potential for experimentation, a dispelling of many barriers to growth and achievement, and an exhilarating mobility of both the body and spirit. The dark side is anomie, alienation, and a sense of homelessness within the cosmos. As Camus has written, "In a universe suddenly divested of illusions and lights, man feels a stranger. His exile is without remedy since he is deprived of the memory of a lost home or the hope of a promised land to guide him" (1960, p. 5).

I think it appropriate to view Ellis's work as a project similar to that taken on by the existential philosophers. Given the modern world and its attendant modern consciousness described above, what kind of practical guide for living can we fashion. If there is no God and we can establish no credible basis for any belief not based on scientific observation, yet we are unwilling to lapse into nihilism and require some foundation upon which to predicate our actions, what, then, are we to do? Ellis provides answers, explicit answers. He does so, in part, because he realizes what is at stake and in what universe of discourse he is operating. He is out to create a personal philosophy of life for a world in which only science has authority.

But just what kind of personal philosophy is viable in a world characterized by Nietzsche's "weightlessness of all things," or one in which, as Marx put it, "All that is solid melts into air?" Of course, the basis upon which Ellis founds his views is that of pragmatic efficacy. As do all therapies, RET offers not goodness for the sake of goodness, nor truth for the sake of truth. The payoff in therapy is happiness. And RET claims to be a science of personal happiness. The tenets of RET require for justification only the proposition that if they are believed and acted upon, the pain of life will be attenuated and happiness will ensue. But within this last assertion may lie the rub. For perhaps there are limits on the abilities of individuals to fashion meaningful world views and happy lives in terms of the epistemological and moral categories provided by scientific culture.

Happiness itself is not an unproblematic concept. For what, after all, is meant by *happiness*? Is this concept so lacking in ambiguity that it can be readily quantified on a single dimension and entered into a hedonic calculus? Or is it the case there are qualitatively distinct kinds of happiness which can only be chosen among by means of value judgments or ethical choices that cannot themselves be derived from a rationalized or purely pragmatic calculus? It does not seem self-evident that a secular happiness grounded in personal pleasure and satisfaction would be necessarily greater (or more admirable) than, say, a sacred happiness bound up with a sense of virtue or with feelings of cosmological communion. How would one even go about comparing the two?

The problem confronting not only RET but the whole of our post-industrial society is whether we can do without a sense of community and a belief that human existence has some meaning beyond the seeking of personal pleasure. Arguing from an impressive data base, Antonovsky (1979) has contended that the maintenance of physical and psychological health requires the ability of the individual to develop and sustain a sense of coherence. Such a sense of coherence necessitates a world view that incorporates a personally meaningful background of community, tradition, and cosmos within which one's coping activities occur. This world view defines the limits of personal control and makes the many uncontrollable and tragic aspects of life "affectively comprehensible." (Note the similarity to Weber's concept of theodicy.) In related empirical research that has confirmed the importance of a meaningful world view, Kobasa and her colleagues (Kobasa, 1979; Kobasa, Maddi, & Courington, 1981; Kobasa, Maddi, & Puccetti, 1982) have shown that the absence of purpose and commitment in one's life, or the presence of feelings of alienation, greatly reduce the ability to tolerate life stress.

The real question is whether RET is part of the problem of modernity or a solution to that problem. It is, no doubt, both. For like most forms of psychotherapy, RET is a product of modernity that also seeks to cure or at least palliate certain of the problems of modern life. A number of commentators (Lasch, 1978; Rieff, 1966) have suggested that the very institution of psychotherapy itself promotes a pathological individualism that culminates in narcissism and the isolation and alienation of the individual. Ellis seems to feel that it is possible to derive a certain kind of commitment to a life of social involvement and responsibility from his fundamental premise of egoistic long-range hedonism. The argument is that if we take into account all those factors that contribute to personal happiness, then clearly the good will, love, and respect of others are important to our psychological well-being. So too is a just and equitable social order:

> The emotionally healthy individual is primarily true to himself and does not masochistically sacrifice himself for others. His kindness and consideration for others are largely derived from the idea that he himself wants to enjoy freedom from unnecessary pain and restriction, and that he is only likely to do so by helping create a world in which the rights of others, as well as his own rights, are not needlessly curtailed. (Ellis, 1973, p. 159)

Therefore, if we want others to care about us, we must care about them; and we are most likely to get good treatment from others if we treat them as we wish to be treated. Despite the apparent similarity to the Golden Rule, there is a key difference between Ellis's maxim and that famous dictum of Christianity. This difference lies in the dissimilarities of the rationales for treating others as we wish to be treated. In religious systems, we are directed to do this because it is the right thing to do. In Ellis's system, however, we take account of others' needs because this is the best way to get our own needs met—a means to an end, rather than an end in itself. One central and unanswered question is whether acts of kindness and generosity performed for instrumental, rather than intrinsic, reasons, will produce the same effects. If one is sensitive only as a device to produce a social exchange of sensitivity, will the recipient of that consideration value it as highly as consideration that flows out of noninstrumental motivation? Will the self-interested basis of one's actions be detectable and vitiate its hoped-for effects?

But perhaps an even more basic question also needs to be answered. Is Ellis correct in his assertion that long-term hedonism is best served by altruism? This would be a difficult question to answer empirically, and different answers might apply to different individuals. Certainly it may be the case that many individuals will decide that being good citizens is less likely to promote personal happiness than a new car or an expensive vacation. If one is fundamentally and primarily for oneself, it would seem that, on assessing long-term prospects for satisfaction, one might just as well resolve to become a very effective psychopath as choose to fashion oneself into an altruistic social democrat. And what about posterity? Once we are gone, the personal hedonic calculus is over. Why should we then care about what comes after us?

It is instructive to compare RET with other kinds of therapy from the standpoint of the human need for a sense of meaning and purpose. It may be true, as Rieff (1966) has argued, that all modern forms of psychotherapy assume and legitimate a certain subjectivism and individualism. Nevertheless, the forms differ in the degree to which they perpetuate (albeit in transvaluated fashion) certain of the underlying assumptions, symbols, and mythic structures characteristic of the premodern world view.

Mircea Eliade (1967), the scholar of comparative religion, has pointed out that the psychoanalytic concept of reviving and living through previously unconscious mental contents is in certain respects "homologous with the experience of the sacred" (p. 17). Thus, for example, the recollection of the supposedly crucial events of early childhood is reminiscent of the return to the primordial time of myth, the time of the gods that is supposed to have preceded the fall into history. In this way, the psychoanalytic theory of development offers a kind of master narrative or metanarrative that retains aspects of mythic or religious consciousness though it does this, of course, in a modernized fashion, having psychologized older symbol systems into a myth of the individual. This quasireligious aspect may account for a certain dogmatism that has long plagued psychoanalysis. However, once one recognizes the importance of a sense of meaningfulness, one must also grant that this aspect could be of considerable therapeutic value.

It is true that a more purely rationalistic psychotherapeutic approach like that of Ellis also provides a source of meaning and an organizing perspective on life, that of secular pragmatism. Pragmatism and its close relative, skepticism, are, after all, value-laden perspectives that can both serve to structure experience and make it coherent, as well as to orient one's conduct in the world. The kind of skeptical pragmatism that pervades Ellis's work (and much of the contemporary scientific–technological sensibility) is, however, dissimilar to those belief systems that characterized premodern consciousness. For one thing, it lacks a certain kind of rhetorical power, that quasi-esthetic resonance that can reside in mythic forms, whether *Oedipus Rex* or the Oedipus complex. For another, it can encourage a certain relativistic outlook on life. Ellis has quite rightly emphasized how the development of some degree of skepticism can free one from self-destructive patterns. One wonders, however, whether he has been sensitive enough to its dangers and disadvantages—the way it can foster Neitzsche's homogenized "weightlessness of all things."

Ellis's psychotherapy offers, on the one hand, a set of problem-solving techniques and, on the other hand, a general pragmatic–rational criterion of worth. What it does not offer—indeed, what it refuses to offer—is the kind of overarching sense of meaning and legitimation, the theodicy, that can come from a master narrative. In this sense, Ellis's RET is very much a product of modernity. In fact, if what has been called the "postmodern condition" can be defined as "incredulity toward metanarratives" (as Lyotard, 1984, p. xxiv, has said), then Ellis's views, with their explicit encouragement of skepticism, are perhaps more actively postmodern than are the forms of psychoanalysis that retain mythic elements, or than other contemporary forms of therapy that have less to say about the disadvantages of belief.

RATIONALITY ANALYZED

As we have seen, RET can be viewed as encompassing a personal philosophy of life that places the ultimate premium upon rationality as a criterion. Central to Ellis's therapeutic aims is the elimination of irrational beliefs. Rationality seems, then, to serve as the transcendent value or ultimate goal in Ellis's philosophy. Just what this means is, however, more problematic than it may appear. For, as numerous writers in philosophy and the social sciences have pointed out, rationality is a rather slippery and problematic concept, and one that cannot uncritically be assumed to be isomorphic with the principles of RET. Lukes's (1970) study of rationality identifies five partially overlapping definitions of the term *irrational*. Beliefs are irrational if they are

1. illogical (self-contradictory or derived from invalid inferences)
2. wholly or partly false
3. nonsensical
4. situationally specific and not generalizable
5. dogmatically derived or held.

Lukes goes on to describe other uses of the rationality–irrationality dimension as it applies to actions. Actions are termed rational, under various schemes, if they are

1. goal-directed
2. in reality, the most efficient means to reach a particular goal

3. according to the agent's belief, the most efficient means to reach a particular goal
4. able to further or consistent with the agent's long-term goals
5. pursuant of goals that are appropriate for the agent or the agent "ought" to have.

It is clear from Lukes's discussion that rationality refers to no simple concept, but rather has a plurality of meanings. He nevertheless wishes to suggest that at least some of these senses of rationality apply universally or are a necessary precondition for any form of inquiry or social activity.

A more relativistic conception of rationality emerges in the work of Peter Winch. Operating out of a post-Wittgensteinian framework, Winch (1958) has proposed that criteria of rationality themselves are not immutable and do not transcend culture and history. Standards of rationality are no more fixed and eternal than are human values or other social creations. They are, in fact, context- or culture-dependent: "We start from the position that standards of rationality in different societies do not always coincide; from the possibility, therefore, that the standards of rationality current in S [society] are different from our own" (Winch, 1958, p. 97).

Finding a culture with different standards of rationality, so Winch's argument goes, does not mean that such a culture is epistemologically backward, only that it is different. There is an internal "logic" and coherence to such primitive practices as magic that is different from that found in Western science. But these practices, which we Westerners commonly consider bogus and which tend to be denigrated by Ellis, are legitimized by those local norms of social regulation and by shared standards for the evaluation of social institutions. So also do they represent integral features of that culture and its guiding *Weltanschauung*. Even logical consistently itself, presumably one universal criterion of rationality is questioned:

Criteria of logic are not a direct gift of God, but arise out of, and are only intelligible in the context of, ways of living and modes of social life. It follows that one cannot apply criteria of logic to modes of social life as such. For instance, science is one such mode and religion is another; and each can be logical or illogical: in science, for example, it would be illogical to refuse to be bound by the results of a properly carried out experiment; in religion it would be illogical to suppose that one could pit one's thoughts against God's, and so on. (Winch, 1958, pp. 100-101)

Recent philosophical work has suggested that even science itself may not provide us with examples of a universally applicable method of rational inquiry and evaluation of claims. Revisionist philosophers of science (Feyerabend, 1975; Kuhn, 1970) tell us that this is because scientists themselves often do not follow these procedures and, in many instances, scientific progress has resulted from "irrational" activities, values, and beliefs of scientists. Rigid adherence to such tenets as empirical verification of hypotheses, for example, would actually have impeded the advance of science in some instances. One rather glaring example of this kind of situation is the initial Copernican heliocentric theory. Though essentially correct in its description of the solar system, it contained some key problems (e.g., the assumption that planetary orbits are circular rather than elliptical). Had ruthless empirical standards been applied to it, the theory would have been rejected out of hand, because the best Ptolemaic theory of the time fit the astronomical data better and made better predictions. Similarly, it is often the obdurate stubbornness and apparent irrationality of investigators that keep them doggedly pursuing lines of investigation that reason would indicate to be initially unprofitable but that subsequently prove to be major revolutionary contributions.

Thus the status of rationality itself is a subject of much controversy within contemporary philosophy. The absolute status and epistemological superiority of modern Western thought seemingly cannot be defended as conclusively as the thinkers of the Enlightenment supposed. Nor does there seem to be any consistent pattern of method or decision-making that is the precursor and necessary ingredient in all scientific progress. A universal scientific method seems not to exist. Rationality itself, under many of its definitions, seems inseparable both from value positions and particular sociohistorical contexts. Rationality would thus appear to be a somewhat muddled concept with a multiplicity of possible denotations. Therefore, when Ellis advocates the abolition of irrational beliefs, he cannot be seen as appealing to some transcendental, ultimate standard by which all thought and action can be evaluated. Rather, he is advancing a value position that advocates the most expedient pursuit of happiness, a happiness defined totally in the terms of a personal hedonic calculus.

A Critique of Rational–Emotive Theory of Personality

Daniel J. Ziegler

INTRODUCTION

The cognitive–behavioral movement within contemporary psychology is profound, deep, and far-reaching. It has touched virtually every major area of psychology, and it is most especially visible in clinical psychology, where cognitive theories flourish and cognitive–behavioral therapeutic strategies abound (Mahoney, 1977c). Yet unlike the psychoanalytic movement, which dominated clinical approaches during the first half of this century, today's cognitive–behavioral movement does not as yet have an underlying systematic, comprehensive theory of personality. This is in spite of laudable, empirically grounded, and very promising steps in that direction (e.g., Bandura, 1969, 1977b). If the cognitive–behavioral movement is to reach its full potential as a scientifically based, systematic account of human behavior, then such a comprehensive personality theory at its base is sorely needed.

Albert Ellis is in a unique position vis-à-vis cognitive–behavioral psychology. A careful inspection of his writings (e.g., Ellis, 1962) clearly reveals that his expression of the central concepts of this movement predated its rise to prominence in American psychology and predated by

27

some time the unambiguous recognition of Ellis as one of its major legitimate pioneers. Moreover, Ellis (1974, 1978b, 1979e) has developed at least the beginnings of the kind of theoretical structure here envisioned as a necessary and desirable personological base for the cognitive–behavioral movement.

The purpose of this chapter is to serve as a critique of the present status of Ellis's rational–emotive therapy (RET) theory of personality. As such, it passes no judgment on the merits or demerits of RET per se, but only on the current state of the personality theory presumed to underlie it. Moreover, the orientation of this chapter is to address what is missing in RET theory as a personality theory rather than to dispute its fundamental assumptions and conceptions. That is, if one were to accept Ellis's basic assumptions concerning human nature and determine what he has thus far asserted about personality, what elements still need to be addressed by Ellis and/or his followers in order for RET theory to become a more fully developed, comprehensive personological system?

The chapter is organized as follows. First, Ellis's concept of personality is briefly examined. Next, using a framework that has already been employed to assess other personality theorists such as Freud, Adler, Skinner, and Rogers (Hjelle & Ziegler, 1981), Ellis's basic assumptions concerning human nature are identified. Within this basic assumptions framework, what currently seems missing in RET theory is in each case addressed. Finally, again using a system previously applied to other personality theories (Hjelle & Ziegler, 1981), six major criteria are employed to assess the current status of RET theory as a scientific theory of personality. And again, within this criterion format, what seems missing in RET theory is briefly examined.

ELLIS'S CONCEPT OF PERSONALITY

It is difficult (but not impossible) to take to task for what is "missing" in his theoretical position a man whose publications number over 500 papers and 49 books and monographs (American Psychological Association, 1986). Undaunted, however, I begin. If we assume that a good personality theory should include a clear, specific, and detailed definition of precisely what is meant by the term *personality*, then we immediately encounter the first gap in RET theory. While the term *personality* is invoked often throughout Ellis's prolific writings, there appears to be no single, explicit, consistent, and, above all, precise definition of the term, one which would specify clearly the hypothetical constructs included under the rubric of the term and, at least by implication, those factors excluded.

Instead, one finds in Ellis's writings the term employed in a general, probably over-inclusive, and sometimes inconsistent fashion. At various points in his writings, Ellis uses the *personality* in conjunction with beliefs (e.g., Ellis, 1979e, p. 17), traits (e.g., Ellis, 1975), attitudes, values, preferences, and a whole host of other hypothetical constructs that scores of personality and social psychologists have spent decades attempting to precisely define and differentiate from one another (e.g., Fishbein & Ajzen, 1975). A precise definition would permit a more consistent and "boundaried" use of the term and clarify the psychological referent in mind.

Included under this definition of personality should be a precise specification and definition of the hypothetical constructs posited and their interrelationships, that is, what are the most meaningful personality dimensions that underlie behavioral stability over time and across situations as well as account for salient individual differences? As RET theory now stands, beliefs appear to constitute Ellis's central construct in this regard. While there have been laudable attempts to specify the nature of this construct more exactly (Ellis, 1985b; Ellis & Bernard, 1986), greater such efforts are needed. That is, building on this previous theoretical work, a much greater specification of the properties of beliefs is desirable. Over the years, Ellis has done a marvelous job of elucidating the contents of beliefs, especially irrational beliefs. Now it is time for a detailed analysis of their properties as well. What is envisioned here is the type of analysis to which other major personality theorists have subjected their central hypothetical constructs, e.g., G. A. Kelly's (1955) description of the formal properties of constructs; G. W. Allport's (1966) listing of the defining criteria of a trait; Henry Murray's (1938) treatment of the criteria by which needs can be recognized. If Ellis and/or his colleagues could systematically develop this type of analysis for beliefs, RET theory would take a distinct step forward as a unified, coherent personality theory.

In defense of Ellis, nowhere does he claim to have a complete theory of personality. Indeed, the very titles of some of his major works on the topic serve as disclaimers in this regard, e.g., Ellis (1978b) "*Toward* a theory of personality"; Ellis (1979e) "*Toward* a new theory of personality" (italics mine). And in these works, Ellis often speaks of a theory of personality change rather than of personality per se. Moreover, Ellis (1982b) explicitly acknowledges that he has not yet tried to formulate RET into a formal theoretical model. Nonetheless, should Ellis and/or his colleagues decide to formulate such a model, a precise definition and specification of the term *personality*, along with the hypothetical constructs (and their properties) subsumed by the term, would be an excellent place to start.

Let us now turn to the assumptions concerning human nature at the base of RET theory.

ELLIS'S BASIC ASSUMPTIONS CONCERNING HUMAN NATURE

It is here argued that every personality theorist holds a set of basic philosophic assumptions concerning human nature and that these assumptions, whether explicitly recognized by the theorist or not, play a major role in his or her theory construction. That is, probably rooted in a theorist's own personality makeup and life experience are a set of basic assumptions (implicit or explicit) about what human beings fundamentally are: these assumptions are necessarily at the foundation of theory construction and potently guide the directions of theory building. Elsewhere (Hjelle & Ziegler, 1981), nine such basic assumptions have been identified:

Freedom	Determinism
Rationality	Irrationality
Holism	Elementalism
Constitutionalism	Environmentalism
Changeability	Unchangeability
Subjectivity	Objectivity
Proactivity	Reactivity
Homeostasis	Heterostasis
Knowability	Unknowability

The assumptions are here depicted as monistic bipolar continua although, philosophically, the issues intrinsic to them may be dichotomous, e.g., human behavior results from either some degree of freedom or is totally determined. Nonetheless, portrayal of these assumptions in this fashion allows discernment of the degree to which a theorist may lean in one assumptive direction or another, e.g., the degree to which a theorist emphasizes freedom or determinism in his or her personality theory. Ellis's positions on these assumption dimensions tend to be clear and, perhaps more than any other personality theorist, explicit.

Finally, it is here also argued that a theorist's basic assumptions concerning human nature function simultaneously to broaden and to narrow his or her perspective on personality. Again, take the freedom–determinism dimension as an illustration. If a theorist assumes freedom, then he or she will be inclined to emphasize, examine, and develop theoretically those aspects of human functioning which suggest that human beings are indeed relatively free agents, e.g., highly developed cognitive capacities that allow humans to see alternatives and thus make choices. Yet such a theorist would also be inclined (at least implicitly) to downplay, not examine thoroughly, and fail to develop theoretically those factors suggesting that human behavior is ultimately determined, e.g., childhood conditioning experiences. Thus, one's theoretical perspective on the totality of human personality and behavior is both broadened and narrowed via necessarily viewing it through the goggles of one's basic assumptions. And since no one, regardless of degree or diversification of talent, can be a theoretical person for all seasons, there is, practically, bound to be something substantial missing from any systematic account of human personality.

Let us now consider Ellis's positions (depicted in Figure 3.1) on each of the nine posited assumption dimensions.

Freedom–Determinism

The age-old freedom–determinism issue focuses on the degree of internal freedom, if any, that humans actually possess in directing their own behavior. Do people truly have choice, or is their behavior actually determined by a whole host of factors, some outside the sphere of conscious awareness? Wherever Ellis squarely addresses this issue (Ellis, 1977a, 1978b, 1985c; Ellis & Bernard, 1986; Weinrach, 1980), he explicitly comes down on the side of a moderate degree of freedom in human conduct. Eschewing both extreme poles of this assumption dimension as untenable, Ellis concludes, "A soft determinism, or the belief that humans have some degree of choice that is limited by environmental situations and by innate biological predispositions, seems much more realistic" (Ellis, 1985c, p. 286). Elsewhere, describing the unique features of RET, he says, "It particularly emphasizes the importance of will and choice in human affairs, even though it accepts the likelihood that some human behavior is partially

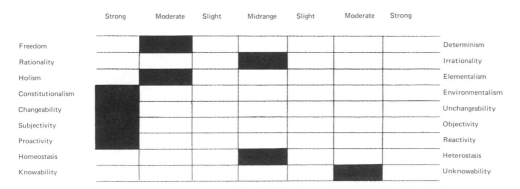

Figure 3.1 Ellis's position on the nine basic assumptions concerning human nature. The shaded areas indicate the degree to which Ellis favors one of the two bipolar extremes.

determined by biological, social, and other forces" (Ellis & Bernard, 1986). So in RET theory we find an underlying commitment to some degree of free will and choice in human makeup, but certainly not the kind of absolute, untrammeled freedom one typically encounters in existential theories. Rather, in RET theory, human choice is clearly limited by a variety of mitigating factors.

What are some of the reflections in RET theory of Ellis's underlying assumption of moderate freedom? Consider the historical centrality of cognitive processes in RET theory; with the exception of G. A. Kelly (1955), Ellis (1962) was routinely talking about these processes long before other personologists were. Especially as Ellis conceptualizes them, cognitive processes are precisely those features of human personality that permit free choice to operate. In outlining the RET position on this issue, he writes, "It hypothesizes that the more rationally people think and behave, the less deterministic they act" (Ellis, 1978b, p. 307). And a major goal of RET itself is to help people alter their cognitive processes—to rid themselves of their irrational beliefs and to begin to think "straight"—such that they may at least partially rise above their determined circumstances and freely, rationally, and continuously choose to move in the direction of greater mental health.

But Ellis's commitment to freedom also seems to result in a downplaying of possible adult personality-relevant factors that assuredly would be more salient for a deterministically oriented theorist. As an illustration, consider the role of childhood experience in adult personality formation and behavior. While Ellis certainly acknowledges that childhood experiences help "indoctrinate" maladaptive behavior, he appears to place more emphasis upon the subsequent and continuous process of "reindoctrination" in this regard, a process that individuals daily choose to continue (Ellis, 1962). However, the details of precisely how this original process of indoctrination takes place are not spelled out, nor are details of the cognitive–learning mechanisms that make possible the hypothesized reindoctrination process. And, finally, there is no pointed, cogent explanation of the relationship between original indoctrination and subsequent reindoctrination. Again, an important point here is that a theorist's basic assumptions about human nature (in this case, freedom–determinism) incline him or her to perceive clearly certain aspects of human behavior while simultaneously having theoretical blind (or at least hazy) spots for certain others.

Rationality–Irrationality

The basic issue underlying the rationality–irrationality dimension is the degree to which human reasoning powers can or do actually influence everyday human behavior. Are humans primarily rational creatures who direct their behavior through reason, or do human actions principally result from irrational forces? Again, Ellis is clear on this issue. In his seminal work, *Reason and Emotion in Psychotherapy*, and back in the days when RET was called RT and humans were called man, he asserted, "The central theme of RT is that man is a uniquely rational, as well as a uniquely irrational, animal" (Ellis, 1962, p. 36). In numerous subsequent writings, he strongly and emphatically has reasserted the position that the duality of rationality and irrationality is the inherent human condition (Ellis, 1974, 1976a, 1978b, 1979e). On the rationality–irrationality assumption dimension, then, Ellis stands squarely in the middle.

My experience is that critics of RET often do not understand precisely what Ellis means by the terms *rational* and *irrational*, for it is not the standard meaning of the terms. To wit: "The term *rational*, as used in RET, refers to people's (1) setting up or choosing for themselves certain basic values, purposes, goals, or ideals and then (2) using efficient, flexible, scientific, logico-empirical ways of attempting to achieve such values and goals and to avoid contradictory or self-defeating results" (Ellis, 1979g, p. 40); "Rationality, then, is a method or technique of effectively gaining certain values; it does not exist in any intrinsic or absolutistic sense" (Ellis, 1974, p. 311). As for irrational: "*Irrationality* means any thought, emotion, or behavior that leads to self-defeating or self-destructive consequences—that significantly interferes with the survival and happiness of the organism" (Ellis, 1976a, p. 145). Thus, a critically important point for appreciating the RET position is that "rational" and "irrational" are relativistic, human, goal-oriented concepts and have no independent existence or meaning in RET outside of this framework. And throughout his writings, Ellis argues that each has equal weight in influencing human behavior.

However he defines rationality and irrationality, Ellis's middle-ground position on this assumption allows him to address and articulate aspects of human nature downplayed by personality theorists taking more extreme positions on this issue, for example, Freud. When one considers Freud's life-versus-death instincts in relation to Ellis's rationality (rational beliefs) versus irrationality (irrational beliefs), there are some intriguing similarities. Both theorists see the human being as forever in conflict between two diametrically opposed and very basic forces. And in both theories the forces themselves are biologically based, specieswide triggers to behavior and fundamentally related to human survival and happiness. But, as the subsequent development of ego psychology within the psychoanalytic movement attests, Freud's basic assumption of irrationality prevented him from properly recognizing and addressing the more rational (ego) components of human nature. Ellis's more moderate position on this assumption dimension allows him to do precisely that, via cognitive processes and rational beliefs.

On the other side of this issue are humanistic theorists such as Maslow and Rogers, who clearly assume rationality (Hjelle & Ziegler, 1981). Commenting on Maslow and Rogers in relation to this issue, Ellis, in his own inimitable fashion, says, "But what tenderhearted humanists like these unrealistically forget is that we are also born—yes born—with several highly irrational, self-sabotaging human tendencies—such as the easily nourished tendency to damn ourselves, devil-ify and deify others, and whine about (instead of moving our asses to rectify) life's hassles (Weinrach, 1980, p. 154). Precisely. And because Ellis takes a more moderate position on the rationality–irrationality dimension, he is able to describe irrational beliefs and, in an article entitled "The Biological Basis of Human Irrationality" (Ellis, 1976a), actually list and categorize 259 major human irrationalities! Thus, Ellis's middle-of-the-road position on this assumption allows him to develop a more balanced, although not necessarily thorough, account of human personality. Subsequently, what appears to be missing in his theoretical account of both rational beliefs and irrational beliefs is addressed.

Holism–Elementalism

Are human beings best understood as individual totalities (holism), or is human behavior better comprehended by breaking it down into its component parts (elementalism)? On this assumption dimension, Ellis is moderately inclined toward holism. He addresses the issue as follows:

> While RET sees people as having units or elements (e.g., high sexuality or low energy) that influence their whole lives, it also sees them as having interacting parts (including cognitions, emotions, and behaviors) that cannot be separated, and it primarily sees them as having a holistic or central "consciousness" or "will" that tends to direct these various parts. (Ellis, 1978b, p. 306)

And on the interplay among the important parts, he says, "Human cognition, emotion, and behavior do not constitute separate entities but all significantly interrelate and importantly affect each other" (Ellis, 1977a, p. 6). Thus, Ellis recognizes component parts of personality but clearly sees their holistic interrelatedness as being more central in understanding human makeup.

The emphasis on holism may lead Ellis to neglect a detailed analysis of the component parts themselves and a detailed account of their precise interrelationships. Cognitions, emotions, and behaviors, after all, are distinctly molar constructs in need of more refined analysis, perhaps of the kind Ellis (1985b) seems to have begun in later writings. (Ellis, 1985b).

The hypothesized interrelationships among these parts also cry out for more precise theoretical description. While Ellis has cited voluminous evidence for his hypothesized interrelationship of cognition, emotion, and behavior (Ellis, 1977a, 1977d), what is missing are his own careful, systematic, and detailed summary, conclusions, and implications of this evidence in RET theory–germane terms. That is, beyond the general observation that changes in one of these components (e.g., cognitions) tend to produce changes in the others (e.g., emotions and behaviors), precisely what might this evidence tell us in RET terms about human personality? Finally, in the above quotation, Ellis alludes to a holistic or central ''consciousness'' or ''will.'' What is this? Elsewhere in his writings this concept does not appear to be spelled out, and a personological construct of this presumed centrality really should be.

Constitutionalism–Environmentalism

How much of human personality results from constitutional factors and how much is a product of environmental influences? How much is nature and how much nurture? On this issue, Ellis leans strongly, although not totally, in the direction of constitutionalism. While in numerous writings he clearly acknowledges the importance of both constitution and environment in personality formation (Ellis, 1974, 1977a, 1978b, 1979e), Ellis practically never misses an opportunity to instruct his readers on the more basic and much greater influence of the former. For example,

> Although almost all contemporary schools of psychotherapy and personality formation take a different view, it seems probable that the main influence on human personality comes from hereditary sources.... My RET-oriented theory of personality says that probably 80% of the variance in human behavior rests largely on biological bases and 20% or so on specific environmental training. (Ellis, 1979e, p. 17)

And further, he asserts that human irrationality is rooted in basic human nature (Ellis, 1976a), that the related ''real'' causes of human disturbance are largely innate (Ellis, 1979e), and even that the human ''conditionability'' which permits the environment to have personological impact is innate (Ellis, 1974).

Given Ellis's strong commitment to the constitutionalism assumption, a present glaring omission in RET theory is a careful, systematic, and detailed account of the origin of irrational (and rational) beliefs in terms that are compatible with and, if possible, grounded in the known facts of genetics and neuroscience. It is one thing to argue convincingly for the biological basis of human irrationality (Ellis, 1976a); it is quite another to hypothesize in scientifically acceptable detail the precise biological under-pinnings for the origin, development, and maintenance of irrational (and rational) beliefs. This point is critically important for RET theory in par-ticular and for cognitive–behavioral theory more generally. In his argu-ment for the powerful biological basis of human personality and dis-turbance, Ellis may well be onto something significant that others in the cognitive–behavioral movement, precisely because of their environmen-talism assumption, do not and cannot see.

Other writers and researchers have noted that the human tendency toward irrational thinking is left unexplained in RET theory (DiGiuseppe, 1986). Still others have taken Ellis to task for failing to specify the inborn nature of irrational beliefs to the satisfaction of geneticists (Mahoney, 1977a) and for not taking systematically into account how environmental influences contribute to the development and maintenance of irrational beliefs (Eschenroeder, 1982). While Ellis has explicitly acknowledged the latter shortcoming in RET theory (Ellis, 1982b), it is here argued that this shortcoming is a logical consequence of his position on the constitutionalism–environmentalism assumption dimension. Ellis's strong constitutionalist leanings lead him to downplay, relatively speaking, careful attention to potentially important specific environmental influences in per-sonality development. For example, precisely what specific environmen-tal influences affect the development and maintenance of rational versus irrational beliefs and precisely how do these influences exert their effects? Environmentally speaking, why does one person end up consistently more ''rational'' than the other? Regardless of Ellis's own commitment to con-stitutionalism, RET personality theory could be substantially strengthened by a more explicit account of the nature and operation of whatever environmental influences are posited in personality development.

Changeability–Unchangeability

The basic issue involved in this assumption is the degree to which human beings are seen as capable of fundamental personality change throughout life. Can an individual's basic makeup really change substan-tially over time? Or are the surface changes observable in human behavior merely that—superficial behavioral changes that occur while the basic underlying personality structure remains unalterable and intact? On this assumption dimension, Ellis appears strongly committed to changeability. He says, ''The RET theory of change holds that, no matter how humans originally get certain personality characteristics and no matter what developmental processes they go through in connection with these characteristics, they can almost always significantly change them'' (Ellis,

1979e, p. 28). And Ellis has spent a rich and extraordinarily productive professional lifetime helping people to do precisely that—change their basic personality characteristics as he conceptualizes them to be.

Significant personality change is possible in RET theory, but it is not easy. Throughout his writings, Ellis repeatedly makes the point that if people really want to change, they will need to "*think* and *work* hard" (Ellis, 1984d, p. 208) and that, in fact, most people have a natural tendency to resist basic personality change (Ellis, 1979g). Despite the persistent difficulty, however, Ellis argues that substantial personality change can and does take place, that cognitive awareness and philosophic restructuring are the most elegant ways to bring about such change, and, not surprisingly, that RET is the preferred therapeutic vehicle of choice in such matters (Ellis, 1979e, 1979g).

While Ellis has written volumes explicating how RET itself helps powerfully to change people's personalities and behavior, what is missing in RET personality theory is a detailed account of precisely how personality develops and changes throughout the life span without RET intervention. Presumably the countless individuals who do not seek, want, or need RET nonetheless experience significant personality change. How? And since beliefs, both rational and irrational, are so central in RET theory, precisely how do they develop and change "normally," sans RET intervention? Based on all of Ellis's writings, one would assume that some sort of self-initiated and maintained cognitive restructuring process could be postulated as central (along with behavioral and emotional corollaries), but the details of any such processes, or any other constructs accounting for personality change, need to be spelled out.

Should Ellis and/or any of his followers choose to address this issue, they could seize an excellent opportunity to advance cognitive–behavioral theory by integrating both cognitive and more traditional behavioristic accounts of change within an RET framework. In the realm of beliefs, for example, one could envision a Piagetian-type account of their early development, combined with at least elements of classical conditioning (e.g., see P. L. Russell & Brandsma, 1974), operant conditioning, and modeling. This, of course, is not the only theoretical road to follow. The major point here is simply that, given Ellis's strong commitment to the changeability assumption, a detailed theoretical description of personality development and change, in the normal course of events, would greatly strengthen RET theory as a comprehensive personality theory. After all, the durability of Freudian personality theory in twentieth century psychology in no small measure rests on its detailed account, however empirically invalidatable, of personality formation and development. There is no a priori reason why cognitive–behavioral theory could not offer a better, and empirically testable, account.

Subjectivity–Objectivity

Do individuals live in a highly personal, subjective world of experience that is the major influence upon their behavior? Or is human behavior influenced primarily, if not exclusively, by external, objective factors? On this assumption dimension underlying theories of personality, Ellis comes down strongly on the side of subjectivity.

In discussing the philosophic precursors of RET (e.g., Ellis, 1984d), Ellis seems fond of quoting Epictetus, who in the first century A.D. wrote in *The Enchiridion*, "Men are disturbed not by things, but by the view which they take of them." To underscore the importance of this point for RET theory, Ellis himself says, "From its inception RET has taken the humanistic and existentialistic position that people create their own world by the phenomenological *view* they take of what happens to them" (Ellis, 1979g, p. 47). Indeed, a bit of reflection reveals that the entire ABC theory rests on this premise. Again, Ellis: "My personality-change hypothesis makes B, the individual's Belief System, the crucial issue. A does not determine C; rather, B does!" (Ellis, 1979e, p. 16). So in RET theory, it is clearly the individual's subjective beliefs (rational and irrational), rather than objective, external factors per se, that most potently influence his or her behavior. Ellis's commitment to the subjectivity assumption could hardly be stronger.

As with other theorists in the phenomenological tradition such as Carl Rogers, Ellis pays a price for his strong emphasis on subjectivity. Just as in Rogers's person-centered theory, in RET theory, there is little in the way of a detailed account of objective factors that may contribute to personality development and current functioning. And unlike some other theorists generally associated with the cognitive–behavioral movement, there is comparatively little attempt in RET theory thus far to anchor all internal constructs to objective, observable factors. Take Bandura's social-learning theory, for instance. In Bandura's (1977b) theory, there is considerable effort, wherever possible, to tie internal constructs to objective, observable factors precisely because, via his doctrine of reciprocal determinism (Bandura, 1978), he takes a midrange position on the subjectivity–objectivity issue (Hjelle & Ziegler, 1981). To remain theoretically consistent, Bandura must account for both subjective and objective factors contributing to behavior, as well as their interactions. Ellis's position on the subjectivity issue in effect relieves him of any such theoretical responsibility and, as a result, RET theory currently lacks a systematic, detailed account of objective factors in personality development and functioning. How serious such a theoretical deficiency is judged to be, of course, depends upon the basic assumptions concerning human nature of the individual doing the judging.

Proactivity–Reactivity

The proactivity–reactivity assumption is concerned with locus of causality in human behavior. Do people generate their behavior internally or is their behavior actually a series of responses to external stimuli? On this issue Ellis comes down strongly on the side of proactivity.

An examination of Ellis's ABC theory clearly reveals that A's (activating events) alone practically never directly trigger human behavior. Ellis speaks to this issue as follows: "RET holds that humans are purposeful, or goal-seeking creatures. . . . The RET theory of personality and of personality disturbances begins with people's trying to fulfill their Goals (Gs) in some kind of environment and encountering a set of Activating events or Activators (As) that tend to help them achieve or block these Goals" (Ellis, 1985b, pp. 314-315). Elsewhere it is noted, "Activating events virtually never exist in a pure or monolithic form but almost always interact with and partly include beliefs (B's) and consequences (C's). *People bring themselves* (their goals, thoughts, desires, and physiological propensities) *to bear on activating events*" (Ellis & Bernard, 1986). And even the first of three important "insights" recommended for RET clients to achieve is the understanding that self-defeating or disturbed consequences stem mainly from the irrational beliefs that people bring to the activating experiences occurring in their lives (Ellis, 1979g). Thus, Ellis is unmistakably committed to the proactivity assumption.

It might be argued that, because Ellis is strongly committed to proactivity, he tends to overlook the potentially important reactivity components of his theory (e.g., A's) and their subtle, complex interrelationships with the proactive components. Such a criticism, while logically consistent with my basic assumptions thesis here, is unwarranted in this instance. The fact of the matter is that, especially in recent times, Ellis and his colleagues have addressed this issue. For example, Ellis (1985b) has made a pointed attempt to articulate further the interrelationships among A, B, and C in his theory. Grieger (1986) has offered a contextual, rather than a linear, model of the ABC's of RET. And R. A. Wessler and Wessler (1980) have proposed an impressive eight-step model of an emotional episode in terms intended to expand the original ABC paradigm. Such efforts, while not violating Ellis's fundamental commitment to the proactivity assumption, serve to move RET theory in the direction of becoming a more comprehensive, detailed account of human behavior. They bode well for the future of RET as a personality theory.

Homeostatis–Heterostasis

The homeostasis–heterostasis assumption is fundamentally concerned with human motivation. Are humans motivated primarily or exclusively to reduce tensions and maintain an internal state of equilibrium a la Freud's (1915–1917) homeostatic pleasure principle? Or is their basic motivation directed toward growth, stimulus seeking, and self-actualization a la Rogers's (1959) heterostatic actualizing tendency?

Perhaps the best way to depict Ellis's position on this dimension is mid-range because (1) he appears to accord about equal weight to homeostatic and heterostatic elements in his system, and (2) neither homeostasis or heterostasis per se is central to his concept of motivation. In describing people's motivation, Ellis says, "They have predispositions...to be creative...and to actualize their potentials for life and growth. They also have propensities...to be short-range hedonists...and to avoid actualizing their potentials for growth" (Ellis, 1984d, p. 196). Moreover, he asserts that practically all people are motivated by four basic human values: (1) to survive, (2) to be relatively happy (satisfied and free from unnecessary pain) while surviving, (3) to live in and get along with members of a social group or community, and (4) to relate intimately (and satisfactorily) with a few selected members of this group (Ellis, 1974). Ellis further argues that the desires associated with such values are biologically based and that human hedonism, i.e., staying alive and seeking happiness, is likewise biologically rooted (Ellis, 1979e, 1979g). Finally, he makes the point that people are motivated by desires and tendencies, not needs or necessities, unless "people foolishly *define* them as such" (Ellis, 1984d, p. 209).

All of the above constitute a good start toward a systematic account of human motivation. But if RET is to become a more comprehensive theory of personality, then a much more precise and detailed description of what motivates people is required. There have been some moves in this direction (e.g., Ellis's 1985b brief listing of the main subgoals as people strive for happiness), but what is needed is a more substantive, thorough, detailed, and systematic theoretical description of human motivation within RET theory. Furthermore, the precise nature of Ellis's motivational constructs needs to be clarified. For example, Ellis notes that "RET sees people as having instinctoid tendencies rather than fixed instincts" (Ellis, 1978b, p. 307). What precisely is an "instinctoid tendency"? While admittedly the term is also found in the writings of Abraham Maslow (1962), it has no clear meaning within traditional comparative psychology. Thus, if RET is to postulate biologically based motivational constructs to account for behavior, then the nature and properties of these constructs need to be described in terms compatible with the rest of scientific psychology.

Knowability–Unknowability

The final basic assumption poses a question: Ultimately, is human nature fully knowable in scientific terms or for some reason does it transcend the potential of scientific understanding? Despite the frequent invocation of scientific, logicoempirical approaches and methods throughout Ellis's writings, a careful inspection of these same writings reveals an almost paradoxical, and at least moderate, commitment to the unknowability assumption. There appear to be at least two major reasons for this seeming paradox: (1) virtually nothing is absolute in Ellis's thinking (including the powers of reason and science, and indeed even RET itself), and (2) personality (and, by implication, human nature) is simply too complex to be captured by any one approach—even that of science.

Concerning the limits of reason, Ellis says, "RET looks skeptically at anything mystical, religious, transpersonal, or magical, when these terms are used in the strict sense. It believes that reason itself is limited, ungodlike, and unabsolute" (Ellis, 1984d, p. 210). And elsewhere Ellis has pointedly argued that personality is too complex and varied to be entirely encapsulated by a single theory comprising empirically testable concepts (Ellis, 1978b, 1979e). Indeed, he strongly questions the usefulness of personality theorizing itself: "Is theorizing about personality, then, a rather hopeless and futile pursuit? To some extent, yes. For we probably won't for the present—and perhaps never will—arrive at precise and satisfactory hypotheses that cover all or most of the observed data" (Ellis, 1979e, p. 27). Instead, Ellis argues that personality theorists would do better to accept his own RET hypotheses as a starting point and then try to "determine the nature of people in the here and now, in their interactions in life, and in therapy, and do so under controlled clinical and experimental conditions" (Ellis, 1978b, p. 310). Thus, while Ellis holds little hope for a comprehensive account of personality and human nature via scientifically based personality theories, some elements of human nature appear potentially knowable through science.

Ellis's apparent commitment to the unknowability assumption has serious consequences for the potential development of RET as a comprehensive personality theory. It probably lies at the root of why RET is presently an incomplete personality theory. If one is basically pessimistic about the prospects of ever fully understanding human nature via a scientifically based, comprehensive personality theory, then it does not make much sense to devote a disproportionate amount of one's time trying to develop and refine one. His unknowability assumption notwithstanding, however, Ellis has given RET and the cognitive–behavioral movement an excellent start in the direction of an eventual comprehensive account of personality and human behavior. To move further in that direction in the future, colleagues and successors with a stronger inclination to the knowability assumption and a more optimistic view of personality theorizing seem required.

Let us now consider the current status of RET theory as a scientific theory of personality.

CURRENT STATUS OF RET THEORY
AS A SCIENTIFIC THEORY OF PERSONALITY

How well does RET theory, in its current state of development, fare as a scientific theory of personality? To answer this question, six criteria used elsewhere to evaluate major personality theories (Hjelle & Ziegler, 1981) are employed here: verifiability, heuristic value, internal consistency, parsimony, comprehensiveness, and functional significance. No attempt at exhaustive analysis is made here. Rather, the judged current position of RET theory on each criterion is briefly described along with a brief account of the major reasons for each judgment. Throughout this discussion the focus continues to be upon the current status of the personality theory associated with RET, not RET itself.

Let us now consider the position of RET theory (depicted in Figure 3.2) with respect to each criterion.

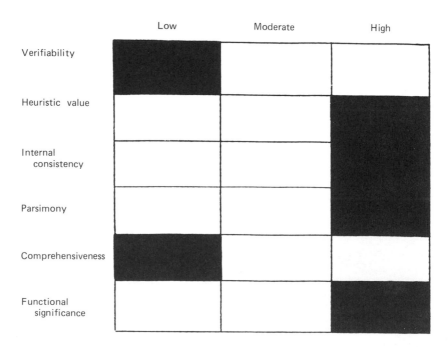

Figure 3.2 The position of RET theory on the six criteria for evaluating theories of personality. A designation of ''High'' indicates that the theory generally meets the criterion in question.

Verifiability

The criterion of verifiability requires that a theory's concepts be clearly and explicitly defined, logically related to one another, and thus amenable to empirical validation. The current position of RET theory must be judged low on verifiability. Critics of RET theory have noted that it is overinclusive (T. W. Smith, 1982), imprecise and general (Meichenbaum, 1977b), loosely related and poorly elucidated (Mahoney, 1977a), and in need of more precise formulation (Ewart & Thoresen, 1977). While Ellis himself sees empirical testing as a major future direction for RET theory in the next quarter century (Weinrach, 1980), its personological concepts first need to be more precisely defined and carefully related to one another before meaningful empirical testing can take place.

Heuristic Value

The criterion of heuristic value is concerned with the degree to which a theory directly stimulates research, and here RET theory fares quite well. Although many studies relating to Ellis's theory may not represent precise tests of his personological concepts (due to the low verifiability of the theory), there are nonetheless a large number of such studies within psychology. Indeed, Ellis has been credited with stimulating research interest in cognitive processes generally (Mahoney, 1977a), and it is here argued that his own formulations have directly led to considerable research germane to RET theory. This is especially the case in regard to the role of irrational beliefs in causing emotional distress (T. W. Smith, 1982), a formulation central to Ellis's personological system.

Internal Consistency

The internal consistency criterion stipulates that a theory should not contradict itself, that it should account for whatever phenomena it encompasses in an internally consistent fashion. RET theory can be judged as high in this regard. Ellis's system is based on a clear-cut set of assumptions about human nature, leading to a limited network of theoretical concepts which account for human behavior in an internally consistent way. Other theorists and researchers may disagree with the explanation of behavior provided by RET theory, but it must be acknowledged that the explanation is nonetheless grounded in theoretical concepts logically consistent with one another.

Parsimony

The criterion of parsimony refers to the number and complexity of theoretical concepts required to account for personality—the fewer and simpler, the better. Here RET theory ranks high. Ellis's fundamental ABC theory contains exceptionally few basic concepts, they are relatively straightforward, and these core concepts support the entire RET theoretical structure.

But sometimes Occum's razor can be taken too far. The ABC schema has been criticized for being insufficient as a scientific theory largely on the grounds of its simplicity (Eschenroeder, 1982). Given the utter complexities of human behavior, the original ABC formulation may just be too simple to encompass these. But almost never caught off guard, Ellis, to his credit, acknowledges this theoretical shortcoming (Ellis, 1982b) and makes efforts to remedy it (Ellis, 1985b; Ellis & Bernard, 1986). Further, others associated with RET likewise have attempted to expand and refine its basic theoretical model (e.g., DiGiuseppe, 1986; Grieger, 1986; R. A. Wessler and Wessler, 1980; R. L. Wessler, 1986b). The basic point here is that RET theory could profit enormously from continued, concerted efforts to expand and specify more precisely the ABC model and its constituent elements. What might be lost in parsimony would be more than made up for in completeness.

Comprehensiveness

The comprehensiveness criterion refers to the range and diversity of phenomena encompassed by a theory; the more comprehensive a personality theory, the more behavioral ground it covers. In its present state of development, RET theory must be judged low in this regard. Ellis explicitly states that "RET is interested not so much in constructing a theory of personality that will explain exactly why humans behave the way they do in practically all respects as it is in constructing a theory of personality change" (Ellis, 1979g, p. 42). This emphasis on personality change, while of unquestionable value for clinical and counseling psychology generally, results in a personality theory currently lacking in comprehensiveness.

As noted earlier in this chapter, major areas of human behavior, such as the precise role of childhood experience in adult personality formation, personality development throughout the life span, and the precise nature of human motivation, remain unaddressed in any systematic, detailed fashion. And when Ellis attempts to address such broader concerns, he sometimes does so in scientifically imprecise language, leading to criticisms by others of "conceptual laxness" in RET theory (T. W. Smith, 1982). Thus, if RET theory is to become a more comprehensive account of personality, then such major areas of human behavior as those noted above must be addressed in scientifically acceptable, systematic, detailed, and precise terms. The theoretical seeds are there; they badly need to be sown by Ellis and/or his followers for RET theory to improve its scientific standing as a comprehensive theory of personality.

Functional Significance

The criterion of functional significance refers to how useful a theory is in helping people (psychologists included) to understand everyday human behavior. Not surprisingly, RET theory rates quite high in this regard. To anyone remotely familiar with the RET movement, such a rating requires little explanation or justification. A glance at Ellis's prolific writings (American Psychological Association, 1986) reveals the staggering number and variety of practical human concerns that he has addressed. His applied work at the Institute for Rational–Emotive Therapy in New York City is practically legendary, and affiliated institutes can be found in countries throughout the world. RET is available to the general public through numerous books, tapes, pamphlets, and even songs (Walen *et al.*, 1980). And RET is the fundamental expression in psychotherapy of Ellis's basic personological concepts. Since its inception in 1955, RET theory has touched the lives of countless human beings. There is every indication that it will continue to do so.

CONCLUSION

As a developing personality theory, RET theory is off to a good start, but clearly it has some way to go to become a more comprehensive and empirically verifiable theory within scientific psychology. To attain this objective, RET theory will require much more precise, detailed, and thorough theoretical development, addressing the kinds of issues raised in this chapter. Such future theoretical development might best be envisioned as a combination of continued pioneering work by Ellis and/or his followers and more integration and incorporation of theoretical concepts from other areas of the cognitive–behavioral movement. RET theory is in a unique position within this movement and, if properly developed, could serve as the central personality theory at its base. If so, then RET theory could occupy at least as important a place in personality theory during the next century as Freudian psychoanalysis did in the field during the first half of the present century. It is hoped that this chapter will help to move RET theory in that direction.

Cognition and Emotion
from the RET Viewpoint*

Richard S. Lazarus

INTRODUCTION

Albert Ellis and I have several things in common, which adds a trace of sentimentality to the task of writing about cognition and emotion from the RET viewpoint. First, we are contemporaries, having both entered psychology during the post-World War II ascendancy of positivism and drive theory, which was then followed in the 1970s by a dramatic shift to cognitivism. Second, we think of ourselves as pioneers, arguing against the mainstream for a cognitive approach to emotion (Ellis, 1957c, 1962;

*An early draft of this chapter was sent to Albert Ellis for his comments. This interchange resulted in numerous changes and additions in the interests of clarity and accuracy in reflecting his viewpoint. The revision was returned to Ellis for further comments, which were assimilated into the text. I want to thank Ellis for the promptness, verve, care, and thoughtfulness he displayed in these time-consuming interchanges, which impressed me very greatly and strengthened my own commitment to clarity and accuracy. As a result, I believe the chapter is far better as an exposition of Ellis's viewpoint than it might have been, though I must be held responsible for any remaining inaccuracies and for my emphases and critique. Overall, I found much more consonance than dissonance in the way both of us think about emotion.

A similar role was played by editor Michael E. Bernard at a later stage of manuscript preparation.

R. S. Lazarus, 1966). Third, we have both seen the field change toward our way of thinking, which makes us prescient or lucky. Finally, we have produced overlapping theories of emotion (Ellis & Bernard, 1985b; R. S. Lazarus, in press; R. S. Lazarus & Folkman, 1984; R. S. Lazarus, Kanner, & Folkman, 1980), though we seed different soil, he in psychotherapy and I in academe.

When I began my work I did not realize that the voices moving the field inexorably away from positivism and drive theory in the 1950s and 1960s were the advance guard in the demise of an outlook in which I had been educated. These early voices included David McClelland (1951), Harry Harlow (1953), George Klein (1958), Robert White (1959), George Kelly (1955), Julian Rotter (1954), and Fritz Heider (1958). There were also those who could be remembered as grandfathers of current cognitivists, such as Kurt Lewin (1935) and Henry Murray (1938). And there is a third generation of cognitivists: Donald Meichenbaum (1977a), Aaron Beck (1976a), Marvin Goldfried (1980b), Michael Mahoney (1980a), and others. Ellis is a progenitor of this latter group of cognitive–behavior therapists.

Explicitly cognitive formulations of emotion theory are promulgated today by Mandler (1984), Averill (1982), R. C. Solomon (1980), Weiner (1985), Epstein (1983), Leventhal (1984), Scherer and Ekman (1984), Roseman (1984), C. A. Smith and Ellsworth (1985), R. S. Lazarus and Folkman (1984), and R. S. Lazarus et al. (1980). If one looks at emotion theory historically, and takes a broad view of cognitivism, one sees that a cognitive tradition has existed for a few thousand years. Ellis would be quick to acknowledge the older philosophical, cognitive approaches to emotion, since he cites many early philosophers as soulmates (see Ellis & Bernard, 1985a). Among therapists there are also early cognitive formulations in Horney (1937) and Adler (1927, 1929) and, of course, among the existentialists. Many other psychological writers could be said to be cognitively oriented but have not been explicit about applying that orientation to emotion.

My strategy for discussing RETs (or Ellis's) approach is first to identify the hallmarks of cognitive theories of emotion, as I see them, and then to test Ellis's thinking against them. Although mostly I refer to Albert Ellis as the progenitor and chief spokesperson of RET, it should also be noted that his collaborators and associates have played an important role in disseminating programmatic ideas, as illustrated by a book by Bernard and Joyce (1984) on RET with children and adolescents. Although Ellis does not write in the style familiar to psychologists who think in terms of variables, because he is clear in what he writes one has no difficulty making the translation into the more formal language of theory.

WHAT IS A COGNITIVE THEORY OF EMOTION?

Philosophers and psychologists have long juggled three facets of mind, motivation, cognition, and emotion, in their efforts to explain human and animal behavior and have conceived of their interrelationships in quite different ways (see Hilgard, 1980). One can, for example, treat them as separate faculties of the brain, each subject to its own rules of operation and capable of influencing the others (see R. S. Lazarus, Coyne, & Folkman, 1982); one can dismiss them as artificial constructions, or disclaim their independence and argue that their separation is tantamount to psychopathology. And if one treats each facet as separate, then the ordering of their mutual influence expresses quite different psychodynamic emphases. One can, for example, examine how emotions affect thoughts and desires, or, alternatively, how thoughts affect emotions; one function can even be subsumed under another, as when motivation is regarded as essentially cognitive and its directional aspects rather than its energetics are emphasized.

Those who adopt a cognitive approach regard emotion as a response to personal meaning, which comes down to judgments about oneself and the world. Different judgments result in different emotional qualities and intensities. Cognitive theorists have always regarded emotions, as Sartre (1948) and Heidegger (1962) did, as expressions of how one apprehends one's place in the environment. They differ, however, in how meaning is produced psychologically, and whether cognitive activity is regarded as a necessary or simply sufficient condition of emotion.

My own theory utilizes two concepts, cognitive appraisal and coping, which constitute for me the basic concepts necessary to understand the psychodynamics of an emotional reaction. Certain metatheoretical ideas are also important; these include transaction and process, which make emotions responsive to the situational context and, therefore, give them the capacity for flux. I summarize these ideas briefly before moving on to Ellis's position and current controversies about cognition–emotion relationships.

Cognitive Appraisal

Appraisal has become a widely used term to refer to evaluative judgments about events. However, use of this term is often careless and fails to distinguish between two related but different cognitive processes, knowledge and appraisal. Knowledge refers to understanding or beliefs about what is going on. In order to survive and flourish we must have knowledge that is reasonably accurate. Cognitive psychologists try to discover how we obtain and process observations from the environment.

Appraisal is an evaluation of knowledge, an additional step required to convert knowledge of the world into its personal significance. To act adaptively we need both observations about what is happening, knowledge about how it affects us, and decisions about whether and how to react to it. As such, appraisal is a kind of meaning (Kreitler & Kreitler, 1976). Appraisal of the significance of an encounter for one's well-being is an essential feature of emotion. The first blush of emotion occurs at the point of this appraisal, its content and intensity reflecting the initial, sometimes hasty, evaluation of the appraised significance of the transaction; following this, coping and further reappraisals may change the emotional state as the transactional flow and cognitive–emotional activity continue.

Coping

One of the major shortcomings of emotion theory is an absence of systematic concern with the coping process. This conceptual lack applies not just to RET but to emotion theory in general, even when it is cognitively oriented. A possible reason for this is the long tradition of associating coping with psychological stress. Although stress theory overlaps extensively with emotion theory, psychologists have created two separate literatures for stress and emotion, and the overlap has not always been appreciated. Another reason is that psychology has long treated coping as a response to emotion rather than a causal factor, as when the presence of anxiety as a drive is said to activate conditioned instrumental or ego-defensive processes (Dollard & Miller, 1950). In contrast with this view, my colleagues and I have been arguing (R. S. Lazarus, 1966; R. S. Lazarus & Folkman, 1984) that the coping process generated by the appraisal of harm, threat, or challenge can modify the original appraisal and thus change the subsequent emotional state. Indeed, much of the flux in emotion stems from coping processes that precede the emotion and change the terms of the troubled or potentially troubled relationship between a person and the environment and the way it is appraised.

In our writings (e.g., R. S. Lazarus & Folkman, 1984) we have distinguished between two major functions of coping, problem-focused and emotion-focused. The former involves actions to modify the environment or one's behavior toward it; this can change the actual person-environment relationship, and, thereby, the appraisal of its significance and the emotional state. In contrast, emotion-focused coping does not affect the actual relationship, but it can indirectly affect the emotions generated by it either by modifying the pattern of attention (as in avoidance) or by modifying the appraised meaning of the relationship (as in denial or distancing); when this succeeds, it changes the way the person thinks about what is happening—although the realities have not changed—and so a change in the emotional reaction must follow. Because emotion-focused coping depends mainly on cognitive processes, we also call it *cognitive coping*. Since the two functions of coping, like appraisal itself, mediate between the encounter and the emotional reaction, a theory of emotion cannot afford to ignore the coping process.

Transaction and Process

Two crucial ideas are expressed in these terms. *Transaction* means that emotions are the result of constantly changing two-way encounters with an environment. An emotion usually involves ongoing commerce with another person. Although an emotion can occur in the physical absence of other persons, what is being appraised is usually a relationship with others, its memory and implications triggered by something in the present.

Neither the environmental nor the internal event is sufficient by itself to explain an emotional reaction; an emotion reflects the joint contribution of both. Thus, appraisals of harm or benefit, threat or challenge do not depend solely on qualities of the person or on qualities of the environment; they are transactional concepts which reflect and require the interplay of both. This is the core meaning of transaction as opposed to interaction. In interaction, the separate sources of variance remain independent and can be decomposed; transaction, on the other hand, takes the interplay of two systems, the person and the environment, to a higher order of analysis (as in threat or challenge) in which the whole cannot be taken as equal to the sum of its parts any more than a bodily organ is describable simply as a collection of individual cells. An organ, such as a stomach, operates as an organized system of cells whose identities give way to a new set of coordinated functions characteristic only of the stomach. These functions cannot be predicted from the cellular level but can only be understood top-down, by reference to the organizing principle or principles.

Process expresses the idea that emotion is always in flux temporally and across diverse encounters. Although people may tend to respond with a similar kind or intensity of emotion, one characteristic of emotion is that today—or in this situational context—the person feels angry, but tomorrow—or in that situational context—the person feels happy, proud, or guilty. Furthermore, in the same situational context a person may feel angry today, yet feel proud, happy, or guilty tomorrow. In other words, not only is emotion related to the situation, but it is also related to the inner state of the person in that situation, which may vary within an individual as a result of physiological factors, mood swings, and outlook.[1]

Emphasis on the flux of emotion, based on a changing person–environment relationship, turns us toward contextualism (Pepper, 1942; Sarbin, 1985). Emotions arise from particular kinds of encounters and they change over time and from encounter to encounter depending on the dramatis personae of the moment. This feature of emotions, as *situated actions*, has been emphasized by Sarbin (1985):

> To avoid involvement in futile controversies centering on the question "what is emotion?" it would be better to take a slice of life, a specific episode in the lives of people. The questions to be asked are like those of the reporter of the news. Who are the principal actors? What did they do? Where? What were the surrounding circumstances? What are the features of the setting that instigate or maintain concrete acts? etc. Suppose we observe the conduct of Mr. Smith who is the object of Mr. Jones' gesture of insult. If Mr. Smith has been acculturated to the concept "insult," to the meaning of the gesture as communicating "insult," and if he has the epistemic skill to make a judgment about the intentions of Mr. Jones, then he is faced with a problem of maintaining self-respect (because insult is by definition a degradation of identity). At the same time that Smith formed the concept of insult, he learned also that retaliation or punishment was an integral part of the concept, and that the appropriate response was the enactment of a specified role vis-a-vis Jones, namely, *anger*. (pp. 8–9).

We must also recognize that the concepts Sarbin speaks of as learned are influenced by innate tendencies as well, a position emphasized by those interested in the phylogenesis of emotion. No matter how humans are raised, they will have some tendency to experience anger whenever they have been insulted. In some degree these tendencies have to do with innate neurophysiological characteristics onto which are grafted the individual and cultural experiences that affect the meaning of social transactions.[1]

Certain emotions can also be regular occurrences for a particular person; such recurrences are a feature of a life plot in which there are consistent themes, roles, and motives. If we emphasize stable person properties and

---

[1]This paragraph, and a few others similarly footnoted, are examples of additions to the manuscript, sometimes stated in a fashion quite close to the way he put it, that came from my correspondence with Ellis about drafts of this chapter.

recurrent emotions, we nicely capture sameness and perhaps pathology (irrationality) but lose the novelty, context, and flux with which any theory of emotion must also grapple. However, if we emphasize the contextual quality, we capture the flux of emotional encounters but lose the story line of the actor. Neither outlook is sufficient in itself to permit a total understanding of our emotional lives. A theory of emotion must be able to handle both stability and flux with equal virtuosity.

Emotion is, I believe, best regarded as a system of interdependent variables that consist of person and environmental *antecedents, mediating processes* such as appraisal and coping, and *multileveled response* patterns that include action impulses, emotional thoughts (often referred to as *affects*), and physiological changes. What is happening to these variables is constantly changing and depends on the transactions of each moment. The task of emotion theory and research is to spell out their pathways of influence in the emotion process (R. S. Lazarus & Folkman, 1984; R. S. Lazarus, DeLongis, Folkman, & Gruen, 1985).

The basic variables for a complete theory of emotion and a comprehensive language include how we read situations (appraisals), the goals and wishes of the person, the person's beliefs or assumptions about life, and the counterproductive coping decisions that get the person into trouble. They need to be woven into an analytic system in such a way as to permit us to understand intraindividual emotional flux as well as interindividual emotional variation. A theory of emotion must address many other difficult issues about how the emotion process works, its developmental origins, the definitional boundaries of emotion concepts, the social and cultural factors that shape both the long-term character of the person's emotional life and the immediate contextual influences, and the role of expressive and physiological changes in emotion. To facilitate comparison between Ellis's and my approach, the above system is schematized in Figure 4.1.

ELLIS'S PERSPECTIVE ON EMOTION

Ellis is without a doubt a cognitivist. From the start he has argued that beliefs about oneself and the world shape emotions (Ellis, 1957c, 1958a). His dominant interest has been irrational beliefs and the disturbed emotions and dysfunctions they create. He conceives of treatment as the process of getting the troubled person to reevaluate irrational beliefs. This conception is expressed as follows (Ellis & Bernard, 1985b, p. 5):

The main subgoals of RET consist of helping people to think more rationally (scientifically, clearly, flexibly); to feel more appropriately; and

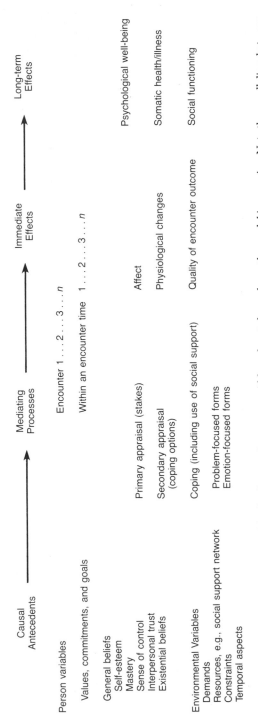

Figure 4.1 Illustrative system variables for the emotion process. Although not shown here, the model is recursive. Note the parallelism between long-term and immediate effects.

to act more functionally (efficiently, undefeatingly) in order to achieve their goals of living longer and more happily. Consequently, RET defines rationality, appropriate feeling, and functional behavior in terms of these basic goals; and it tries to be as precise as it can be about these definitions.

What does Ellis mean by rational or irrational thoughts and feelings? The key principle is that rational feelings help us live longer and more happily because they help us in achieving goals and avoiding contradictory or self-defeating activities. Some negative feelings (e.g., sorrow, regret, annoyance, frustration, and displeasure) are appropriate reactions when goals are blocked and frustrated, because the premises on which they are based are rational. Other negative feelings (e.g., depression, anxiety, despair, and worthlessness) are inappropriate reactions because the premises on which they are based are irrational and they make obnoxious conditions and frustrations worse. Some positive feelings (e.g., love, happiness, pleasure, and curiosity) are appropriate when goals are realized, and they increase human longevity and satisfaction. Other positive feelings (e.g., grandiosity, hostility, and paranoia) are inappropriate because they are based on faulty premises and although they might make people feel good in the short run, sooner or later they lead to interpersonal conflict, ill-considered risk-taking, homicides, and wars. All human goals are appropriate even when they are not easily fulfilled, but all absolutistic commands, demands, insistencies, and musts are inappropriate and self-sabotaging.

How do emotional disturbances arise? The process involves an activating event, thought, or memory (A) that either helps people achieve their goals or blocks them. The emotional disturbance is generated by cognitions (B) about this event which strongly influence the cognitive, emotional, and behavioral consequences (C). In effect, B's or cognitions about A, what is happening, serve as mediators of C, the disturbed emotional response, in the classic S–O–R pattern of modern neobehaviorism. Thus, three basic sets of variables are causally implicated in Ellis's view of emotion: a goal disposition, an encounter with the environment that either thwarts or facilitates goal attainment, and expectations and interpretations of what is happening.

Among these three sets of variables, Ellis has paid the most attention to the cognitive, that is, the beliefs that cause dysfunctional emotions and behavior. They include thoughts present in awareness, thoughts not in immediate awareness, and general beliefs that constitute the assumptive framework by which people appraise what is happening to them and form conclusions about it. Some beliefs are inherently irrational. They fall into three major categories (Ellis & Bernard, 1985b, pp. 10–11): (1) I must do well and win approval, or else I am a rotten person; (2) others must treat me considerately and kindly in precisely the way I want or they should be severely damned and punished; and (3) conditions under which I live must enable me to get what I want comfortably, quickly, and easily, and to get nothing I don't want. A more detailed list of the 12 famous irrational beliefs that are regarded as pathogenic had been published very early (Ellis, 1958a).

Irrationality does not stem from erroneous reasoning about the encounter with the environment, but from errors in the basic assumptions people carry around as features of their personalities. They are erroneous because they trap the person into inappropriate negative and positive emotions. This is, of course, circular reasoning because irrationality is defined largely by the negative outcome, namely, emotional disturbance and dysfunction, and this negative outcome is explained by the offending assumptions. Ellis concedes (personal communication) that one can be illogical and unrealistic without necessarily being disturbed. He maintains, however, that it is almost impossible to cling inflexibly to absolutistic musts, to use his language, without being emotionally disturbed or behaviorally dysfunctional. Rigidity is thus a prescription for emotional and adaptational disaster.

Beliefs, in Ellis's account (Ellis & Bernard, 1985b, p. 11), refer to "people's appraisals and evaluations of their interpretations, expectations, and inferences concerning reality." The usage is somewhat careless here because Ellis and Bernard fail to distinguish between generalized beliefs which people presumably carry around with them, contextual beliefs, and situational appraisals (see Folkman, 1984); the latter are influenced by the actual conditions being faced. Rotter's (1966, 1975) concept of *locus of control*, which consists of generalized expectancies, illustrates stable cognitive concepts that are analogous to Ellis's irrational beliefs or assumptions about life; Bandura's (1977b, 1982; Bandura & Adams, 1977) concept of *efficacy expectations* illustrates situational appraisals, which are characterized by variability across encounters.

Ellis also argues that the thinking involved in emotional disturbances is inherently self-defeating, and there are four common types of such thinking: (1) awfulizing; (2) I-can't-stand-it-itis; (3) self-worthlessness; and (4) other unrealistic overgeneralizations from a bad experience. These pathological and pathogenic ways of thinking overlap quite closely with Beck's (1976b) depressive cognitive styles. They also are a product of what Ellis calls *absolutistic should, ought,* or *must.* As Ellis says (personal communication),

If you treat me badly, I think that you should not and hence what you have done is awful. If, on the other hand, I thought it preferable that you not treat me this way, and that you have a perfect right to as a fallible human being, I would probably wind up by telling myself that bad treatment is unfortunate but not awful.

The problem is that the latter cognitive position is difficult to adopt and stick to.

How do Ellis's views on emotion compare with mine? The comparisons are threefold. First, Ellis's analysis of the ABC's of emotional disturbance adopts a traditional cognitive position in which there are precipitating events, thoughts and beliefs that pertain to them, and emotional and behavioral outcomes. Beliefs (and goals) are key person antecedents of the emotional reaction to an encounter. The person's appraisal of what happens in that encounter is a key part of the process whereby emotion is generated, and these appraisals are influenced by generalized beliefs. So far there seems to be basic agreement.

Second, although the ABCs of emotion seem to be transactional and process-centered, Ellis's main interests center not on process, that is, the changing emotional encounter per se, but on the stable, irrational beliefs that result in the recurrent, dysfunctional emotions for which treatment is indicated. These irrational beliefs are the main targets of RET; they should be vigorously disputed and the client induced to change them.

Third, as with most other cognitive theories of emotion except mine, no systematic attention is paid to the coping process, which must shape the emotional response by virtue of its effect on the realities of the person–environment relationship and/or a change in the meaning of what is happening. On the other hand, some of the cognitive techniques used in RET or formulated by the client seem geared to confidence building (e.g., "I thought to myself that if I just relaxed, I could do it"; "I know I am good enough to succeed") as well as distress reduction; they are also capable of strengthening positive emotions, which may have great value in sustaining the person under stress (R. S. Lazarus et al., 1980). There is also a significant overlap between Ellis's therapeutic concept of disputation and my emphasis on cognitive coping; RET clients are taught to dispute what seems to make them overly and irrationally upset, and to ask themselves, for example, "Why must I do very well?" "Where is it written that I am a bad person?" "Where is the evidence that I can't stand this?" Thus, certain kinds of cognitive coping are built into the RET method.

Nevertheless, as I have said, Ellis does not say much about the contextual processes of coping, whether effective or ineffective, though he has written brief comments about the hazards of teaching coping statements without showing people why these are rational and helpful (Ellis & Abrahms, 1978).

ELLIS AND THE COGNITION–EMOTION DEBATE

There is vigorous argument among emotion theorists about how to understand cognition–emotion relationships. The focus of this argument centers on three interlocking questions, the answers to which divide theorists into two broad camps that could be characterized as separatist and holist.

The first question concerns how the mind is organized: Are emotion and cognition best regarded as separate sets of processes or do they work as an organized unit? The second question concerns whether appraisal of the significance for one's well-being of what is happening in an encounter is a necessary or merely sufficient condition of an emotion. The third question is whether more than one mechanism is needed to encompass emotions in infants and infrahuman animals as well as in human adults.

Separatists, similar to the way Fodor (1983, 1985) views perception and cognition, are inclined to separate mental activity into independent systems. This is reminiscent of faculty psychology in the past (see Hilgard, 1980) and akin to the emphasis on localization of function in the brain in contrast to mass action. The wave of interest in split brain research (Fox & Davidson, 1984) is an example of separatism applied to emotion. A separatist might say, as Zajonc (1980, 1984) does, that "separate anatomical structures can be identified for affect and cognition" (1980, p. 119).

Separatists, perforce, answer the second question about whether appraisal is necessary to emotion in the negative. As Zajonc argues, emotion can come into being without cognitive activity and cognitive activity can occur without emotion. Rejection of the idea that appraisal is necessary to emotion is expressed clearly by Hoffman (1985): "We gain very little by postulating in advance, as Lazarus does, that cognitive evaluation is always necessary."

Separatists give a positive answer to the third question, arguing that an infant can experience emotions even before it is capable of engaging in cognitive appraisal. This position is taken by Izard (1978) and Leventhal (1984; Leventhal & Tomarken, 1986). Leventhal regards emotional processing in infants and young children as largely innate, and points to the newborn's receptivity to specialized social cues such as tone of voice and the human face. He writes that "The variety of expressive reactions produced just hours after birth provide fairly strong evidence to the preprogrammed nature of expression and its associated set of emotional experience, though evidence for the latter half of the assumption is lacking" (Leventhal, 1984, p. 275). The latter qualification is the standard reply of the holists to the claim that infants react with emotion before they can appraise the significance of environmental events. The holists point out that the early smile of the infant is not social at all but that in the first months of life it is a reflex and not an emotional response (Emde, 1984). Moreover, since cognitive appraisal can occur in primitive as well as complex, symbolic versions (R. S. Lazarus, 1986; LeDoux, 1986), it probably also occurs far earlier in life than is usually assumed by those who argue for hard-wired affect programs.

In contrast to separatists, holists argue that appraisal is a necessary condition of emotion. Meaning is said to underlie all emotion and is automatically available in every transaction with the environment. The significance of an encounter for well-being is apt to depend on the person's goals and how what happens affects the fate of these goals. From the holistic standpoint, separation of cognition and emotion is not a biological principle nor normative and occurs mainly in ego defense or disease. Models of the mind that depend on separation are therefore distortions of how things usually operate in healthy adults.

Buck (1985) has added an interesting idea to the debate by proposing that there may be more than one way of producing meaning. One is by a process he calls *analytic cognition*, which is the linear, sequential organization of digital information. The other, *syncretic cognition*, does not require a transformation of input but instead involves directly perceived analogue information. Syncretic cognition is surely closer to the process the holists are thinking of, which automatically draws on memory, belief, and motivation. The person's history and personal agendas create perceptual and attentional sets that yield an immediate sense of whether something is at stake in the encounter, whether it implies harm or benefit, and in what particular way. So we see that even if we regard personal meaning as the essential core of an emotion, we can entertain different conceptualizations of how that meaning is generated.

Who are some of the separatists and holists in emotion theory? Among the holists, some of whom are almost contemporary, we might number Lashley (1926), Sartre, Heidegger, and Dewey, and the best choice of neo-Freudians would be Adler. Among the more visible contemporary holists, present company excepted, are R. C. Solomon (1980), Heider (1958), Weiner (1985), Sarbin (1985), Epstein (1983), Roseman (1984), and De Rivera (1977, 1984). Separatist ancestors include Gall, Descartes, Cannon (1932, 1939), Darwin (1973), Spencer (1901), Comte (1893), and J. B. Watson (1930); one notes that many in this group are concerned with neurophysiology. With respect to current separatists, Zajonc (1980, 1984), Tomkins (1962, 1963, 1981), and Izard (1978) should surely be listed, and those whose work centers on split brain methodology, such as Fox and Davidson (1984); ironically, perhaps, the progenitor of split brain research,

Sperry (1982), should be excluded since he has argued that there is rapid integration between the hemispheres at a primitive neural level.

I am confident that Ellis belongs in the holist category. In a comment (Ellis, 1985a) about the Lazarus–Zajonc debate (R. S. Lazarus, 1982, 1984; Zajonc, 1980, 1984) in which he summarized his views about the relationship of cognition to emotion, he made the following points:

1. "Rarely, if ever, do disturbed emotions exist independently of cognitions" (p. 471). It is difficult to interpret "if ever"; on the one hand, it seems to suggest that there are exceptions that would undermine the argument that cognition is a necessary condition of emotion. On the other hand, "rarely" suggests that he regards these exceptions as possible but unlikely and unimportant, an interpretation he has confirmed in personal correspondence.

2. Thoughts and feelings affect each other. To this I would add the caution that since feelings always contain thoughts, the interaction is not that of two separate systems but is temporal, as when a feeling results in a change in a subsequent thought.

3. When people change the way they think their feelings also change.

4. Not all thoughts that affect feelings are conscious; many are unconscious, but these usually can be brought into consciousness so that they can then be changed; this seems similar to Freud's view of treatment as making what is unconscious conscious. RET stresses, however, that most unconscious thinking is easily brought into consciousness if we look for it.

5. When emotional disturbances, such as depression, are precipitated by physiological processes, the latter always interact with cognitions, which is another way to say that cognitions are always involved.

6. Although RET attempts to treat emotional disturbances by changing cognitive activity, these attempts are more effective when supplemented with efforts at changing behavior and emotions.

R. S. Lazarus and Folkman (1984) have noted the latter point in reviewing cognitive behavior therapies; despite the central role of cognitive activity in cognitive therapies, their strategies of change are *multimodal*, to use Arnold Lazarus's (1981) term. Few if any cognitively oriented therapists today, including Ellis, restrict themselves to attempts to change only cognitive activity, regardless of what they say programmatically about cognition as the basis of disturbed emotion and psychopathology. Many, such as Wachtel (1977), would say that intellectual insight alone is inadequate to produce therapeutic change and must be supplemented by behavioral struggles that involve distress in order to generate emotional insight.

I believe Ellis would accept the assertion that there is one basic cognitive mechanism of human emotion, though he waffles a bit on this (probably he learned as I have that one must always be wary of words like *always* and *never*). He has informed me that he believes there could be a few minor exceptions to this rule.

I have found two places in Ellis's writing in which his holistic ideas are stated clearly and forcefully. The first is a reply to R. M. Schwartz's (1984) review of conceptual issues in cognitive–behavior modification. There Ellis (1984, p. 216) wrote,

> RET assumes that human thinking and emotion are *not* two disparate or different processes, but that they significantly overlap and are in some respects, for all practical purposes, essentially the same thing. Like the two other basic life processes, sensing and moving, they are integrally integrated and never can be seen wholly apart from each other. Instead, then of saying that "Smith thinks about this problem," we should more accurately say that "Smith senses–moves–feels–THINKS about this problem."

In the above comment Ellis quoted himself from Chapter 2 of *Reason and Emotion in Psychotherapy* (Ellis, 1962). However, the holist stance is evident in even his earliest writings on RET. In an article that, he tells me, several clinical journals of the day showed no interest in, he wrote (Ellis, 1958a, p. 2),

> It is hypothesized, then, that thinking and emotion are closely inter-related and at times differ mainly in that thinking is a more tranquil, less somatically involved (or, at least, perceived), and less activity-directed mode of discrimination than is emotion. It is also hypothesized that among adult humans raised in a social culture thinking and emoting are so closely interrelated that they usually accompany each other, act in a circular cause-and-effect relationship, and in certain (though hardly all) respects are essentially the *same thing*, so that one's thinking *becomes* one's emotion and emoting *becomes* one's thought.

Ellis's insistence that unconscious processes are accessible to therapeutic inquiry is an antidote to the Freudian iceberg analogy that most of the mind is unconscious and inaccessible. It is also a useful device for assuring clients that they can exert control over their emotions rather than being defeated by an interminable search for the wellsprings of their troubles. One can visualize a continuum of emphasis or deemphasis on unconscious processes among clinically oriented theorists ranging from the Freudian stance to the other extreme in which unconscious processes are either denied or considered epistemologically incapable of disconfirmation. In any case, Ellis thinks that although most of our basic disturbance-creating outlooks, especially our musts, are outside of awareness, they can easily be brought into view in the interests of producing therapeutic change.

THE RELATIONAL ASPECTS OF EMOTION

I said earlier that the essence of a cognitive approach is that emotion is a response to judgments and beliefs about oneself and the world. The thoughts that underlie emotions are not just any thoughts but are always about a relationship between the person and the environment which is relevant to well-being. For all intents and purposes, relationship and transaction are interchangeable concepts, though the former emphasizes more the confluence and organic unity of person and environment whereas the latter emphasizes the dynamic interplay of both sets of variables. If the relationship is judged by the person as harmful, then the emotion will be a negative one. If the relationship is judged as beneficial, then the emotion will be a positive one. Each emotion quality expresses the specific way in which the person feels harmed or benefited. An important task of emotion theory and research is to examine the chapter and verse of this *cognitive–relational principle.*

On what basis can people be harmed or benefited? The answer must lie in individual, cultural, or species characteristics, and in the diverse conditions of our lives which arise from our habitat. The most important individual characteristics consist of values and goal hierarchies, especially those to which we have become committed. This is the *motivational principle,* which means that because harms and benefits are defined by the strength and patterning of our goals, one person will be greatly threatened in a situation in which another person will be pleased or indifferent. Actually, Ellis's treatment of irrational belief is as much motivational as it is cognitive in that such beliefs center on what people think they want and have. He writes, for example (Ellis & Bernard, 1985b, p. 6),

> Appropriate negative feelings are defined in RET as those emotions that tend to occur when human desires and preferences are blocked and frustrated.... Appropriate positive emotions result when particular goals or ideals are realized and when human preferences and desires are satisfied.... One of the main assumptions of RET is that virtually all human preferences, desires, wishes, and longings are appropriate, even when they are not easily fulfillable; but that practically all absolutistic commands, demands, insistences, and musts, as well as the impositions on oneself and others that usually accompany them, are inappropriate and usually self-sabotaging.

The cognitions relevant to emotions consist, in effect, of appraisals about how the person is faring in the world with respect to long- and short-term goals. How well do the person's appraisals match what is actually happening and its implications? Ellis is concerned largely with the irrational and stable assumptions that lead again and again to inappropriate and hence dysfunctional emotions; these assumptions are more or less fixed in contrast with the flux of moment-to-moment appraisals of how things are going, and they constantly affect the appraisals. It is, of course, irrational in some sense to have beliefs that make us feel bad when there is no good reason to, but at the same time, if we have inflexible beliefs about what should be true, or if our goals are unreasonable and foolish, then failure to gratify them will make us feel bad, which is not illogical given the premises under which we are operating.

As Sarbin (1985) puts it,

> Contrary to the traditional view that emotional behavior is by defini-
> tion irrational, identity roles follow a logic. It is the logic built into the
> self-narrative that dictates the course of action. The logic is the plot of
> the story, the origins of which are not necessarily remembered. Just as
> we may criticize a novel because the acts of the protagonist are not con-
> sistent with the plot structure, so may we criticize dramatic role enact-
> ments as appropriate or stupid, well-conceived or reckless, wise or
> idiotic. It is not until a narrative episode is concluded that a critic can
> evaluate the effects of the enactments. (pp. 17–18)

RET does not tell us much about the garden-variety process of emotion generation or the accuracy of the person's appraisals of daily encounters with the environment. In addition to stable beliefs that affect recurrent or characteristic emotional responses, we need a set of principles about how the person goes about judging how things are going at any given moment.

Although Ellis does not provide such principles, he does acknowledge in personal correspondence that there are different degrees to which people hold irrational beliefs, and that irrational negative beliefs such as "I must do well, or else I will be worthless" are apt to begin with a rational negative belief, for example, "I would highly prefer to do well, or else I will suffer disadvantages." Ellis's assumption is that people easily and frequently jump from a weak and more or less rational version to a strong or rigidly irrational version. The person's difficulties begin when rational negative beliefs escalate to irrational negative extremes, which are the basis for recurrent emotional disturbance and dysfunction.

Ellis and I began our professional lives during a period of psychology's history in which there was a vigorous debate about the nature of percep-
tion. Classical perception theorists were preoccupied with how it is that people perceive the environment the way it is. After all, to survive we have to be pretty accurate about what we see, hear, smell, and so on, and about the inferences we draw from this. Efforts to examine this cognitive

activity had three characteristics: They were normative in that the focus was placed on how people in general perceived the world; they were veridical in that the interest lay in the match between knowledge, action, and the objective environment; and they were cold rather than hot, meaning there was little interest in emotionally relevant environmental displays.

During the 1950s, however, personality, social, and clinical psychologists also became interested in perception and began to ask a different question, namely, how it was that each of us perceives the same environmental display differently. Their "new look" theoretical and research efforts were centered on individual differences rather than being normative, as in classical efforts; instead of being veridical in emphasis, the new look interest lay in distortions of reality produced by defense mechanisms, personal needs and goals, and individual differences in cognitive styles; and they dealt with hot perceptions rather than cold, that is, conditions of personal importance to the person doing the perceiving, hence potentially emotional. Although both approaches to cognitive activity addressed legitimate sets of concerns, they were never integrated into a common perception or cognitive theory (see F. H. Allport, 1955). The gap between them remains, though one finds occasional voices attempting to bring cognition and emotion together (Bower, 1981; Erdelyi, 1974; Neisser, 1967).

How can the above difference in approach to perception and cognition be reconciled? We must identify to what extent and in what respects information about matters relevant to well-being, and how it is appraised, depends on environmental realities and person factors. Above all we need principles about how these two sources of information are brought together and integrated in emotion-relevant meaning.

Neither Ellis nor I take the purely phenomenological position that meaning lies exclusively in the eye of the beholder or that merely thinking something makes it so. From a purely phenomenological standpoint, what occurs objectively in the environment is of no interest. On the other hand, neither of us would say that meaning lies completely in the objective stimulus configuration or that our adaptational task is solely to fathom the external order of things by means of cognitive activity. We both know that survival as a species, or as individuals, would not be possible if our appraisals were in poor fit with the environmental realities, or, for that matter, with our personal agendas. Therefore, the primary task of appraisal is to integrate what is in the objective world with our personal requirements for living without going overboard in the direction of personal agendas (which is tantamount to autism), or in the direction of the environment (which is to abandon our personal identity).

Ellis shows he subscribes to such a balanced view by distinguishing between appropriate and inappropriate emotions and yet by supporting the legitimacy of personal goals and wishes. Nevertheless, he emphasizes the importance of reality testing, which is a strong traditional clinical value. He does not subscribe to the theory of the positive value of emotion-focused coping (e.g., denial and illusion) by means of which, as I have argued (R. S. Lazarus, 1983), even psychologically sound people regulate their feelings when nothing can be done to change negative conditions of life. More than I, Ellis wants people to be relentlessly realistic in the way they see things as the best guarantee of psychological soundness.

CONCLUDING SUMMARY AND CRITIQUE

It would be stretching things to say that Albert Ellis has presented a fully elaborated theory of emotion. Probably no one has. However, he has provided the beginnings of such a theory, a programmatic statement for which we often use the modest phrase "toward a theory," which involves a set of useful basic principles about the pathology of the emotional life and how to correct it. These principles must be expanded and constantly tested against observations if we are to achieve the full understanding to which we aspire. Studies have shown, for example, that people who are more disturbed tend to acknowledge having more irrational beliefs than those who are not disturbed (Baisden, 1980), and there have been other efforts to test RET principles (Ellis & Whiteley, 1979). What is most lacking in Ellis's writing, however, is a close examination of how the emotion process works.

Beliefs that shape emotional dysfunction, as Ellis discusses them, are largely static, structural variables rather than processes that are in flux from encounter to encounter and moment to moment. Ellis does recognize that beliefs are also contextual. In recent correspondence he gives as an example, "I like your being nice to me and dislike your not treating me fairly; and I like a lot of money and dislike a little money." Then he adds that beliefs such as these also must have an implicit context, since a person would rarely say, "I must have you act unfairly to me and I must not have you treat me fairly"; nor would a person be apt to say, "I must not have a lot of money and must have a little money." However, beliefs, even when contextually appropriate, have a tendency to escalate into fairly static, structural variables, and this very rigidity or absolutism is what makes them irrational and hence self-defeating. Thus, although Ellis concurs with a view of emotion as transactional, and he has said so quite early (Ellis, 1958a), this is not where his therapeutic emphasis lies.

Stability is, perforce, the core of Ellis's vision of psychopathology and dysfunction; he wants to explain why people mess up their lives, are unhappy, and keep on doing and being so; he wants to help such people manage their lives better. Knowing that a person has a seemingly insatiable need for love, to use Horney's (1937) phrase, or that certain people believe they are not worthy unless constantly approved of or admired, to use Ellis's language, help them understand what is wrong in their emotional lives. We need to know this to help people straighten out their lives. Nevertheless, to explain the content and intensities of emotions requires examination of the changing transactions which lead them to be sometimes anxious, angry, sad, guilty, joyful, happy, loving, relieved, and so on. Although stable beliefs contribute importantly to psychopathology and recurrent distress, they cannot provide an explanation of this flux. What is also needed is a way to explain the emotions of the moment, and the appraisals that account for them.

Ellis responded to this point in a very interesting way in a letter:

> RET could go into examining the changing transactions leading to disturbed emotions more than it does. But the question might then be raised: Would it then be a more adequate *explanation* of what is going on—and a less effective *therapy*? It could be argued that RET is efficient partly *because* it glosses over many *affecting* and *appraising* processes and mainly focuses on what may well be the more important *essences* of disturbance—musturbatory thinking. This would be a fascinating hypothesis to investigate!

The issue of stability versus flux also points up a general problem that arises from using psychopathology as the starting point for general theory. One begins with an attempt to explain problem behavior and dysfunctional emotions. However, in making it apply to other kinds of functioning, the theory gets overextended: The focus on disorder or dysfunction underemphasizes the extent to which even in troubled people there are large areas of healthy functioning, which one neglects to describe and to explain how they work. There is a limit to what one can understand about healthy emotions from the standpoint of the pathological.

Pathology-centered analyses also leave us without a clear borderline between an affective disorder and appropriate distress. The concept of disorder is often overextended to include all instances of distress (see R. S. Lazarus, 1985). Although Ellis distinguishes between appropriate and inappropriate emotional reactions, I remain somewhat unclear about how this might work. Rather than put this as a criticism, which would not really be fair, it seems more useful to point up the problem for all of us to ponder.

Much dysphoric or depressed mood is thoroughly justified by the changing circumstances of a person's life, for example, loss of loved ones, sickness, and the loss of roles and functions in aging which once helped make life attractive. To be depressed about this, perhaps even angry, is not disorder unless one wants to argue, ironically, that health requires keeping a stiff upper lip in the face of adversity or engaging in positive thinking (or denial), whereas sickness is giving in to reality. The medical model, very commonly applied to depression, also creates a disposition to regard recurrent or chronic emotional distress as a biological disease without ever actually pointing to diseased tissue. Ellis is not prone to this kind of pathology-centered reduction.

If we use the word *pathology* as a metaphor rather than as signifying actual tissue disease, is it appropriate to see dysphoric affect, such as depression, as pathological? Surely depression, brought about by severe loss, cannot be considered pathological per se, though one could argue as Ellis does that when one's expectations are unreasonable the person is vulnerable to depression and this should be corrected by changing the expectations. Nevertheless, a person who has had much and who loses it does not have unreasonable expectations, though that person will ultimately have to scale these expectations back in the face of the new reality. This is what normal grieving presumably entails.

This line of reasoning takes us to the following conclusion: Depression is not inherently pathological but only becomes so when the person is unable to accept the new reality comfortably (see also Klinger, 1975). Time is therefore a critical criterion of pathology. How long the process, which we call grieving, should take, and how long the distress should last, is difficult to say (it seems to take longer normatively than it was once thought); obviously, the longer it takes the more prolonged is the impairment of the quality of life.

This points to a second criterion of pathology, namely, that even though depression or other dysphoric moods are not by definition pathological, they often have very destructive consequences such as the inability to function adequately in social and work roles, or damaging spinoffs such as alcohol abuse and suicide.

Therefore, these two criteria, the duration of the distress and its destructive consequences, constitute what is mainly pathological about so-called mood disorders without regard to their mechanisms. In seeking explanations one should look either for neurophysiological diseases that might be genetic, or for patterns of thinking that increase or sustain the person's vulnerability, or both. In any case, distressing emotions, per se, should not be thought of as pathological, especially if they have some justification in the actual conditions of life.

Theorists and practitioners need to be more precise when using the terms *pathology* and *disorder*. These terms are constantly used without concern about the boundaries and limitations (e.g., Depue & Monroe, 1986). We are also probably on a sounder basis when we substitute the words *inadequate wisdom* or *suboptimal coping* for the word *disorder*. We seldom gain by using the latter term, or by implying it by other words, when we wish to help troubled people.

Ellis wisely seems to avoid the term *disorder* but seems to embrace its functional implication in the concepts of irrationality and dysfunction. In his correspondence about this chapter, he distinguished between disorder and pathology by saying that all humans are biologically inclined to order their lives in a self-defeating way, in other words, to display disorder. Since we all do it, we should not call this pathology, except when disorder occurs in the extreme, as in severe depression. Ellis also believes that humans are biologically inclined to actualize themselves and to reorder things when they are disordered. When this tendency is not present or is minimal, we could call it pathology.[2]

Ellis's system of thought also contains many values that call for examination. I like these values, but it is important to question them. For example, how should we judge well-being? Should we take into account how happy people say they are, or is happiness irrelevant? Is positive thinking a proper end in itself, or can even a misanthrope make some claim to psychological health? Should we consider the success with which the person has used his or her resources to achieve personal or social ends? How should we qualify an assessment of success in life by the opportunities or lack of opportunities in the social structure that either block or facilitate it? Should we regard psychological health as a continuum or, as has often been suggested, a qualitatively different condition than its absence? These issues need careful examination.

The danger I see in RET is not that it contains anything particularly egregious but that it could come close to being an unquestioned system, a kind of cult, with protagonists and users who may stop thinking about important issues of both science and value. Knowledge can only advance through attempts to evaluate the utility of the questions we ask and the validity of the answers that emerge. RET can add to knowledge by seeking further to systematize its concepts and constantly testing them against clinical and research observation. This would guarantee that it remained a vigorous, dynamic approach to emotion and the treatment of dysfunction long after its founder could no longer guide its fortunes.

---

[2]This paragraph, and a few others similarly footnoted, are examples of additions to the manuscript, sometimes stated in a fashion quite close to the way he put it, that came from my correspondence with Ellis about drafts of this chapter.

An Evaluation of the Rational–Emotive Theory of Psychotherapy

Michael J. Mahoney
William J. Lyddon
Darlys J. Alford

INTRODUCTION

The impact of cognitive theories and therapies upon contemporary approaches to personal development and human change processes has been substantial (Beck, 1985; Cormier & Cormier, 1985; Guidano & Liotti, 1983, 1985; Hollon & Kriss, 1984; Kendall, 1983; Mahoney, in press-a, in press-b; Mahoney & Freeman, 1985; Meichenbaum, 1985; Reda & Mahoney, 1984; Stone, 1982; Werner, 1984). A significant force which has helped to establish cognitive therapies as a viable approach to psychological services has been rational–emotive therapy (RET) as developed by Albert Ellis (Ellis, 1958a, 1962, 1973, 1985b; Ellis & Grieger, 1977; Ellis & Whitely, 1979). Since the late 1950s the pioneering efforts of Albert Ellis have served to inspire the trend toward more cognitively oriented methods and have established RET as one of the most prominent and popular approaches to counseling and psychotherapy.

Ellis's support for a critical appraisal of RET is commendable, particularly in view of the divergent perspectives represented by the contributors to

69

the present volume. Critical evaluation is essential to continued development and refinement of theory. To quote Weimer (1980),

> Criticism, as the essence of rationality, is a rhetorical process that never
> seeks final form or ultimate proof. Instead it seeks to articulate and assess
> the merits of a position within its unique context, and both the nature
> of the position and the form of the criticism are likely to change as a
> result of that articulation and assessment. (p. 386)

It is within this spirit of pan-critical rationalism (Bartley, 1962) that the
present appraisal of RET theory is offered. Following a brief historical overview of some of the significant strands of influence that have helped to
shape contemporary rationalist approaches to psychotherapy and human
change processes, this chapter (1) outlines the basic theoretical assumptions and assertions about human change as set forth by RET in its original
and expanded forms; (2) evaluates the current adequacy of RET as a theory
of psychotherapy; and (3) proposes a number of challenges and issues
facing RET and its future theoretical and practical development in late
twentieth-century psychology.

BASIC ASSUMPTIONS AND ASSERTIONS
ABOUT HUMAN CHANGE

Historical Contexts

> The intellect, by its native strength, makes for itself intellectual
> instruments, whereby it acquires strength for performing other intellec-
> tual operations, and from these operations gets again fresh instruments,
> or the power of pushing its investigations further, and thus gradually
> proceeds till it reaches the summit of wisdom. (Spinoza, cited in Randall
> & Buchler, 1960, p. 76)

Classical Rationalism

The general contours of traditional rationalist philosophy are founded
in the belief that knowledge emerges from self-evident, a priori truths that
are independent of experience with the world. In addition to the domains
of logical and mathematical analyses, these "truths" most importantly
include those which are thought to derive from the analysis of the *cogito*—
that class of truths which constitute the power of reason and knowledge
of the contents of the conscious mind (Collins, 1985). This view, epitomized
by classical rationalists like Descartes, Spinoza, Leibniz, and Kant, draws
a primary distinction between thought and experience and assumes

thought to be superior to sense and most powerful in determining experience. The idea that the intellect is more powerful than perceptual experience has appealed to practitioners and clients of psychotherapy for centuries.

Aristotelian Logic

Some of the earliest roots of rationalist ideology may also be traced to the philosophy of Aristotle. As Coulter (1977) has documented, Aristotelian logic and cause-and-effect relations have formed the cornerstone of rationalist approaches to therapeutic method. The Aristotelian system of therapeutics described symptoms and treatment in terms of various opposing qualities, the hot, the cold, the wet, the dry, or a combination thereof. Once a diagnosis was made, determination of the appropriate treatment was logically deduced to be the one with the opposite quality. This "contrary medicine" was later reflected in the medical practice of seventeenth-century latrochemists and latromechanists. While the former substituted laboratory chemistry ("acids" and "alkalines") for Aristotelian symptom-treatment qualities, the latter viewed the human organism as a mechanical (hydraulic) system. Latromechanical specialists ascribed disorders to "obstructions" in the veins and arteries and selected medicines on their ability to "dissolve" these hypothesized obstructions. Contemporary medical interventions designed to counteract certain microorganisms believed to be causally related to various disease states are a recent expression of rationalist therapeutic doctrines (Coulter, 1977; Weil, 1983).

Rationalist approaches to psychotherapy have followed a similar path in developing the view that intense negative emotions are symptomatic of disorder and psychopathology. According to this view, emotional equilibrium and order may be reestablished through appropriate "contrary" interventions designed to counteract, eliminate, or control specific behaviors and thoughts presumed to be causally related to such disorganizing emotional expressions. While mainstream behaviorally oriented rationalists have tended to intervene at a behavioral level (e.g., counter-conditioning, reinforcement of competing responses, punishment of undesirable behavior), cognitively oriented rationalists have focused upon changing beliefs and thoughts (e.g., covert conditioning, self-instructional training, cognitive restructuring).

The "Mind-Cure Movement"

At the turn of the century, the seeds of contemporary cognitively oriented rationalist approaches to counseling and psychotherapy were evident in what William James described as the *mind-cure movement*. This popular movement echoed the early Stoic philosophies of Epictetus and Marcus Aurelius and looked to the power of optimistic thought and healthy-minded attitudes as being the primary path toward happiness in human affairs. Commenting on the proponents of this "religion of healthy mindedness," James (1902/1958) noted, "The leaders in this faith have had an intuitive belief in the all-saving power of healthy-minded attitudes as such, in the conquering efficacy of courage, hope, and trust, and a correlative contempt for doubt, fear, worry, and all nervously precautionary states of mind" (p. 84). Advocating the inherent "curative" power of "positive," "right," and "rational" thinking, the progeny of this early movement include a number of influential writers and thinkers: Du Bois (1906, 1908, 1911), Coué (1922), Bain (1928), Carnegie (1948), Maltz (1960), and Peale (1960). Perhaps no single contemporary theory has done more to further advance the rationalist approach to psychological counseling, however, than the rational–emotive theory of Albert Ellis (Mahoney, in press-a,b).

Ellis and the Original ABC Model

Originally outlined as a "reformulation of the basic principles of psychoanalysis" (Ellis, 1956) and termed *rational psychotherapy* (Ellis, 1958a), the first formal statements of the rational–emotive model (Ellis, 1962, 1971b, 1973) provided an explicit formulation of the hypothesized role of irrational beliefs as mediating the relationship between environmental events and emotional distress. The basic postulate in these early presentations is expressed by Ellis's ABC model of the relationship among perception, cognitive judgment, and behavioral–affective reactions.

According to this model, individuals filter their perceptions of particular activating life events, activities, or agents (A) through the beliefs (B) they hold about themselves and the world which, in turn, lead to the experience of a variety of emotional and behavioral consequences (C). Within this linear ABC formulation, points B and C are further subdivided into rational and irrational categories. According to Ellis (1973), a rational belief (rB) about A is a reasonable or logical interpretation that "can be supported by empirical data and is appropriate to the reality that is occurring, or that may occur, at point A" (p. 57). It is this "realistic" evaluation that is thought to be associated with an appropriate rational consequence (rC) characterized by healthy, well-adjusted emotion and behavior. In contrast, an irrational belief (iB) lacks empirical support, is inappropriate to the ongoing reality, and is associated with dysfunctional emotion and behavior, or an irrational consequence (iC). The cognitive–evaluative emphasis of Ellis's conceptualization of emotion essentially embraces Arnold's (1960,

1970) cognitive appraisal of emotion theory. Ellis (1962) states, "Much of what we call emotion is nothing more nor less than a certain kind—a biased, prejudiced, or strongly evaluative kind—of thought" (p. 41). Accordingly, a client's feelings of rejection, anxiety, worthlessness, or depression represent "disturbed," "neurotic," or "overreactive" symptoms instantiated and maintained by his or her own belief system. At least two different lists of specific iBs presumed to constitute one's potential repertoire of irrational self-statements have been set forth in these earlier formulations of RET (Ellis, 1962; Ellis & Harper, 1975). A causal relationship between iBs and iCs has also been explicitly advanced:

> These are the premises that *literally cause* them [clients] to feel and behave badly; that they keep endlessly reiterating to themselves without effectively challenging; and that they must persistently in theory and practice work, and work, and work still harder against to disbelieve if they are ever to overcome their basic anxiety and hostility. (Ellis, 1973, p. 153, emphasis added)

Two basic assumptions about human change processes emerge from Ellis's original ABC model:

1. the assertion that thought can rule feeling and action (founded in the philosophical tradition of the Stoics, particularly Epictetus)
2. the assumption that emotional distress, disorder, and dysfunction reflect instances of "irrational" thinking (which lie at the heart of most psychological disturbance)

The logical therapeutic implication of these foundational premises entails treating unreason with reason. Representationally, the ABC model is extended to include D–Es, whereby the primary goal of RET is to teach clients to identify and dispute (D) the irrational and illogical notions that underlie their disturbing symptoms in order to arrive at point E, a set of sensible cognitive effects (cEs) and appropriate behavioral effects (bEs). Congruent with the "contrary" doctrines of rationalist therapeutics (Coulter, 1977), the principal task of the RET therapist is to extirpate the basic cause of the client's emotional difficulty through methods designed to oppose and counter his or her irrational belief system. According to Ellis (1962), the rational–emotive therapist engages in a concerted attack on the client's irrational philosophies by serving as a "frank counter-propagandist" who forthrightly contradicts and denies the illogical and self-defeating beliefs that the client has learned and continues to employ (p. 95). In Ellis's words, the client "must continually—and I mean *continually*—question and challenge and uproot this negative thinking until it really—and I mean *really*—is killed off" (p. 357).

Although the therapist–client relationship itself and various empathic-supportive and insight-interpretive methods are acknowledged as playing a part in RET, such relationship-enhancing techniques are viewed as secondary to the more active and directive methods—logic and reason, suggestion, teaching, deindoctrination, indoctrination, persuasion, and confrontation—that have become the hallmark of RET. In describing his personal approach, Ellis (1973) states,

> I am deliberately not very warm or personal with my clients, even those who crave and ask for such warmth, since, as I quickly explain to them, their main problem is usually that they think they need to be loved, when they actually do not; and I am there to teach them that they can get along very well in this world *without* necessarily being approved or loved by others. I therefore refuse to cater particularly to their sick love demands. (p. 155)

While the original ABC formulation of RET emphasizes cognition, reason, and verbal persuasion, it also recognizes the importance of "motor counterpropagandizing" activity (Ellis, 1962). As a result, the RET therapist actively tries to persuade, cajole, and occasionally insist that the client perform specific homework assignments of a behavioral nature as an integral part of the therapeutic process.

The Expanded Model

The growth and popularity of RET has been accompanied by a trend involving a continuing elaboration of the model itself and of the therapeutic techniques incorporated into the model (Dryden, 1984a; Dryden & Ellis, 1988; Ellis, 1977b, 1980d, 1984b, 1984e, 1985b; Ellis & Grieger, 1977; Ellis & Whitely, 1979; Maultsby, 1984; R. L. Wessler, 1984). Ellis (1977b) has presented 32 clinical and personality hypotheses which he suggests are fundamental to RET and other modes of cognitive–behavior therapy. Although this "expanded" model remains consistent in its commitment to the central role of iBs as mediators of emotional disturbance, its practical utility and heuristic value have been questioned. The most salient criticisms have suggested that this elaboration of rational–emotive theory and practice is exceedingly vague and general, contains few specific and disconfirmable hypotheses, and incorporates such a wide spectrum of behavior change methods that it bears little correspondence to the original model (Ewart & Thoresen, 1977; A. A. Lazarus, 1979; Mahoney, 1977a; Meichenbaum, 1977b). In responding to his critics, Ellis (1977c) contends that his theory exists in an "elegant" and "inelegant" form. According to Ellis, elegant or specialized RET is the preferential form and corresponds to his initial theoretical formulation, while the inelegant version is more general in nature, nonpreferential, and is essentially thought to be synonymous with broad-based cognitive–behavior therapy (CBT).

Ellis (1980d) has further differentiated these two forms of RET by outlining some of the major cognitive, behavioral, and emotive differences between specialized RET and CBT (or general RET). According to Ellis, some of the features that distinguish specialized RET from CBT are that the former has a distinct philosophic emphasis, contains an existential–humanistic outlook, favors long-lasting rather than symptomatic change, strives to eliminate all client self-ratings, stresses "antimusturbatory" rather than antiempirical disputing methods, recognizes the role of secondary and tertiary symptoms in emotional distress, discriminates between appropriate and inappropriate negative emotions, uses vigorous and forceful interventions to counteract irrational philosophies and behaviors, employs punishment as well as reinforcement procedures, and favors the use of *in vivo* desensitization and flooding methods rather than gradual desensitization strategies.

Recent Formulations of iBs

Elaborations of RET theory have been associated with evolving conceptualizations of iBs. Ellis (1985b) has recently defined iBs as "those cognitions, ideas, and philosophies that sabatoge and block people's fulfilling their basic or most important Goals" (p. 314). According to RET theory, the most basic rational human goals include (1) staying alive and (2) being reasonably happy and free from pain while alive. It is apparent that irrationality and rationality are not defined in any absolute sense in RET theory. In addition, rather than providing a list of specific irrational beliefs, recent presentations of RET theory have offered a number of categories of irrational thinking which subsume specific exemplars of self-statements (Dryden & Ellis, in press; Ellis, 1984a, 1985b). Perhaps the broadest categorical distinction Ellis makes (1984a) is among *cold cognitions* (nonevaluative inferences and conclusions), *warm cognitions* (preferential and nonpreferential evaluations), and *hot cognitions* (absolutistic and necessitous evaluations). Couched in the form of dogmatic *musts, have to's, got to's, shoulds,* and *oughts,* it is this latter category of evaluative hot cognitions that are posited to lead to most emotional disturbances characterized by intense feelings of anxiety, depression, inadequacy, rage, grandiosity, and manic states. Common cognitive derivatives of such highly evaluative thinking include the subcategories of disturbed ideas (e.g., awfulizing, I-can't-stand-it-itis, and damnation) and logical errors and unrealistic inferences (e.g., all-or-none thinking, jumping to conclusions and negative non sequiters, fortune telling, focusing on the negative, disqualifying the positive, minimization, emotional reasoning, labeling and overgeneralization, and perfectionism).

While Ellis's subcategories of evaluative thinking are distinctly similar to the cognitive distortions advanced by other cognitive therapists (Beck, Rush, Shaw, & Emery, 1979; Burns, 1980), it is an emphasis upon the musturbatory ideation of the client that is thought to uniquely define RET and set it apart from other cognitive approaches:

> The essence of human emotional disturbance, according to RET, consists of the absolutistic *musts* and *must nots* that people think *about* their failure, *about* their rejections, *about* their poor treatment by others, and *about* life's frustrations and losses. RET therefore differs from other cognitive-behavior therapies. . . in that it particularly stresses therapists looking for client's dogmatic unconditional *musts*, differentiating them from their preferences, and teaching them how to surrender the former and retain the latter. (Dryden & Ellis, in press)

Dryden and Ellis emphasize that client adherence to a philosophy of musturbation is at the core of most psychological disturbance while a philosophy of relativism or desiring is a central feature of psychological health.

A Cognitive Primacy or an Interactionist Theory?

One issue that has become a focus of debate is whether RET may be better conceptualized as a cognitive primacy or an interactionist theory of personality and human change (Ellis, 1984c; R. M. Schwartz, 1982, 1984). In a recent review of conceptual issues in cognitive–behavior modification, R. M. Schwartz (1982) has endorsed a unified–interactional approach to therapeutic theory and practice that incorporates a reciprocally interactive or multicausal view of cognition, behavior, and affect. While Schwartz's interactionist position represents an articulation of a relatively recent trend in psychology toward integration and reciprocal determinism (Arnkoff, 1980; Bandura, 1978; A. A. Lazarus, 1971, 1976; R. S. Lazarus, Averil, & Opton, 1973; Mahoney, 1977a; Meichenbaum & Butler, 1980; Staats, 1981), his analysis does not include Ellis and RET as being representative of this view. Rather, according to Schwartz, RET may most adequately be described as a cognitive primacist theory of personality and human change. Ellis (1984b) has objected to being placed in the cognitive primacy fold and has suggested that RET has embraced a unified–interactionist position since its inception. Ellis contends that although RET does hypothesize a central role for irrational beliefs in the creation of emotional and behavioral disturbance, it has always been an integrated cognitive–affective–behavioral theory:

Because humans are innately predisposed to think, emote, and behave interactionally, and virtually never disparately, they rarely make and sustain fundamental cognitive changes unless they also forcefully (and usually uncomfortably) work on their feelings and unless they consistently (and also uncomfortably) practice, practice, and practice new behaviors. RET—which is not idly named rational-*emotive* therapy—therefore stresses cognitive, affective, and behavioral techniques and encourages therapists often (not always) to present these techniques in an active-directive, encouraging manner. (Ellis, 1984b, p. 217)

In a reply to Ellis, R. M. Schwartz (1984) contends that while Ellis in principle may claim an interactive position, an examination of his basic tenets justifies the cognitive primacist stamp. As Schwartz points out, 14 of the 16 etiological hypotheses set forth by Ellis (1977b) place cognition in the role of independent variable and emphasize its causal and/or mediating role in affective (Hypotheses 1 and 3), behavioral (Hypotheses 2, 4, and 9), behavioral and affective (Hypotheses 5, 10, and 11), and physiological (Hypothesis 7) domains as well as being the prime mover in emotional disturbance (Hypotheses 12, 13, 14, 15, and 16). The remaining two hypotheses include a general interactional statement (Hypothesis 6) and a statement concerning the effect of innate characteristics on behavior and affect (Hypothesis 8). Schwartz notes that not a single specific hypothesis delineating a causal role for either affect or behavior is contained within these core tenets. Based on this finding and examination of Ellis's (1971b) verbatim transcripts which reveal an almost exclusive focus on the self-statements, beliefs, and philosophical positions of the client, R. M. Schwartz (1984) concludes,

Despite the inclusion of a general interactive statement, the lack of specific hypotheses that place affect or behavior in a primary role suggests that RET is in actuality a cognitive primacy theory with a formally undeveloped interactionist stance. This position tends to result in unicausal analyses of a cognitive primacy nature, to reduce affect to cognition, thus discouraging further conceptual distinctions, and to limit therapeutic practice by promoting a "uniformity myth." (p. 224)

Recent accounts of RET theory have acknowledged the shortcomings of the ABC model and have begun to espouse a position which views cognition, emotion, and behavior as highly interdependent and interactive psychological processes. However, as Dryden and Ellis (in press) contend,

A model which emphasizes the interactive and interdependent nature of intrapsychic and interpersonal processes does not have to take the position that all have equal explanatory variance in accounting for human psychological disturbance. Indeed, RET has become renowned for the central role it has given to cognition in general and to evaluative beliefs in particular in its theory and practice.

Although Ellis's recent acknowledgments of the complexities in causation and treatment represent a step away from billiard ball determinism and unicausal analyses (Ellis, 1984a, 1984b, 1984c, 1985b), it would appear that RET's emphasis is clearly cognitive in both theory and practice.

ADEQUACY OF RET AS A THEORY OF PSYCHOTHERAPY

We begin our evaluation of RET theory by summarizing what we believe to be its foundational assertions about human change processes. Following a discussion of some of the philosophical and epistemological limits of these basic premises, an appraisal of RET's current empirical status is offered. We conclude our critical assessment with a practical and less formal exploration of the popular appeal of RET.

Foundational Assertions about Change Processes

1. *Rational supremacy and explicit awareness.* Perhaps the most basic premise of RET is that of *rational supremacy,* the assertion that behavioral and emotive processes can and, in most cases, should be governed or controlled by rational thought (Mahoney, in press-a, in press-b; Mahoney & Nezworski, 1985). It is clear from Ellis's writings that this ''governance through reason'' is accomplished by making a client aware of his or her self-statements, actively evaluating their logical implications, and consciously restructuring the irrational beliefs to reflect reality. Ellis would be the first to argue that most people are not explicitly cognizant of their irrational thoughts and that explicit conceptual awareness of such self statements is one prerequisite for change. Thus RET's emphasis on cognitive content rather than process and surface structure particulars rather than deep structure personal meanings seems to clearly set it apart from other cognitive approaches of a more structural nature (Guidano, 1984, 1987; Guidano & Liotti, 1983; Mahoney, 1988a, 1988b).

2. *Argumentation and rationalist interventionism.* Argumentation as a method of arriving at the ''truth'' has a long and influential history in our judicial system and is Ellis's primary technique in therapy. Because irrational beliefs are thought to be the basis of human distress and a restructuring of them the apparent solution, a logical argumentative approach seems sensible. A reliance on the therapist's abilities to recognize irrational thinking processes and to actively intervene and persuade clients to change their thoughts from irrational to rational is an essential feature of RET.

3. *"Negative" emotions as problems.* Ellis's view of negative emotions is one shared by most rationalist approaches to psychotherapy (Mahoney, in press-a, in press-b). In essence, negative and intense feelings are perceived as problems to be controlled and/or eliminated. In RET terms, if no obvious precipitating catastrophic event is evident, such distress is thought to be clearly dysfunctional and indicative of certain perceptual–cognitive errors on the part of the client. Conversely, when negative emotions are not present, one might assume that the person is in control and, therefore, psychologically healthy.

The Limits and Legacies of Rationalism

Reappraisals of the Nature of Rationality

An increasing recognition of the complexities associated with the study of psychological and social phenomena has been accompanied by a philosophical and epistemological view that suggests that there are inherent constraints upon the nature of our knowledge and ultimately upon formal rationality itself (Hayek, 1952, 1964, 1967, 1982; Weimer, 1982, in press-a). One such limitation is intimately tied to the degree of explanation available when studying complex phenomena. The distinction here is between what Weimer (1982), in his overview of the theoretical and philosophical essays of Friedrich von Hayek, has termed *explanation of the particular* and *explanation of the principle*. He notes that while the successes of the physical sciences have been a function of their ability to explain and predict the particulars of simple phenomena deductively subsumed under cause-and-effect laws, this approach to science is not applicable to the realm of complex phenomena whose understanding is confined to a more abstract level of explanation—explanation of the principle. In other words, it is explanation of the general, abstract principle (as opposed to the precise particular) that provides the context of constraint which not only delimits the understanding that one may expect to attain in a given domain of complex phenomena (e.g., the nervous system, psychological, social, and cultural phenomena), but also questions the viability of imposing any form of rational planning and centralized control upon a complex system.

This latter conclusion is based upon the argument that because it is not possible to know all the relevant information in a dynamic, complex system, such a system is not subject to rationalized plans of intervention and control (Weimer, 1982). Furthermore, Hayek (1967) has argued that the desire to subject human affairs to rational control, rather than exemplifying the maximal use of reason, actually represents

an abuse of reason based on a misconception of its powers, and in the end leads to a destruction of that free interplay of many minds on which the growth of reason nourishes itself. True rational insight seems indeed to indicate that one of the most important uses is the recognition of the proper limits of rational control. (p. 93)

Another constraint upon human knowing and knowing processes concerns the limited role of conscious thought in human experience and the fundamental primacy of unconscious, tacit processes (Guidano & Liotti, 1983, 1985; Hayek, 1952, 1964, 1982; Mahoney, 1980b, in press-a, in press-b; Polanyi, 1958, 1966; Weimer, 1977, 1982). This difference has been explicitly represented by a number of philosophers, in particular James (1890) and B. Russell (1945), who differentiated between *knowledge by description* (or explicit, propositional knowledge) and *knowledge by acquaintance* (or tacit, procedural knowledge). Polanyi (1966) has pointed out that because "we can know more than we can tell" (p. 6), most knowledge is tacit rather than explicit. The primacy of the tacit realm is revealed in all domains of human experience and action. Whether motoric, perceptual, or conceptual in nature, the common denominator is our inability to fully explicate how we accomplish such acts. As Weimer (1982) asserts, "Our consciousness and explicit awareness, and the rationality that depends upon them, are a thin veneer upon the tacit dimension that, although it operates according to complex rules of determination, *is not consciously rational*" (p. 245). Contrary to traditional conceptions of rationality which assume that it must be explicitly and consciously specifiable, Weimer (in press-b) has argued that "rationality in complex orders is never fully explicit nor instantly specifiable."

Challenges to Rationalist Interventionism

The constraints imposed upon our knowledge and conscious rationality by explanation of the principle and the role of tacit processes in human and social affairs hold clear implications for the practice of counseling and psychotherapy. Because no counselor or psychotherapist can ever come to know or predict all the relevant particulars of a client's life, therapeutic interventions with an algorithm to modify clients' thinking and behavior toward preconceived ends are doomed to experience limited success (Weimer, 1982). As Weimer (in press-b) contends,

In the complexity of our unpredictable world no instant rational assessment is possible—*rationality emerges only in the long run as a result of following abstract rules* that provide a context of constraint in terms of which we cope with the unknown and unforeseen.... Rationality (the task of being rational) is a means, a never-ending or standing obligation, not an end. It is a matter of following general principles in the constant flux of unanticipated occurrences—not a matter of specifying in advance particular ends to achieve.

Thus, rather than prescribing rational particulars (specific and explicit thoughts, beliefs, and self-statements) for the client with the purpose of somehow inoculating him or her to the vicissitudes of life experience, the core argument here is for the rationality of helping clients generate for themselves very general and abstract principles that can be applied to an indefinite number of particular problems they may encounter (Burrell, 1987). Central to this metacognitive perspective is also an inherent trust in the directionality and rationality of a client's tacit processes and in the wisdom and self-knowledge that may be culled through a process of self-exploration and personal discovery within a therapeutic context that respects the unique personal and social realities construed by the client (Guidano, 1987; Guidano & Liotti, 1983, 1985; Mahoney, 1988a, 1988b). Such a view clearly points to the potential "tyranny of technique" (Mahoney, 1986; Raimy, 1975) and challenges the prudence of rationalist intervention into open and dynamic complex systems, of which the psychotherapeutic relationship is but one obvious example (Mahoney, 1988a, 1988b).

An Alternative View of Negative Emotions

Emotions have often been defined as biologically primitive mechanisms or evolutionary residuals that have a functionless, disorganizing effect on goal-directed behavior (Kuiper & MacDonald, 1983). This view of emotions may have contributed to Ellis's belief that "negative emotions such as depression, anxiety, anger and guilt are almost always unnecessary to human life" (Ellis, 1962, p. 52). Research in neurobiology has indicated that lower and midbrain structures are, indeed, pervasively involved in emotional processes, but the evidence does not suggest that emotions, negative or otherwise, are unnecessary (Melzack & Casey, 1970; Plutchik, 1977; Plutchik & Kellerman, 1980; Pribram, 1970; Scherer & Ekman, 1984; Stanley-Jones, 1970). On the contrary, the extant theory and research point to emotional processes as critically important elements in phylogenetic and ontogenetic development (Arnold, 1970; Candland et al., 1977; Costello, 1976; Plutchik, 1966, 1970, 1984). From a developmental perspective, emotions serve as primitive and powerful "knowing processes" and, as Costello (1976) points out, ought to be considered important evolutionary developments in their own right.

Guidano (1987) and Mahoney (1988a, 1988b) have begun to describe the functional and adaptive role that emotional intensity may play in human developmental processes. According to their presentations, intense feelings are indicative of a significant shift away from affective equilibrium which may be associated with an identifiable stressor (although sometimes no apparent stressor is present). If such disequilibrium (affective disorder) is sufficiently intense or persistent, it may motivate (literally "move") the individual to seek equilibration through his or her available coping skills. If emotional equilibrium is reestablished, the episode is over and life returns to "business as usual." If the individual's attempts to cope and reequilibrate are unsuccessful, however, a personal crisis may ensue (Mahoney, 1980b). The typical scenario then entails cycles or waves of emotional, cognitive, and behavioral disorder. Some individuals become stuck or entrenched in these repetitive cycles, presumably due to limitations in their resources and abilities for psychological reorganization. A successful resolution of this dilemma requires the emergence of higher-order knowing structures that are capable of accommodating the challenges associated with the ongoing crisis. As this transformational reorganization evolves—and it often involves substantial time, experience, and distress—the individual emerges as more differentiated and developed. A new and more complex level of emotional equilibrium is established and maintained until the next lifespan episode of disorder.

The views proposed by Guidano and Mahoney describe a process of psychological reorganization that differs dramatically from Ellis's restructuring of irrational beliefs. Whereas Ellis has emphasized replacement of surface structure content and the elimination of negative emotions, these constructivists propose a dynamic and highly personal emergence of innovations in cognitive development which result from a complex functional interdependence between varying emotional intensities and deep structural cognitive transformations.

RET and the Rhetoric of Science

Appeals to Evidence and Evidence of Appeals

The first attempted demonstration of the utility of rational psychotherapy was provided by Ellis (1957b) in a review of his own effectiveness as a therapist during three different phases of his professional career in which he consecutively practiced within orthodox psychoanalysis, directive psychodynamic, and rational modes. An examination of client records revealed that each successive shift in orientation was associated with both an increased improvement rate among clients and shorter therapy time. Despite its serious methodological flaws (e.g., a lack of experimental controls for incremental development of therapeutic skills, therapist's differential expectancy about the three approaches, and the use of sub-jective and changing criteria of improvement), Ellis has cited this study as both supportive of his original statement of a 90% improvement rate for clients treated for 10 sessions or more with rational therapy (Ellis, 1962, p. 38) and indicative of a controlled experimental study demonstrating RET's clinical effectiveness (Ellis, 1971b, p. 11).

While such claims clearly demonstrate Ellis's personal enthusiasm and desire to scientifically justify RET, they do not unequivocally establish the clinical viability of RET. Indeed, one of the most salient features characteriz-ing debates about the scientific status of RET has been the glaring discrepancy between the enthusiastic claims made for its clinical efficacy by its proponents and the dearth of compelling evidence for its basic tenets cited by its critics. The following quotes illustrate the degree of these disagreements:

> Of all the scores of methods that are variously advocated and employed, RT is probably one of the *most effective* techniques that has yet to be invented. (Ellis, 1962, p. 119)

> The rational–emotive approach to psychotherapy is not only unusually effective clinically but it is now backed by a considerable amount of experimental evidence which almost consistently supports its phenomenological tenets and indicates that human emotions and behavior are enormously influenced by cognitions. . . . There is clinical, experimental, and other support for rational–emotive therapy. (Ellis, 1973, p. 27)

> Experimental research evaluating the efficacy of [RET] has been sparse, methodologically poor, and summarily modest in its implications. . . . This, of course, means that the clinical efficacy of RET has yet to be ade-quately demonstrated. (Mahoney, 1974, p. 182)

> A vast amount of research data exists, most of which tend to confirm the major clinical and personality hypotheses of RET. (Ellis, 1977b, p. 2)

> We simply cannot accept Ellis' claim that his methods are supported by large numbers of well designed, scientific studies. While this can be said for some of the hypotheses he offers. . . most of the RET statements offered are very ambiguously related to research data or are not sup-ported at all. This is particularly true for those aspects of RET that do not overlap other cognitive behavior therapies (e.g., the emphasis on rational disputation as the primary means to effect change). (Ewart & Thoresen, 1977, p. 55)

> A growing body of literature in many related areas. . .does provide

support for the efficacy of the rational–emotive psychotherapy approach. (DiGiuseppe & Miller, 1977, pp. 88–89)

Considering the mixed results and limitations regarding the few experimental studies of RET using clinical populations, the lack of internal validity in unsystematic case studies, and the lack of demonstrated external validity of analogue studies, the clinical efficacy of RET has yet to be adequately demonstrated. (Zettle & Hayes, 1980, p. 161)

RET. . .strives to state its basic theoretical constructs in testable ways. . . . Because its theories are relatively simple, direct, and clear, they have been subjected to literally hundreds of controlled scientific experiments which have largely tended to support them. (Ellis, 1984a, p. 20)

The theory of RET is insufficient because of formal and empirical reasons; the concept of rationality is ambiguous; the definitions of appropriate and inappropriate emotions are based on circular reasoning; the analogy between the process of uncovering and disputing irrational beliefs and the methods of science is rather weak. Rational–emotive therapy is not very rational itself. I doubt if a slight modification of the theory of RET is sufficient to correct its anomalies. (Eschenroeder, 1982, p. 389)

It is our conclusion that the degree of support for basic hypotheses of the [RET] model is not consistent with the popularity and purported effectiveness of the therapeutic procedures. (T. W. Smith & Allred, 1986, p. 65)

Although it is not uncommon to find divergent interpretations of data by competing perspectives in science, it is less common to encounter such disparate views about the existence of those data. In our opinion, experimental data documenting the efficacy of RET are not considerable, vast, or consistent, and they do not warrant the strong claims asserted by Ellis. The fact remains, however, that RET has grown in visibility and practice since the early 1960s. If this growth cannot be attributed to its demonstrated empirical warrant, how can it be explained?

What Is the Appeal of RET?

One of the appeals of RET may be its simple format and clear-cut methods. According to Ellis (1962), the fundamental procedures of RET are clearly detailed and may be easily taught to any open-minded therapist. In fact, he states that "a good deal of the *modus operandi* of RT is more clear-cut and specifiable than most schools of therapy" (p. 337). We agree that therapists, especially therapists in training, who face complex dilemmas in their daily practice might, indeed, find the straightforward structure of RET appealing. RET imposes its ABC structure on nearly any situation so that it becomes more manageable for all involved. The practitioner can memorize a list of irrational beliefs and begin identifying iBs from the very first session. Logically arguing with clients about their beliefs provides the therapist with a perpetual strategy of intervention. Moreover, this approach to counseling may ostensibly simplify the often troublesome problem of client resistance (Ellis, 1985d). Since RET specifies that the true source of resistance lies within the client's beliefs, the therapist can strategically side with the client to actively combat his or her irrationality rather than explore sources of fear that often accompany personal change.

The procedural methodology of RET is not only clearly specifiable, but it also reflects a very basic, *formistic* thinking style (Pepper, 1942) which may be appealing to therapists and clients alike. According to Pepper, formistic thinking is essentially categorical in nature; things and events are classified in a binary, either–or fashion. Similarly, RET separates thoughts and emotions into two distinct categories: rational/irrational thoughts and positive/negative emotions. The separation of experience into these dichotomous classes constitutes a rudimentary kind of thinking that is ironically similar to the cognitive errors often challenged by RET. The reliance of RET on a formistic style of thinking may be particularly attractive to clients who feel overwhelmed by their emotions or circumstances and are presented with the clean and logical explanation that irrational thoughts lead to negative feelings and rational thoughts bring about emotional relief. The simplicity of the explanation is very powerful and seductively attractive to the distressed client. Compared with other cognitive techniques which require the client to explore the source of their emotions, identify the problem, investigate information from their environment, generate possible solutions, take action often involving interaction with other people, and then evaluate their own successes and failures, RET is much less complicated for the client. The tendency to look for the cognitive shortcuts is referred to in social psychology as the *cognitive miser* perspective (Fiske & Taylor, 1984). There is considerable evidence that people often compromise thorough investigations of their environment and opt for speed and efficiency rather than engage in cognitive work.

The current focus on cognition in psychology is unfortunately associated with an almost exclusive emphasis on the thinking process of the individual and an accompanying deemphasis on the interpersonal quality of human experience. RET is no exception. The RET client is told that the emotional difficulties they are currently experiencing are essentially "all in your head." Even though many of those seeking psychotherapy are experiencing interpersonal problems, the solution presented in RET is intrapersonal in nature. The intrapersonal approach to solving inter-personal problems, although logically questionable, presents certain advantages to the client and the therapist. It obviates, for example, the need for significant others to join the client in therapy. Rather, the client may adjust certain thoughts with the guidance of the therapist and resolve the problem singularly. The inadequacy or powerlessness the client may have been experiencing in negotiating the intricacies of interdependent relationships is replaced with a sense of accomplishment in making rational thought adjustments. The shift away from changing the relation-ship to changing the self may, indeed, result in a lessening of pressure that brings about dramatic changes in the relationship. This process may confirm the client's belief that the resultant change was due to the simple replacement of irrational thoughts rather than to complex changes in the dynamic properties of the relationship as a system.

Another factor that may help account for the popularity of RET is its eclectic incorporation of diverse therapeutic techniques. Over the years Ellis has integrated a wide range of cognitive, behavioral, and emotive techniques into the practice of generic RET. As a result of this technical infusion, RET may have garnered a broad base of support from other pro-fessionals who endorse these various techniques. While serving to shade the distinctions between RET and cognitive–behavioral therapy, this expan-sion, nonetheless, may have brought many new converts into the RET fold. This expansion of RET may have also provided its own practitioners with more flexibility to deal with a broader range of problems and thereby increased their confidence in the merits of RET.

On a broader level of analysis, these numerous and logically based prescriptions coupled with the directive, authoritative nature of RET, clearly find much appeal within the socially sanctioned role of therapist as healer and provider of specific curative remedies (Frank, 1974). The therapist's role of healer in society holds certain ramifications for clients: Their passive acceptance of the offered "remedies" facilitates the work-ings of the healer–patient model. There is evidence from the attribution literature that clients might be particularly susceptible to being told in a directive manner by the RET therapist the specific causes of their distress. Nisbett and Wilson (1977) suggest that people are rarely aware of the causes of their behavior but readily supply answers to "why" questions. The answer to "why" (for example, "Why do you feel upset?") is based on "implicit causal theories" or "judgments about the extent to which a par-ticular stimulus is a plausible cause of a given response" (Nisbett & Wilson, 1977, p. 231). When people are experiencing severe emotional upset and cannot provide a plausible cause, they are likely to seek professional assistance and be particularly susceptible to persuasive approaches which pinpoint the causes of their problem. For distressed clients, the explanation that irrational thoughts are the cause of negative emotions and that rational thoughts will bring about positive affect is quite plausible.

In summary, we suggest that a number of features associated with the current practice of RET may hold appeal for therapists and clients alike. These include

1. a high level of visibility and exposure
2. a clear and specifiable procedural format that can be easily learned and quickly put into practice
3. a formistic thinking style which reduces complex phenomena to simple, dichotomous categories
4. an emphasis on intrapersonal sources and solutions to a range of interpersonal difficulties
5. a significant degree of practical flexibility and professional support stemming from an incorporation of numerous cognitive, behavioral, and emotive techniques
6. a direct, persuasive, and authoritative approach that conforms to culturally sanctioned doctor–patient roles and
7. a plausible and ostensibly logical rationale regarding the etiology and logical remediation of human emotional distress.

RET AND THE FUTURE OF PSYCHOTHERAPY

RET and the History of Modern Psychotherapy

The history of modern psychotherapy has been rendered quite differently by various historians (e.g., Alexander & Selesnick, 1966; Ehrenwald, 1976; Ellenberger, 1970). The majority of these histographies fail to even mention RET and the cognitive therapies. This may not be surprising, however, given the relative recency of these approaches. More surprising perhaps is the failure of recent volumes on the ongoing cognitive revolution in psychology to acknowledge the clinical contributions to that development (e.g., Baars, 1986; H. Gardner, 1985). Modern handbooks of therapeutic approaches and practices rarely neglect the cognitive approaches, however, and some have even suggested that these cognitive perspectives may represent the wave of the future in psychotherapy. According to one recent analysis (Mahoney, 1988a), there are at least 18 different cognitive therapies. Moreover, a review of surveys of the theoretical preferences of American clinical psychologists between 1961 and 1982 suggests that cognitive psychotherapies represent the primary theoretical orientation of more than 10% of those who responded (and more than 20% of those who specified a theoretical preference rather than eclecticism).

When Abraham Maslow was helping to establish humanistic psychology as a viable approach to the conceptualization and facilitation of human experience, he referred to it as the "third force" in psychology. The first and second forces, of course, were psychoanalysis and behaviorism. These three fundamental approaches have spawned a host of differentiations, resulting in the 280 distinguishable versions of modern psychotherapy (Herink, 1980; Mahoney, in press-b). Recently, and some would say increasingly (Capra, 1983), there has been talk of a fourth force or a new paradigm in our views of ourselves and our worlds. Indeed, it is quite common for new perspectives to hail themselves as a major improvement on and a preferable alternative to the traditional views that dominate at any given time. Thus, claimants to the honor of being the new wave in psychological thinking include the cognitivists, transpersonalists, integrationists, and systems specialists. These and other emerging themes represent an "essential tension" (Kuhn, 1977), the perennial tension that characterizes the relationship between changing and unchanging aspects of an open, developing system.

In our opinion, there is little doubt that Albert Ellis and RET should, in future histories, be given substantial credit for helping to pioneer the formal resurgence of cognitive perspectives in late twentieth-century psychology. Ellis's contributions join those associated with Beck's (1976a) cognitive therapy and the collective cognitive–behavioral contributions of such people as Bandura (1977a), Breger (1977), Davison (Davison, Feldman, & Osborn, 1984; Davison, Robin, & Johnson, 1983), D'Zurilla (1988), Goldfried (1982), Hollon (Hollon & Beck, 1986), Kendall (1983, 1984), A. A. Lazarus (1971, 1976), Mahoney (1980a), Marlatt (Marlatt & Gordon, 1985), Meichenbaum (1977), and Raimy (1975). What is less clear, however, is the overall direction these cognitive perspectives are taking us. It has taken more than a century, but there is now both conceptual and empirical warrant for the assertion that human experience, whatever its content and "feel," involves mediational or representational (cognitive) processes.

Issues in the Development of Future Psychotherapies

The therapies of the immediate future seem to be converging on a few transtheoretical themes that reflect basic assumptions about human nature and human change (Goldfried, 1980b, 1982; Mahoney, in press-b; Prochaska, 1984). Practitioners of these therapies are beginning to acknowledge the importance of understanding fundamental principles and processes in psychological change. An example is the growing acknowledgment of Jerome Frank's (1985) emphasis of the 3 R's of helping—rationales, rituals, and relationships. The available data suggest that our theoretical orientations (rationales) and our therapeutic techniques (rituals) are far less important in predicting successful outcome than are the client's psychological characteristics and the quality of the attachment (relationship) between client and counselor (Bergin & Lambert, 1978). Another example of the growing emphasis on basic principles and processes is the transtheoretical acknowledgment that novelty and novel experience play an important role in successful psychotherapy (Goldfried, 1980b). There is, in this sense, a legitimately "meta" aspect to emerging psychotherapies, and a corresponding interest in what features are shared by purportedly different perspectives.

Even though our theoretical orientations may not contribute as much to the outcome variance as our individual personalities and the quality of the relationships we develop with our clients, conceptual and theoretical issues continue to influence what we do and how we approach our work as helpers. In reviewing the array of 280 modern psychotherapies and the changing popularity of the major schools, it is clear that conceptual and practical issues influence what is practiced. Complex, esoteric, and abstract theories, for example, are less popular than simple, mundane, and concrete approaches. Likewise, models that offer clear, prescriptive, and teleological techniques tend to be more popular than those that do not. This suggests, among other things, that the complex-systems approaches may face an uphill battle in the teaching and training of professional helpers. Complexity is not easily taught and is even less readily translated into practical dimensions. Thus, it would appear that simple, concrete, and prescriptive approaches are more likely to enjoy popularity than their more complex, abstract, and proscriptive counterparts. This trend or tradition is relevant to our appraisal of RET in the light of future psychotherapies.

To the extent that psychotherapies of the future continue to reflect a valuation of simplicity and concrete, how-to-do-it perspectives—in other words, to the extent that future psychotherapies continue to endorse what have been called "rational interventionist metatheories" (Hayek, 1978, 1982; Weimer, 1982, in press-a)—Albert Ellis and RET will have a secure place. So long as counseling and therapy apprentices long for a monolithic system of rationales and rituals, RET will remain a major contender. Insofar as future psychotherapies acknowledge the importance of personal beliefs in quality of living, RET will continue to be credited with a pioneering contribution. All of these assertions may appear to be warrantable predictions about the futures of RET and psychotherapy. Whether RET will survive as a formal and distinguishable system, however, is another question, and its specificity requires a corresponding degree of caution in our conjectures.

From our perspective, RET is a modern expression of the ancient philosophies of rationalism and Stoicism. The rationalism is perhaps most apparent in the contention that thoughts are capable of influencing feelings and actions. "As you think, so shall you feel" is the assertion, and negative affect is considered to be the result of faulty thinking. It is, indeed, the nature and function of this thinking that determines the quality of one's life. This is the fundamental assertion of classical rationalism, which propagates the belief that thought is superior to sense. The pioneer of this theme in Western civilization is Pythagoras (Aristotle, Kant, Plato, and Socrates were all Pythagoreans). In elevating the intellect to a position above the realms of sensory/affective experience and volitional action, rationalism came to express the tacit assumption of cerebral primacy that continues to pervade multidisciplinary models of human development (Gould, 1977). This assumption is usually expressed in the idea that the brain leads and dominates the body and, in the classically rationalist version, that the higher (rational, logical, symbolic) brain processes can and should direct their more primitive counterparts (feeling, sensing, and acting).

Early Greek Stoicism was one of the first expressions of what might be called "classical rationalism." It was an appeal to the primacy and power of explicit and concrete expressions of the "higher" aspects of intellect or intelligence. As he has repeatedly acknowledged, Albert Ellis has been significantly influenced by the Stoic philosopher Epictetus. Epictetus was a slave who authored a manual (the *Enchiridion*) designed to help other slaves deal with their plight. Its opening words are as follows:

> Of things some are in our power, and others are not. In our power are opinion, movement towards a thing, desire, aversion, and in a word whatever are our own acts; not in our power are the body, property, reputation, offices, and in a word, whatever are not our own acts. . . .
> Remember then that if you think the things which are by nature slavish to be free, and the things which are in the power of others to be your own, you will be hindered, you will lament, you will be disturbed, you will blame both gods and men: but if you think that what is another's, as it really is, belongs to another, no man will ever compel you, no man will hinder you, you will do nothing involuntarily, no man will harm you, you will have no enemy, for you will not suffer any harm. (Epictetus, undated/1956, pp. 169–170)

It is therefore not surprising that Epictetus stated that "Men are not disturbed by things, but by the views they take of them." This is a foundational assumption of RET which, like classical Stoicism, seeks to ease our emotional burdens by rationalizing our lives and practicing detachment from everything in our power. Logic and the principles of rational intercourse were thought to lead toward appropriate action, and an important epistemological distinction was drawn between knowledge and the mental impressions on which knowledge was based. Not unlike the Eightfold Path of Buddhism, Stoic guidelines for the "good life" emphasize "right" thinking and rigorous detachment:

> I must die. But must I die groaning? I must be imprisoned. But must I whine as well? I must suffer exile. Can any one then hinder me from going with a smile, and a good courage, and at peace? "Tell the secret." I refuse to tell, for this is in my power. "But I will chain you." What say you fellow? Chain me? My leg you will chain—yes, but my will— no, not even Zeus can conquer that. "I will imprison you." My bit of a body, you mean.... These are the thoughts that those who pursue philosophy should ponder, these are the lessons they should exercise themselves. (quoted in B. Russell, 1945, p. 263)

It may be difficult from our present-day perspective to appreciate the power and appeal of a philosophy that openly asserted its immunity from the likes of Zeus. There should be little doubt, however, that Albert Ellis is a modern representative of classical rationalism and Stoicism. He has clearly asserted the powers of cognition and rational living to mitigate against all forms of social, religious, and internalized oppression. Indeed, he has been a major figure in the attempt to separate "naturalized" humanism from "spiritual" humanism, a debate that lies at the heart of the current controversy over the essence of humanistic psychology (see Moustakas, 1985; T. W. Smith, 1986):

> Is RET a truly revolutionary approach to psychological treatment and to the prevention of emotional disturbance? In some ways, of course, it is not, since it basically stems from the teaching of stoicism, of logico-empiricism, of existentialism, and of humanism, all of which have been around for a good many years and are therefore no longer too revolutionary. But in some of its specific applications of these values and ideas to the field of psychotherapy, rational–emotive psychology is truly innovative and radical. (Ellis, 1973, p. 15)

In the opening pages of *Humanistic Psychotherapy*, Ellis goes on to illustrate how this interpretation of these philosophic traditions transform our understanding of human psychological struggles:

> People do not *get upset* but instead *upset themselves* by insisting that (a) they should be outstandingly loved and accomplished, (b) other people should be incredibly fair and giving, and (c) the world should be exceptionally easy and munificent....

[RET] is one of the few—perhaps the only—method of personality change that provides the person with severe emotional problems with the most elegant, deepest, and nonpalliative solutions of these problems; namely, his learning how to steadfastly refuse to berate himself, as a human, for *any* error; to accept himself, as a living creature, at *all* times; and to rate and measure only his traits and performances, and never his self. RET is the one regular mode of psychotherapy which truly solves the ego problem—by showing the individual how to stop esteeming or disesteeming himself for anything, and thereby eliminating pride or "ego."

It is one of the few systems of psychotherapy that will truly have no truck whatever with any kind of miraculous cause or cure, any kind of god or devil, or any kind of sacredness. Where many other systems deify feeling, experience, self-interest, self-disclosure, relationship, trust, reason, anti-intellectualism, and what have you, rational–emotive therapy deifies nothing, holds no absolutes, and is quite comfortable with the world of probability, uncertainty, fallibility, and even disorder. It teaches people to *desire* and *prefer* many goals; but to *demand*, to *need*, and to *dictate* nothing. In this sense, and quite revolutionarily, it helps free humans of their own anxiety-creating, depression-invoking, and hostility-manufacturing grandiosity and demandingness. . . .

Man is man; he will (in all likelihood) never be more than a man. When and if he fully accepts that reality, together with the reality that there is no supernatural "force" in the universe that gives a damn about him or ever will, he will then be truly humanistic. (Ellis, 1973, pp. 15–16).

The message is clear. Echoing the ideas of Epictetus, Ellis invites us to recognize what little control we have over our lives, to renounce any hope of supernatural meaning or salvation, and to accept our lives as they are. (There is a modern bumper sticker that conveys the same basic outlook: "Life sucks, and then you die.") We cannot change the reality of our slavery (literal or symbolic), but we can change what we demand of life and we can aim toward a rational detachment that will ease our pain.

It has been suggested that the hidden human images that underlie our theories reflect some basic themes of meaning (Friedman, 1974). The psychoanalytic portrayal, for example, depicts humans as anxiously conflicted animals with a penchant for sex and aggression. The behavioristic rendition of human learning would emphasize the *tabula rasa* nature of the unconditioned nervous system and, in agreement with Freud, the fundamentally hedonistic nature of human motivation. If Albert Ellis has an unconscious archetype for the average human being, it must include features of whiny, neurotic demandingness from a sniveling, self-critical wimp. It is, indeed, to this very stereotype that RET markets itself as a remedy. With rational living skills, people's expectations are likely to be lowered and their abilities to "rationalize" their behavior improved. For the most part, the rational skills and lessons imparted through RET should encourage self-acceptance, feelings of increased competence, and/or reduced domination by emotional needs. Much of their intended effect is inhibitory, seeking the reduction of impediments to action. It is from this frame of mind that we are invited to have sex without guilt (which conveys a very different approach to the topic than its rival, the joy of sex). The underlying message is a combination of Stoic detachment and unconditionally positive self-regard, with a heavy dose of rationalist interventionism. Our miseries are self-produced, according to Ellis, and they are remedied only via the rationalizations that characterize RET.

The Challenges Facing RET

Among the challenges facing RET in the decades to come are (1) its apparent overemphasis on thought rather than feeling or action, (2) its lack of a developmental theory of psychological change across the lifespan, and (3) its relative deemphasis on the importance of the helping relationship. To the credit of Ellis and his RET colleagues, they have given priority to critical scientific scrutiny and ongoing refinement. This emphasis on empirical inquiry should encourage the future refinement of RET and should facilitate permanent reappraisals of its foundational assumptions and assertions.

Another factor in the future of RET has to do with the extent to which its popularity has been connected with the persona and personality of Albert Ellis. Although we are not familiar with any formal assessment of his audience effects, we would not be surprised to find that many of Ellis's listeners experience him as an inspiring and charismatic teacher. So long as he remains the "living master," the penultimate authority on RET, it will be difficult to estimate the independent viability of the approach he has pioneered. The twenty-first century should offer a more enlightening vantage point on the endurance and contributions of RET.

CONCLUDING REMARKS

Any balanced evaluation of RET must begin with an acknowledgment of the important role played by Albert Ellis and RET in both the cognitive revolution and in the popularity of rationalist interventionism in late twentieth-century psychology. There can be little doubt that the ideas and clinical techniques developed in the context of RET will continue to have a practical impact over the coming years. At the same time, however, it is our opinion that the primary contributions of RET lie ultimately in (and are necessarily limited by) its roots in classical Stoicism and rationalist interventionism. We concur in the value of some of the contributions rendered via Stoicism and rationalism, particularly the early assertion of equal human rights and the acknowledgment of mediated knowing. Our concerns with these two traditions have to do with their overall inadequacy as philosophical perspectives, their exaggeration of the powers of explicit reason, and their lopsided appeal to the cognitive (versus affective, behavioral, and, dare we say "spiritual?") aspects of human experience. Nevertheless, the writings of Albert Ellis and other RET practitioners have helped to clarify the challenging complexities that continue to face the theories and therapies of the future, and that, in itself, is a valuable contribution.

6

The Practice of Rational–Emotive Therapy

Arnold A. Lazarus

INTRODUCTION

Albert Ellis's categorization of common irrational beliefs; his A, B, and C formulation of activating events, beliefs, and consequences; his incisive and evocative methods of disputing irrational ideas; his writings on human fallibility in concert with a nondemanding, noncondemning philosophy of life; and his views on self-esteem and self-acceptance are among his signal contributions. The foregoing are sufficient in and of themselves to place Ellis at the spearhead of psychotherapeutic inventiveness. As stated by the American Psychological Association in citing reasons for giving him the 1985 Award for Distinguished Professional Contributions, "Dr. Albert Ellis' theoretical contributions have had a profound effect on the professional practice of psychology."

At a time when people like Wolpe (1958) were emphasizing that subcortical hypothalamic brain centers account for human emotion, with little or no connection to cognitive processes (which Eysenck, 1986, still believes), Ellis held the neurophysiologically valid and now widely accepted view that cognitive and affective processes are not disparate but essentially interactive (R. S. Lazarus, 1982; Plutchik, 1980). By elaborating

    95

on a basic theme, that people largely create their own emotional reactions by the ways they interpret or evaluate their environments, Ellis paved the way for an internal locus of control, a cognitive–perceptual realignment, whereby specific and predictable changes are wrought and many types of neurotic miseries are allayed. RET specifically addresses the impact of overgeneralizing, labeling, personalizing, "catastrophizing" and "awfuliz-ing." By proceeding beyond Horney's "tyranny of the should" and highlighting the pernicious effects of categorical imperatives, absolutistic thinking, perfectionism, excessive approval-seeking, and numerous cata-strophic non sequiturs and misplaced attributions, Ellis can lay more than legitimate claim to originality and distinctiveness.

The foregoing laudatory comments notwithstanding, there are numerous points concerning Ellis's writings in particular, and RET in general, with which I take issue. Since Ellis (1957c, 1958a) first propounded rational psychotherapy, his fecundity has given rise to literally hundreds of articles and scores of books. As a forward thinker, he has revised, modified, and amplified several of his earlier conceptions. Any viable treatment orien-tation changes constantly in response to the data and the *Zeitgeist*. Thus, many issues can generate grievous, albeit unwitting, distortion even by careful observers. Before commenting intelligently on a particular nuance or facet, one must ponder, "Did Ellis revise or expunge this particular statement? If he revised it, did he make still further revisions? Does he agree fully, partially, or not at all with modifications offered by other RET practitioners such as Bernard, Broder, DiGiuseppe, Dryden, Garcia, Grieger, Harper, Hauck, Knaus, Maultsby, Oliver, Walen, Wessler, and Wolfe?" Another thorny question centers around the adequacy of the research that has been carried out on RET, despite Ellis's (1979h) asser-tion that "this particular system of psychotherapy has immense—indeed, almost awesome—research backing" (p. 103). Without evading my editorial mandate, I attempt to steer clear of these issues by building my case for and against RET primarily on clinical (procedural) grounds. (For an incisive critique of the research on RET see Kendall, 1984; Rachman & Wilson, 1980; T. W. Smith & Allred, 1986.) Since a three-and-a-half page critique, outlining what I saw as some inconsistencies in RET (A. A. Lazarus, 1979), evoked a five-page anfractuous rebuttal from Ellis (1979h), I select my bones of contention very carefully throughout this chapter.

OVERINCLUSIVENESS

Exactly what is (and is not) RET? How does it differ from the cognitive therapies promulgated by Beck, Burns, Emery, Mahoney, Meichenbaum, and the entire field of cognitive–behavior therapy? Consensus on these

issues cannot be achieved. Too many contradictory opinions are endorsed
by theoreticians and practitioners within and between the different camps.
The boundaries grow murky, and significant differences get lost in the
shuffle of individual personalities competing for originality and superiority.
Nevertheless, as I argue, the distinctiveness of RET lies in its methods
of cognitive restructuring (A. A. Lazarus, 1971).

The theoretical underpinnings of RET are so broadly eclectic and so
pliable that an extremely wide range of methods and principles can be
incorporated into its purview. It encompasses, or has been molded by,
everything from Stoic philosophy, general semantics, the works of Spinoza,
Voltaire and numerous latter-day philosophers, to the seminal writings
of Adler, Coue, Dewey, Emerson, Frankl, Horney, Kelly, Low, Rogers,
Russell, Wittgenstein, and many others. It also spans the entire gamut
of social learning theory (Bandura, 1986) and cognitive–behavior therapy.
Indeed, as Ellis and Bernard (1985a) describe it, RET is humanistic,
behavioral, insight-oriented, and many things besides. Moreover, they
assert that "it has always been multimodal in its use of many cognitive,
emotive, and behavioral methods" (p. 20), a view with which I take serious
issue later in this chapter. I also challenge Ellis's (1979j) statement that
RET's "greatest similarity is with multimodal behavior therapy, with which
general, or inelegant, RET is practically synonymous" (p. 61). Perhaps
the practice of RET is part of a multidimensional or multifaceted treatment plan, but presently I explain why it is not multimodal as I use that
term.

There is nothing to prevent a rational–emotive therapist from drawing
on phenomenology, attribution theory, the placebo effect, cognitive
dissonance, or from offering desensitization, biofeedback, relaxation,
modeling, self-control, social skills training, operant conditioning, paradoxical intention, role-playing, contingency contracting, and so forth—all in
the name of RET! This raises an important question: When using a technique other than rational disputation, shame-attacking exercises, rational-
emotive imagery, or some of the other methods developed by Ellis and/or
his associates, is one still practicing RET? If the answer is yes, it would
seem that RET loses all distinctive meaning or identity and merges totally
with the entire field of applied psychology. The intelligent answer is that
RET is devoted predominantly to parsing errors in absolutistic thinking,
diminishing blaming and damning, eliminating categorical imperatives,
correcting faulty inferences and other cognitive distortions, with the fundamental goal of enabling clients to alter some of their basic philosophies
about themselves and the world. In so doing, disputation is the method
of choice, be it disputing discomfort anxiety, self-condemnation, help-
lessness, low frustration tolerance, or any other crazy-making propensity.
Ancillary techniques that fall within the domain of RET include referenting

(Danysh, 1974; Ellis & Harper, 1975), rational–emotive imagery (Maultsby & Ellis, 1974), coping statements, and empathic self-statements (Ellis, 1977d).

Ellis (1979i) claims that "probably 50 or 60 different kinds of cognitive procedures in therapy now exist, and more appear all the time," and he adds, "RET tries to use, in various ways, almost all these methods" (p. 241). After listening to many of Ellis's therapy tapes, seeing several of his films and videos, and perusing a good deal of the literature on rational–emotive procedures, it seems to me that disputation is employed about 90% of the time. With few exceptions, it would appear that most RET practitioners seldom use methods outside of actively explaining, inter- preting, and disputing clients' irrational beliefs. Ellis and Bernard (1985a) are quite explicit on this subject: "RET emphasizes the use of active disputing as the most elegant, though hardly the only, way of helping people to surrender their irrational beliefs (iBs)" (pp. 16–17).

Nevertheless, let us grant that there are indeed dozens of distinct and well-defined cognitive techniques, and let us further agree that all of these techniques can be seen as legitimate units of RET (Mahoney & Freeman, 1985). However, Ellis (1979i) states, "General RET. . .even makes use of many specialized emotive methods (such as encounter exercises, Gestalt therapy or psychodrama techniques. . .)" (p. 243), and Ellis and Bernard (1985a) also include *in vivo* desensitization, stimulus control, skill train- ing, modeling, and operant conditioning under "general RET." What, then, would not fall under the rubric of general RET? Ellis (1979h) has a section titled "Techniques and Approaches Avoided or Minimized in RET" (pp. 94–97) which eschews (1) lengthy descriptions of activating experiences (e.g., long-winded histories), (2) overemphasis on the client's emotional consequences or feelings (e.g., reveling in affective responses and describing them ad nauseam), (3) abreaction and catharsis (e.g., primal screaming and ventilating anger), (4) psychodynamic techniques (e.g., free association, intense transference interpretations, and dream analysis), and (5) encounter–movement excesses (e.g., using evocative techniques without placing them within a philosophic or problem-solving context). Apart from the foregoing, to which we might add transpersonal dogma, orgone therapy, rebirthing, or downright mystical ideologies such as voodooism, astrology, and prayer, everything else in the psychotherapeutic realm would presumably be considered "general RET."

Let it be understood that I am not critical of (indeed, I applaud) the fact that Ellis and most RET practitioners remain open to a broad spectrum of methods drawn from a wide variety of sources. (How many different tactics are actually employed remains in contention.) This technically eclec- tic stance is one that I have advocated for years as the most viable approach to clinical problems (e.g., A. A. Lazarus, 1967, 1971, 1976, 1981, 1986a, 1986b). It is extremely myopic to adhere to one theoretical perspective and apply it to the myriad problems of human misery. No one approach can have universal applicability, and since the mid 1970s, fewer clinicians report strict adherence and allegiance to a single system. In line with this trend, Ellis and perhaps most other RET practitioners have kept pace with the rise of systematic eclecticism (Norcross, 1986a, 1987). For example, Ellis (1985e) advocates a very wide array of strategies, tactics, and methods in his excellent book *Overcoming Resistance*. Nevertheless, my argument with Ellis *et al.* is that they present RET as a unique, coherent, distinctive psychotherapeutic system, and also contend that it is a broad-based eclectic orientation (no different from the multimodal approach) that attempts to combine "state of the science" with "state of the art" techniques and procedures from many disciplines.

Harper (1959), one of the principal pioneers of rational–emotive therapy, presented a persuasive case in favor of eclecticism. After reviewing the fundamentals of 36 systems he concludes, "Until science brings us definitive answers—if science does—let us try to avoid commitment to a rigid religion of psychotherapy. Let us learn from and constructively employ the arts of many therapies" (p. 156). I read the foregoing as a graduate student; it profoundly molded my own professional outlook. More recently, Dryden (1984b) has adopted a clear-cut eclectic stance, and one that meets with approval and endorsement from Ellis (1984d). As Dryden (1986a) strongly underscored, "*Rational–emotive therapists don't only practice RET.*"

Dryden's observation addresses the core of my major criticism, namely, that when a practitioner of RET draws on operant conditioning, social skills training, *in vivo* desensitization, and so forth, he or she is no longer using RET but has stepped outside the confines of rational–emotive theory and therapy. Thus, when I advise a supervisee to "use RET with this client," what am I implying? That he or she will address matters such as excessive approval-seeking and achievement goals, combined with overreactions to inconsiderateness from others, with a view to excising the demands, the basic "musts" that the client imposes intra- and interpersonally. When you, or I, or Ellis, elect to use deep muscle relaxation, biofeedback, meditation, behavior rehearsal, or contingency contracting, we are not practicing RET. This is so obvious that it would be ridiculous to labor the point were it not for the fact that Ellis *et al.* have called all of these techniques "general RET," or "inelegant RET."

R. W. Wessler (1986a) sees RET as "an assumption about disturbance rather than a prescribed set of procedures for reducing disturbance" (p. 75). Its major premise is that the employment of logical (scientific)

thinking will facilitate the implementation of happiness-producing purposes. The corollary is that disturbed individuals tend to be less rational,
objective, and scientific. Ellis limits the term "elegant or preferential RET"
to the goal of a philosophical realignment that transcends mere pallia-
tion. The elegant or preferential outlook (tantamount perhaps to "self-
actualization") is one that addresses the core of irrationality, the fundamental disturbance-creating philosophies. Here, the goal appears to achieve
a state of veritable undisturbability (rather than merely striving to be less
disturbable). Rachman and Wilson (1980) state, "There is insufficient
evidence that such a massive psychological change is feasible or necessary
for successful treatment" (p. 208).

Before turning to a different topic, I would like to point out that I have
seen many clients who appear free from the common irrational ideas so
eloquently discussed by Ellis and Harper (1975), but whose suffering
stemmed from rather different cognitions, such as happiness is dangerous;
let your anger out; the less personal information you disclose, the better
off you will be; it is generally good to show that you are right; total self-
sufficiency is attainable and desirable (A. A. Lazarus & Fay, 1975).
Similarly, perusal of the RET literature could lead one to conclude that
problems related to worthlessness, overgeneralization, low frustration
tolerance, and "awfulizing" cover the entire gamut of neurotic disorders.
It would enhance the basic edifice of RET if Ellis *et al.* set out to compile
a more exhaustive compendium of irrational beliefs. This might tend to
offset the tendency to employ Procrustean maneuvers—fitting the client
to 11 or 12 preconceived beliefs. Moreover, by including other cognitive
distortions within the basic theory, RET would become more flexible and
applicable to a wider range of subtle disorders. Certainly, in specific contexts, Ellis has listed numerous irrational beliefs (e.g., Ellis, 1981) but many
of these notions have not been incorporated into the mainstream of RET.

AS YOU THINK SO SHALL YOU FEEL AND ACT VERSUS AS YOU ACT SO SHALL YOU THINK AND FEEL

As practicing clinicians, we are convinced that cognitive change leads
to behavior change (and vice versa). The presumed two-way street between
insight and action is one that is heavily touted by clinicians of different
disciplines. Certainly, RET practitioners believe that a shift in logic will
have a corresponding impact on emotion and behavior. Significantly,
however, many years ago, Festinger (1964) was unable to find a single
experimental investigation that actually showed that a change in cognition led, per se, to a change in behavior. Similarly, London (1964)

elaborated on the fact that a change in insight did not necessarily lead to a corresponding change in action. More recently, Rachman and Wilson (1980) stated, "Furthermore, studies that show a significant change in irrational beliefs do not necessarily produce a change in behavior" (p. 203). They cited Trexler and Karst (1972) in support of their thesis, and concluded that "Results of this character are embarrassing for the RET rationale." Their major thesis, well-documented by outcome research, is that " *performance-based methods are more effective than techniques which rely entirely on symbolic induction processes*" (Rachman & Wilson, 1980, p. 155, italics added). The superiority of *in vivo* over imaginal treatment methods was demonstrated by Sherman (1969) and subsequently confirmed across many conditions (Bandura, 1986). In fairness to Ellis, he has long advocated the use of homework assignments, shame-attacking exercises, and other *in vivo* activities. However, in practice (judging by the numerous work samples I have studied) he is too apt to favor disputation and cognitive restructuring.

Several authors (e.g., Bandura, 1986; Rachman & Wilson, 1980; Raimy, 1975) have pointed out that behavioral procedures might be effective because they produce changes in cognitive processes. Emmelkamp, Kuipers, and Eggeraat (1978), in treating agoraphobic subjects, found prolonged exposure *in vivo* superior to cognitive restructuring, but pointed out that their results could at least partly be explained in terms of cognitive restructuring.

> During treatment with prolonged exposure *in vivo* clients notice, for example, that their anxiety diminishes after a time and that the events which they fear, such as fainting or having a heart attack, do not take place. This may lead them to transform their unproductive self-statements into more productive ones: "There you are, nothing will go wrong with me." A number of clients reported spontaneously that their "thoughts" had undergone a much greater change during prolonged exposure *in vivo* than during cognitive restructuring. It is possible that a more effective cognitive modification takes place through prolonged exposure *in vivo* than through a procedure which is focused directly on such a change. (p. 40)

When a client is successfully desensitized to a hierarchy of phobic stimuli and can freely venture into situations that had hitherto been avoided, can there be doubt that cognitive restructuring has been achieved? Systematic desensitization can be conceptualized as a method of cognitive restructuring, no less than one of counterconditioning or extinction. Nevertheless, methods such as desensitization, behavior rehearsal, response prevention, covert sensitization, aversion conditioning, emotive imagery, flooding, contingency contracting, overcorrection, participant modeling, assertiveness and social skills training, relaxation and biofeedback are methods of behavior therapy and not RET, although RET practitioners can and do employ them (Bellack & Hersen, 1985). It may be argued that a change in behavior is one of the best ways of correcting dysfunctional thoughts. While Ellis and his followers would agree with the foregoing statement, perusal of their writings shows that RET often downplays this reality and "prefers, with many individuals, to use active–directive disputing" (Ellis & Bernard, 1985a, p. 18). Suffice it to say that active–directive disputing will, in general, not get very far when treating panic disorders, obsessives, compulsives, severe phobics, most cases of anorgasmia, functional vaginismus, or dyspareunia, or the paraphilias. Likewise, with severe eating disorders (especially anorexia and bulimia), the addictions, and substance abuse, active-directive disputing is more than likely to fall on deaf ears.

I had treated a professional musician whose career was in serious jeopardy because of intense performance anxiety. He was totally unresponsive to my most ardent RET interventions and remained unmoved by my attempts to modify his demandingness, his proclivity to catastrophize, and so forth. Consequently, an elaborate course of systematic desensitization was implemented, replete with a 90-item hierarchy, which took over 3 months to traverse before the client reported the absence of anticipatory anxiety. Soon thereafter he was no longer anxious, even when giving solo performances. After this laborious process, how did the musician account for his progress? He stated, "I now realize that before your treatment I failed to separate my music from my own being. The desensitization made me aware of the fact that a poor performance would not end my life or my career." Thus, a purely cognitive rationale had emerged. There are numerous individuals whose dysfunctional beliefs are not amenable to direct cognitive restructuring but who are able to change their minds upon modifying their behaviors, or after undergoing a course of sensory retraining (e.g., biofeedback, relaxation, and a physical exercise regimen), or through the use of various imagery techniques that far transcend rational–emotive imagery (Bandler, 1985; A. A. Lazarus, 1984a; Robbins, 1986; Zilbergeld & Lazarus, 1987). We are, as Ellis (1962) said, "a sensing-moving-thinking-emoting complex" (p. 47). As already emphasized, it would appear that RET practitioners tend to focus too heavily on the thinking component at the expense of other modalities. At this juncture, it might be appropriate to dispute the contention that general RET and multimodal therapy (MMT) are one and the same.

THE MAIN DIFFERENCES BETWEEN RET AND MMT

While the major philosophic and theoretical propositions, as well as the basic technical strategies, endorsed by RET are entirely compatible with the multimodal orientation, except perhaps for the fact that multimodal therapists pay more attention to general systems theory (see Kwee & Lazarus, 1986), there are several important procedural differences.

1. During assessment, multimodal therapists specifically address the entire BASIC I.D. (behavior, affect, sensation, imagery, cognition, interpersonal relationships, and drugs/biological factors). In so doing, with adult outpatients, extensive use is made of the Multimodal Life History Questionnaire[1] (A. A. Lazarus, 1981). This leads to the development of a Modality Profile, a chart that lists the salient problems and proposed treatments across the client's BASIC I.D., which subsequently serves as a blueprint for therapy. RET practitioners do not systematically assess the BASIC I.D., and they do not construct Modality Profiles.

2. When treatment impasses arise, a typical multimodal tactic is to conduct a second-order BASIC I.D. The problematic item is subjected to a recursive analysis across the entire spectrum, thereby often elucidating more productive avenues of intervention (see A. A. Lazarus, 1981). In RET, this procedure is not employed.

3. Multimodal therapists make use of a procedure called *bridging*, whereby the clinician, when encountering resistance, first joins the client in his or her preferred modality before gently coaxing him or her into other, potentially more productive, avenues of inquiry and treatment. For example, Mr. A is intent upon describing a host of irrelevant interpersonal details surrounding a party he attended, whereas his therapist wishes to know what he was telling himself, which dysfunctional beliefs he was endorsing. Direct inquiries vis-à-vis cognitive content only elicit more examples from Mr. A of who said what to whom at the party. To confront the client about his evasiveness may only engender greater defensiveness, whereas to go along with him for about 5 minutes, asking for even more information about the party per se may then more easily encourage him to move out of this domain, perhaps by first discussing his sensations or images, and then addressing the specific self-talk that the therapist considers clinically productive (see A. A. Lazarus, 1981, 1984b). Skillful rational–emotive therapists may employ this method intuitively, but it is not a specific feature of RET instruction and training.

4. Tracking the ''firing-order'' of specific modalities is a procedure employed by multimodal therapists when clients are unable to account

[1]Obtainable from Research Press, Box 3177, Champaign, IL 61821.

for their disturbed feelings, or claim that they arise "out of the blue." The tracking sequence teaches the client to attend to the antecedents that culminate in negative or untoward feelings or emotions. Thus, Mrs. Smith comes to realize that she typically upsets herself by dwelling first on images of gloom and doom, followed by catastrophic self-talk, resulting in negative sensations (tension, palpitations, dizziness) which escalate into extreme anxiety—an imagery-cognitive-sensory-affective firing order (ICSA). Mrs. Jones, on the other hand, after tracking her firing order, discovers that she usually follows a sensory-imagery-cognitive-affective sequence (SICA). The selection of treatment strategies would be tailored to the client's specific firing order (A. A. Lazarus, 1981, 1984b, 1986a). The literature on RET contains no reference to the tracking procedure.

5. Structural profiles yield a quantitative record of the client's self-ratings across the BASIC I.D. so that one obtains a graph or a bar diagram depicting how active, emotional, sensual, etc., the person perceives himself or herself to be. In marriage therapy, one may also use structural profiles to obtain estimates of how couples think their spouse will rate them, and how they, in turn, would rate their spouse in each modality. These metacommunications often provide significant clues for effective intervention (A. A. Lazarus, 1981, 1984b). Again, in RET, these procedures are not employed.

There are other tactics used by multimodal therapists that are typically not employed by RET practitioners, e.g., the deserted island fantasy test and various time-tripping imagery exercises (see A. A. Lazarus, 1981 and the case example later in this chapter), but the foregoing five procedures are the most salient points of departure between MMT, RET, and all other psychotherapeutic disciplines. Thus, those who allege that "general, or inelegant RET is practically synonymous...with multimodal therapy" (Ellis, 1979h) are seriously in error. Whether there is any merit to the unique procedures employed within the multimodal framework remains an open question. While suggestive data point to the clinical utility of these methods (e.g., Briddell & Leiblum, 1976; Kwee, 1984; Kwee & Duivenvoorden, 1985; Lazarus, 1986a; O'Keefe & Castaldo, 1985), their intrinsic merits have yet to be widely demonstrated. Nevertheless, these procedures set multimodal assessment and therapy apart from all other eclectic, multifaceted approaches and systems. BASIC I.D. assessment is more systematic and comprehensive; it promotes a coherent organization of techniques (and when, and with whom, to use them).

As a final point of clarification, it should be stressed that there is no such thing as multimodal therapy per se. The multimodal orientation points to the advantages of traversing the BASIC I.D. during assessment (if thoroughness is desired) and then addressing the salient deficits and excesses that emerge in each modality (if durable outcomes are to be achieved). The actual treatments employed are those that appear to best fit the clients' unique requirements (be it communications training with a family, and/or systematic desensitization with an individual). The treatments of choice are drawn from a wide range of disciplines, with special emphasis being placed on the outcome literature (e.g., Frances, Clarkin, & Perry, 1984; Rachman & Wilson, 1980). But there is no particular method of treatment that is distinctively multimodal. The multimodal assessment procedures are unique, e.g., the use of modality and structural profiles, second-order BASIC I.D. templates, bridging, and tracking. And to reiterate a crucial point, within this framework, RET is defined as the application of cognitive restructuring, especially the disputation of categorical imperatives. When applying assertiveness training, covert sensitization, contingency management, operant conditioning, modeling, stimulus control, or electrical aversion, neither I nor anyone else is practicing RET. In this vein, when looking to Bernard (1986) for the unique features of RET, the overwhelming majority are cognitive–philosophical, e.g., the emphasis on self-acceptance, the fact that people upset themselves about being upset, the strength of irrational convictions, and people's penchant to "think in overly subjective, absolutistic, rigid, unclear, inaccurate, and self-defeating ways" (p. 52).

ISSUES NOT FULLY ADDRESSED IN THE LITERATURE ON RET

The burgeoning literature on differential therapeutics and treatment specificity (e.g., Frances, et al., 1984; G. S. Howard, Nance, & Myers, 1986; Karasu, 1986; A. A. Lazarus, 1984d) has concerned itself with issues such as how psychotherapy works, specific treatments of choice, and the matching of client expectancies and relationship styles. Thus, G. S. Howard et al. (1986) have endeavored to provide a systematic organization of therapeutic techniques, a conceptual framework for use in selecting a particular therapeutic procedure, and an appropriate therapeutic style for a specific problem or client. They inquire quite explicitly (as do multimodal therapists) how a therapist is best advised to behave with a particular client: when to be directive and when to be nondirective; when to be highly supportive and encouraging and when to be less supportive and more neutral; when to be didactic and instructive rather than pensive and reflective (and vice versa). The implication is that an effective therapist will be flexible and will vary his or her behavior systematically in line with the treatment goals and client response. According to G. S. Howard et al.

(1986, p. 415), "Without a therapist's willingness and ability to engage in a range of behaviors and to employ a range of therapeutic modalities, the therapist, by intent or default, will have to limit his or her practice to clients who fit the specific range of behaviors he or she has to offer." The aforementioned considerations are, at best, lightly alluded to in the literature (books, articles, videotapes, and audiotapes) on RET.

Along similar lines, one might inquire whether RET trainees and therapists incorporate the latest clinical findings about the client–therapist relationship, trust building, and the overall establishment of rapport. The answer is that they do so somewhat cursorily. Ellis (1973, 1977d, 1984f) has stressed that empathic listening, reflection of feeling, and the building of good rapport with clients will facilitate the course of RET. He has also sounded a note of strong caution to avoid therapists' and clients' dire needs for each others' approval. But little attention seems to be devoted to determining the specific cadence of client–therapist styles or the range of interactions that are most likely to augment compliance. My perusal of the RET literature also found little attention given to considering certain personalistic or idiosyncratic factors that might point to the virtues of one specific type of relationship over another (A. A. Lazarus, 1981). Thus, Ellis and Bernard (1985a) state that RET "encourages the therapist to be a highly active–directive teacher who had often better take the lead in explaining, interpreting, and disputing clients' iBs and to come up with better solutions to their problems" (p. 20). Yet any experienced clinician can attest to the fact that certain clients see their therapy entirely as an opportunity to derive benefit from an active listener. They will profit solely from a nonjudgmental relationship and want neither cognitive restructuring nor behavior change. Such clients are tailor-made for person-centered (Rogerian) therapy. Prochaska and DiClemente (1986) point out that whereas some are "ready for action," others are in a "precontemplation stage," and that RET is best suited "for clients in the contemplation and action stages" (p. 170). The point I am stressing in this regard is that RET practitioners are inclined to dispense cognitive disputation to virtually all comers, whether or not the client is precontemplative or in need of a very different treatment for other reasons. Certainly, when watching Ellis demonstrating RET at numerous lectures and workshops since 1966 (including those in which we were co-presenters), I often felt that he was resorting to Procrustean maneuvers to fit the client to his model.

Another important point that seems to be missing from the literature on RET is that some clients require specific preparatory steps, a certain degree of "priming" before they can profit from cognitive interventions (disputation, restructuring, or reframing). For example, I have treated numerous individuals who were so tense, so preoccupied with sensory discomforts, that they required immediate attention to the sensory modality via deep muscle relaxation, biofeedback, and, on occasion, some bioenergetic exercises (Lowen, 1975). After they had "simmered down" and "loosened up" sufficiently to pay attention to cognitive inputs, it was possible to begin to dispute their irrational ideas and dysfunctional beliefs. It is a serious mistake to gloss over the specific impact of nonverbal cues, such as sensory (somatic) inputs. With other people, it is necessary first to deal with interpersonal clashes and family saboteurs (modifying behavioral patterns) before endeavoring to examine and modify the beliefs that may have been at the base of their difficulties. In practice and in theory, RET practitioners are too eager to start cognizing. And while they give behavioral assignments, there appears to be very little attention to nonverbal behavior.

There is also a somewhat meager amount of information about paradoxical interventions in the RET literature, and yet these methods have been applied to the human change process in diverse ways (e.g., Dowd & Milne, 1986; Erickson, 1965; Fay, 1978; Frankl, 1963, 1975). Paradoxical intention (Frankl, 1960) is a particularly useful strategy in overcoming resistance, yet Ellis (1985d) covers the topic in less than 15 lines. There are many different types of paradoxical interventions, and clients who remain utterly impervious to the most elegant cognitive disputations may respond gratifyingly to these techniques. While there are paradoxical implications and innuendos in several of Ellis's methods (e.g., his use of humor, his garland of rational songs), there is nonetheless a basic neglect of recent research and treatment findings that point to the manifold ways in which the systematic use of paradoxical tactics tend to foster therapeutic gains.

A similar criticism can be made about the use of imagery techniques. Whereas multimodal clinicians make use of a wide array of effective imagery procedures (Lazarus, 1984a; Zilbergeld & Lazarus, 1987), RET practitioners seem to rely almost exclusively on rational–emotive imagery (Maultsby, 1971; Maultsby & Ellis, 1974), a specific, stylized method that fleetingly taps into prescribed images to modify dysfunctional self-talk. Ellis and Harper (1975) discuss the uses of negative imagery and positive imagery, but in a somewhat desultory way. Dryden (1984a) draws on a wider range of imagery methods, especially in his use of vivid RET, but he too seems to gloss over or totally bypass many helpful methods of mental training. The point at issue is that comprehensive therapy requires more than the correction of faulty thinking. It goes beyond words, thoughts, talk, and beliefs and also pays serious attention to the brain's right hemisphere which does not normally contribute to language processes in a major way (Gazzaniga, 1985). Clinically speaking, a change in right hemispheric activity tends to generalize to the left hemisphere. A brief vignette might clarify the point.

Case Example

A 32-year-old woman (an unemployed computer programmer, recently married) suffered from depression and anxiety. She was bewailing the fact that her parents had treated her unfairly and had showered unbridled love on her younger brother at her expense. She had already consulted two therapists, a psychodynamically oriented psychiatrist and a cognitive–behavioral psychologist, without benefit. Initially, I endeavored to address her faulty cognitions, her blaming, damning, self-pitying penchant. This resulted in a gridlock. The use of humor (e.g., Ellis's song "Whine, Whine, Whine") and some paradoxical injunctions proved unfortunate. The client failed to see the benevolent intent and retaliated with passive-aggressive, hysterical telephone calls at 3 A.M. She vetoed my suggestion that family therapy might prove helpful. Nor was she enthusiastic about the use of behavior rehearsal as a vehicle for developing an effective method of discussion vis-à-vis her parents. In our sessions, she was constantly dredging up the past, and since my most heroic interventions had backfired, I decided to adopt a nondirective position, simply listening and occasionally reflecting her affective content. This lasted about three sessions, whereupon she commented that I personified the worst aspects of her two previous therapists. A second attempt at rational disputation proved futile once more.

In retrospect, her entire demeanor was so irrational, so blatantly riddled with dysfunctional ideas and beliefs, that I was caught up in her cognitive distortions. Ordinarily, I would have employed imagery techniques much sooner. Nevertheless, when it finally occurred to me that I had bypassed the imagery modality, I decided to use *time tripping*. She had frequently alluded to events that allegedly took place when she was 8 years old, especially of unfair punishment meted out in front of strangers, which led to the following dialogue:

Therapist:	*I'd like us to try out a method called "time tripping." Try to imagine that we have a time machine and that you can travel back in time. You enter the time machine, and within a few moments you have gone back to that incident when you were unfairly punished in front of strangers. As you step out of the time machine, you are your present age, and you see your alter ego, yourself at age 8. Can you close your eyes and imagine that?*
Client:	(Closes her eyes) *Oh yes! I can see the 8-year-old child.* (Pause) *That's me all right. She's hurt and bewildered.* (Pause)
Therapist:	*The 8 year old senses something special about this adult woman who has just entered the picture. She doesn't realize, of course, that you are that same little girl, all grown up, out of the future.*

	Nonetheless, she pays close attention to you. Can you go along with that?
Client:	*I see it as if it happened yesterday. My mother is there with that dreadful woman from next door, and she is shaking and slapping me for interrupting her.* (Becoming emotional) *And that awful Mrs. Anderson is looking over the fence. God! I can see it so clearly.*
Therapist:	*Well, can you say or do something to help that 8 year old?*
Client:	*I'm a lot taller than my mother.* (Pause) *I'd like to kick her!*
Therapist:	*It might set a better example for the child if you simply told your mother off in no uncertain terms.*
Client:	(Opens her eyes) *Does she know who I am?*
Therapist:	*No. But she too senses something very special. So she will listen to you.*
Client:	(Closes her eyes) *I want to say, "Look here, lady, that's no way to bring up a child." And I want to say to the kid, "Forgive her, child, for she knows not what she does."* (Laughs and opens her eyes) *Isn't that a bit ridiculous?*
Therapist:	*It could be profound. How about stepping back in the time machine? Return to the present, and let's review it.*

Similar scenarios were enacted over and over in sessions and the client was asked to use time tripping back to the past at least once daily as homework. Week after week, she would present real or imagined injustices out of her childhood, and she seemed quite content to confront the protagonists in imagery (usually her mother, followed next by her father, brother, other relatives, neighbors, teachers, and peers). She often dwelled on the same scene. "I'm not ready to leave that one yet and move on," she would say. One particularly stubborn scene involved an incident wherein she had apparently been unfairly accused of cheating in school. It required imagery excursions that included her parents, three teachers, and the principal, and culminated in a make-believe court scene (the client's own innovation) in which she served both as defense council for herself at age 11 and as the prosecuting attorney who cross-examined her accusers. This continued for eight sessions, during which she first insisted on repeating all the "facts," together with "forgotten memories" that were generated between sessions. Finally she stated, "Well, I think I've worked that one out of my system. Let's move onto a different image." (I inquired what it meant and how it felt when a particular series of images had been "worked out of her system." Her answer was that she knew instinctively when the "sting was out" but that she could not explain it in words.) This process continued for over 7 months!

I sensed that a turning point had been reached when she arrived for a session and asked if we might spend the hour discussing some job opportunities and, if time permitted, look into certain facets of her marriage. For the first time in many months, we remained present and future oriented. When three more sessions followed a similar trajectory, I made inquiries about the imagery excursions. "I think I've reached a point," she said, "where I'm just sick and tired of digging up the past. If I may say so, I've come to see how stupid my parents were, how badly trained my teachers were, and how poorly programmed my brother is. So why fret about it? I get flashbacks from time to time, but I say: 'Forget it! It's over. It belongs in the past!' It gets harder and harder to get all riled up over it. A lot of things used to really tear me apart. Now when I think of them, I either wonder why I was making such a big deal out of it at the time, or I simply shrug my shoulders and walk away from it." Here we have a poignant instance of imagery (right brain material) leading to a rational shift in cognition (left brain conclusions). Tactics of the foregoing kind led to my being "excommunicated" by mainstream behavior therapists, but RET can accommodate a broad range of imagery techniques both conceptually and in practice. My point is that, to date, the literature on rational–emotive therapy has bypassed a host of effective mental-imagery methods.

The final point I wish to address with regard to issues that RET practitioners tend to gloss over or downplay is the question of conflict. It is my impression that the theory and practice of RET does not appear to accord sufficient importance to conflict and to conflict resolution in the management of clinical cases. While reading transcripts of RET sessions and also while listening to audiotapes, I observed that there was a tendency to examine and dispute irrational ideas at the expense of the ambivalence that often characterized the clients' situations. Thus, while supervising a RET trainee, I critiqued a tape in which he was endeavoring to dispute a man's tendency to awfulize about his wife's behavior. It seemed to me that the husband was in conflict over the viability of the marriage, and I urged the trainee to pursue this path, to allow the man to weigh the pros and cons and try to reach a decision. This was readily accomplished, whereupon it was no longer necessary to engage in cognitive disputation because the faulty cognitions were no longer present. The conflicts to which I am alluding are not the putative unconscious psychodynamic forces that we hear so much about. It was Lewin (1931) who distinguished three patterns of conflict that give rise to a considerable amount of social psychological research: (1) approach–approach, (2) avoidance–avoidance, and (3) approach–avoidance conflicts. I offer the aphorism that it is usually advisable for conflict resolution to precede cognitive disputation.

A NOTE OF PERSONAL IRRITATION

In preparing for this critique, I read much more material than appears in the reference list and noted that over the past 10 years a most unfortunate phrase has crept into most of the RET literature: *had better*. Since the categorical imperatives—*should, ought,* and *must*—are presumed to be at the core of many irrational beliefs, Ellis *et al.* go out of their way to avoid these words in their speech and writing. Instead of *should* or *must*, they employ the term *had better*. The assumption is that the implied imperative of a should, ought, or must is thereby avoided, and a preference rather than an absolutistic demand is conveyed. Thus, a typical passage reads as follows: "To help people change their fundamental irrational beliefs (iBs), therapists *had better* actively–directively use many cognitive–emotive, and behavioral methods; *had better* be scientific and experimental during therapy sessions; and *had better* teach their clients how to use the scientific method in their own lives" (Ellis, 1985b, pp. 178–179, italics added). After checking with several friends and associates, it appears that I am by no means alone in feeling that *had better* carries a threatening tone. As a child, in my home, the violation of a parental edict preceded by *had better* was always far more ominous than the nonobservance of a *should*. "You should try to be home before midnight," suggested that a 30-minute leeway existed, whereas "You had better try be home before midnight" indicated that anything after the stroke of 12 was unacceptable. "You *must* try some of my special meatloaf!" is an enthusiastic host's invitation to sample something really tasty. It readily permits refusal: "Thanks anyway but I'm too stuffed." When my mother said, "You had better eat some meatloaf," the implication was that negotiation was nonexistent.

The problem, of course, is that many words have a variety of semantic meanings. As Dryden (1986b) has pointed out, *should* can mean "I absolutely should," but it can also mean "I preferably should." He goes on, "It also has an empirical meaning (e.g., given the empirical conditions that exist in the world at this present time, the sun should come up in the morning). It can also refer to matters of recommendation (e.g., 'You really should go and see *Chariots of Fire*'). I have on more than one occasion heard novice RET therapists challenge such nonabsolutistic shoulds" (p. 39). Thus, the statement, "Tom's plane is due in at 6:30 so he should be here soon," carries no ominous undertones or implicit demands. "Tom's plane is due in at 6:30 so he had better be here soon" is an implied threat.

Compare the following:

> You should lose some weight.
> You had better lose some weight.
> Al must tell me what Sam said to him.
> Al had better tell me what Sam said to him.

To my sensibilities, "had better" carries an ominous tone; it is an admonition. "I think *it* would be better" rather than "*you* had better" more readily achieves the nondemanding objective. The construction that appeals most to me is "It would be better in my opinion." There are many nonintrusive ways of expressing strong preferences (e.g., "You might be best advised to...," "It is strongly recommended that...") but the mere extirpation of *should*, *ought*, and *must* is not the answer. It is the intent behind the word that determines whether or not it is a command or a suggestion. "You should not talk to your mother that way" can mean (1) you are a rotten and dreadful person for speaking impolitely to your mother, or (2) it really would be nicer for all concerned if you decided to display more tact and diplomacy when dealing with your mother. May I implore RET practitioners to use the words *should*, *ought*, and *must* lovingly, caringly, and essentially in a nondemanding and noninsistent way?

This review has discussed some of the main strengths and weaknesses of RET from a practical perspective. It has addressed the distinctive and general features of the rational–emotive orientation, and in so doing has underscored the eclecticism that characterizes its basic ethos. The principal differences between RET and MMT are outlined, followed by a consideration of certain important areas that are glossed over or ignored by RET practitioners. Since there are no practical, theoretical, or meta-theoretical reasons for the practitioners of rational–emotive therapy to bypass any of the additional tactics, strategies, or techniques mentioned herein, or to neglect the broader and more detailed issues described above, it is hoped that the practitioners of RET will experiment with and refine these addenda to the final benefit of all.

ACKNOWLEDGMENTS

My special thanks to Windy Dryden, Allen Fay, and Bernie Zilbergeld for their thorough and incisive criticisms.

The Client–Therapist Relationship in Rational–Emotive Therapy

Sol L. Garfield

INTRODUCTION

At the outset I should make it clear that if the chapter title were to accurately describe what is to follow, it would have added to it, ''as practiced by Albert Ellis.'' Ellis is the founder and clearly the outstanding figure in RET, and it is not possible for me to speculate on how closely other RET therapists resemble Ellis. Most of what I have to say is based on the writings of Ellis, on a number of tapes made available to me of actual therapy cases seen by Ellis, and a small number of published analyses of Ellis's interactions with patients (Becker & Rosenfeld, 1976; Zimmer & Cowles, 1972; Zimmer & Pepyne, 1971). Before getting down to a discussion of the client–therapist relationship in rational–emotive therapy, with particular reference to Albert Ellis, however, some general and basic aspects of all the psychotherapies should be mentioned, albeit briefly.

One of the interesting, but at the same time bewildering, aspects of contemporary psychotherapy is the diversity evident among the existing schools of psychotherapy. If one reads accounts of these therapeutic orientations, the impression one gets is of rather marked differences, at least among a large number of them (Herink, 1980). Furthermore, the emphasis

113

is placed on theoretical and procedural or technical differences between the different approaches to psychotherapy. Very little, if anything, is said about the potential variability among the practitioners of any given orientation. The comparisons made are generally of the differences between schools of psychotherapy and not of possible therapist differences within each of the therapeutic schools. The implication is that practitioners of one orientation function therapeutically in very similar or identical ways. Thus, if a psychotherapist tells you he or she is a psychoanalytically oriented therapist, a behavior therapist, or an RET practitioner, you are supposed to know exactly how they function in the therapeutic interaction. Kiesler (1966, 1971) has referred to this type of occurrence as the "uniformity myth." Although all men may be created equal, it is extremely doubtful that they (or all women) will be equally effective as psychotherapists. Unfortunately, although there has been a fair amount of research comparing two or more different forms of psychotherapy, there has been surprisingly little research comparing the effectiveness of different psychotherapists (Garfield, 1977). Nevertheless, I believe it is important to keep the possible variability of therapists in mind when we discuss types of psychotherapy. Besides the therapist's orientation and techniques, the skill and personality of the therapist undoubtedly play an important role in the type of outcomes secured.

Another aspect of the development of psychotherapeutic schools that has interested me is the influence of the school's founder on the way the therapy is perceived and practiced. The founder of a therapeutic school undoubtedly has a significant influence on the followers of a particular orientation. This would appear to hold for both the descriptions of the formal aspects of the therapy (theory and techniques) as well as for the personality of the school's founder. The originator of a school of psychotherapy is probably motivated by a number of reasons and experiences to develop his or her own approach to therapy. However, I would hypothesize that one component in this process is that the therapy be congruent with or fit the founder's personality. Persons who have observed the film showing Rogers, Perls, and Ellis interviewing the same "patient" not only can observe differences in the way the therapy is conducted, but they also note that these individuals differ as persons. Beyond these observations, one can also infer without undue effort how the therapists' personalities and value systems seem to go along with the particular types of psychotherapy developed.

I would hypothesize further that at least a number of therapists who opt to follow a given orientation attempt to imitate or model themselves after the founder or the main guru of that approach. With the frequency and availability of meetings and workshops, individuals have an opportunity to observe the school's founder and also to listen to recordings or view videotapes. Thus, the opportunity for possible imitation or modeling is greatly enhanced. Although such activities do provide more direct opportunities for observational learning, do they also influence individuals to copy the personal style of the leader of the school? If so, is this a worthwhile occurrence? What I am getting at here is whether it is desirable for individuals to copy others or whether they should adapt an approach or approaches to their own personal style. I raise this issue since many (or most) creators of psychotherapeutic schools have had very distinctive personalities or therapeutic styles, and this is certainly true of Albert Ellis. It is also something to keep in mind when generalizations are made about RET.

COMMONALITIES AND DIFFERENCES AMONG THERAPEUTIC SCHOOLS

Since the focus of this chapter is on the client–therapist relationship in RET, it is important to point out first certain commonalities among the different approaches to psychotherapy. The therapeutic relationship is certainly one such common and basic aspect. Regardless of the type of therapy being offered, the importance of this relationship would be recognized by most orientations, and this is even true of behavior therapists (Emmelkamp, 1986; Goldfried & Davison, 1976; Wilson & Evans, 1977). There seems to be little doubt that a satisfactory relationship between the therapist and the client or patient is important if therapy is to progress and a desirable outcome secured. Although our knowledge of this relationship and process is by no means complete, attributes of the therapist, the client, and their interaction clearly appear to be involved. We must emphasize the interactional aspect in particular, since it is not just the actual qualities or behaviors of the two participants that are important, but also how each is perceived by the other.

Although the personal attributes of the therapist are considered to be of great importance and lists of desirable qualities have been prepared from time to time, relatively little research has been performed on such variables (Garfield, 1977). Nevertheless, personal qualities such as tact, intelligence, warmth, genuineness, and sensitivity, have long been deemed desirable characteristics (Holt, 1971; Holt & Luborsky, 1958). To the extent that such personal qualities of the therapist may be influential in contributing to positive patient change, they become factors common to most forms of psychotherapy.

In a similar fashion, there appear to be client or patient variables that may influence outcome in psychotherapy (Garfield, 1986). In fact, such noted figures in psychotherapy as Jerome Frank (1979) and Hans Strupp

(1973) have stated their belief that the client is the most important variable in psychotherapeutic outcome. Whatever the degree of importance (Garfield, 1973), the client can be conceptualized as contributing in a significant manner to outcome, regardless of the type of therapy conducted. Some clients are motivated, hardworking, respond well to therapy, keep their appointments, pay their bills, and show positive change. Other clients seem to behave in less positive ways. Although it seems likely that some patients may do better with some forms of therapy than others, there is considerable variability among them and they can be viewed as a common but important variable in psychotherapy.

In other words, the therapeutic relationship is made up of the particular interaction of a specific patient with a specific therapist—and this is true for all forms of psychotherapy. Although the individual therapist may follow a given orientation, the specific therapy may not be of prime importance. What appears to be important is whether the patient responds favorably to the therapist and the therapy. As has been pointed out by Frank (1973) and Garfield (1980), all therapeutic schools provide the patient with some rationale for the therapeutic approach as well as a possible explanation of the patient's problem. These explanations, interpretations, or insights differ from orientation to orientation, but they become therapeutic if the patient accepts them. To this extent such aspects are again common features of the therapeutic process.

Thus, the interaction of patient and therapist takes place in a socially prescribed setting which is influenced by the personalities of the two participants, the skillfulness of the therapist, and the cognitive–behavioral–affective milieu of the form of therapy being utilized. From this perspective, as I have tried to indicate, the commonalities among the psychotherapies are quite impressive and need to be considered and understood before one draws conclusions about a specific therapeutic system. I have described this point of view in greater detail elsewhere (Garfield, 1980), but this presentation suffices for present purposes. Now, having provided the general background for this discussion, I discuss the therapeutic relationship in RET.

THE RELATIONSHIP IN RET

The earlier writings of Ellis (1962) particularly emphasized the rational or cognitive aspects of the therapy as the unique and important features. The ABC formulation and the need to correct disturbed or faulty cognitions were and continue to be the recognized cardinal components of RET. As pointed out in the preceding section, common aspects of psychotherapeutic systems receive relatively little emphasis; features that tend to differentiate the psychotherapies are the ones that obviously receive the major focus of attention. Thus, the relationship in RET did not receive a great deal of recognition or unusual emphasis. However, recent writings do more clearly acknowledge the significance of the therapeutic relationship in RET (Ellis, 1985d). Mentioned specifically by Ellis is the therapist's unconditional acceptance of the client. This formal recognition of unconditional acceptance was somewhat of a surprise to me, since such an emphasis has always been associated with Carl Rogers and his more non-directive approach. However, it reflects both the clear awareness of the importance of the therapeutic relationship on Ellis's part as well as an evident tendency on his part to broaden the RET perspective. This is a very desirable development and is in line with the trend toward integration and eclecticism (Garfield, 1982; Goldfried, 1980b, 1982; Norcross, 1986).

Besides the recognition of the importance of unconditional acceptance, there are other aspects of the therapeutic relationship that can be noted in Ellis's interaction with patients. These features, it should be emphasized, are those that I have observed and consequently are the products of my own inferential–cognitive processes. They, therefore, reflect not only my observations, but also my views of the psychotherapeutic process.

One basic aspect of the interactions that take place between Ellis and the patients he sees is that he is a known authority in the field of psychotherapy and the founder and leading figure in rational–emotive therapy. I am hypothesizing that this is one important feature of the relationship. I assume that this is known to most of the patients he sees and that this feature alone makes the therapeutic relationship with Ellis somewhat different than the relationship with other "ordinary" RET therapists. In fact, one patient in the tapes I heard did refer specifically to the fact that she was somewhat awed at being seen by Ellis personally. Thus, there may be a heightened suggestibility, motivation, cooperation, and general desire to make the most of this opportunity. All of these can be viewed as components contributing initially to a positive attitude toward the therapist and the therapy.

Ellis's personal style is also quite congruent with his role as an acknowledged leader in psychotherapy. He always comes across as confident and assured. There is no hesitation or halting quality to his verbal responses to the patient's comments or queries. They are given in a manner that allows for no doubts whatsoever; and if you discern a note of envy here, make the most of it!

Although Ellis's personal and confident style is emphasized here, it should be pointed out that the assured and authoritative manner of relating to the client is also stressed by Ellis as the modus operandi of RET therapists. This is clearly described in the following passage:

> In several important respects, then, rational–emotive psychotherapy encourages interpretation which is rather different from the kinds that occur in most other forms of therapy. . . . Interpretation is usually made in a highly direct, not particularly cautious, circumlocutious, or tortuous manner. The rational therapist feels that he knows right at the start that the client is upsetting himself by believing strongly in one or more irrational ideas; and he usually can quickly surmise which of these ideas a particular client believes. . . . Where the majority of other therapists tend to be passive and nondirective in their interpretations, the rational–emotive therapist is almost at the opposite extreme, since he believes that only a direct, concerted, sustained attack on a client's long-held and deep-seated irrationalities is likely to uproot them. (Ellis, 1973, pp. 89–90)

Thus, as indicated above, the stance of the RET therapist differs considerably from that of many other therapists and generally reflects a therapist who seems to know what he or she is doing. For many patients, I would hypothesize that such a stance inspires confidence in the therapist and thus contributes to a positive therapeutic relationship. However, not all RET therapists may be able to play this role or engage in such behaviors with equal effectiveness. As stated earlier, although the variability among therapists has received relatively little research attention, there is little basis for doubting that such variability does in fact exist. Those therapists who both believe in the intrinsic validity of RET therapy and who have the personal qualities and persuasiveness to influence the patient positively should be expected to achieve superior results.

At the same time, I would emphasize again that the therapeutic relationship is dyadic, and consequently we should not discuss the role or influence of the psychotherapist in isolation. Some clients are much more likely to respond positively to the rationale of RET and to the directive stance of the therapist than are other clients. Some studies, in fact, have attempted to investigate the effects of client–therapy interaction (Garfield, 1986). In one study, clients with internal and external locuses of control respectively were exposed to relatively directive and relatively nondirective therapies (Abramowitz, Abramowitz, Roback, & Jackson, 1974). In this relatively small study, the "external" clients secured better results in the directive therapy, while "internal" clients did better when receiving the nondirective therapy. One possible implication of this study is that externally oriented clients might respond better to RET and a directive therapist than would internally oriented clients. However, one must be cautious in attempting to apply the results of any single study, and in particular, one should be cautious when generalizing about such constructs as locus of control and therapist directiveness. As Messer and Meinster (1980) have reported, an examination of the studies that supposedly have shown that externals are more responsive to directive therapy and internals more successful with nondirective therapy have had a number of deficiencies. Clearly, then, caution should be observed. Nevertheless, differential response of clients should be expected.

In addition, directive behavior on the part of the therapist can actually be perceived in a number of different ways. Some patients may view the therapist's directiveness as a sign of competence, understanding, interest, and involvement. Others may view such behavior as autocratic, bossy, domineering, and uncaring. Such differences in perception may be due to differences in patients as well as differences in therapists. Not all directive therapists behave in the same manner, and obviously patients' perceptions and evaluations of their behaviors are going to differ. My own appraisal of Ellis is that he equates directiveness with many other possible therapist variables. I have already made reference to his acknowledged status as the leader of RET and to his confident and very assured manner of relating to the patient. In addition, however, I believe that despite this perceived stance, he also is perceived by most patients as being interested in them and in their problems. He does not just sit back and nod or say "Hm, hm." He is active, in fact very active, through the session. Certainly, the patient can not say that Dr. Ellis just sits back and says very little. Although there is only very modest research data available in the area of comparative therapist verbalization, what does exist would indicate that Ellis's verbal output in a therapy session is among the highest (Zimmer & Cowles, 1972). I come back to this point later. However, it does reflect Ellis's interest and involvement with the patient and is undoubtedly perceived that way by a large percentage of patients, although actual research data on this matter apparently are not yet available.

Thus, the emphasis on focusing on the client's irrational thoughts and persistently pointing them out exemplifies to many clients the therapist's efforts to help them. It is a form of engagement regardless of what other values may be attributed to this activity. However, to the extent that the interpretations of the therapist also may have a ring of truth to them, the positive impression of the therapist may be increased. Not only is the therapist trying to help the client, but what he says seems to make sense. Such possible views of the therapist would tend to strengthen the therapeutic relationship.

The use of homework assignments may also have an indirect effect on the therapeutic relationship. Although the emphasis clearly is on the performance of specified activities, the successful performance of such activities may enhance the therapeutic relationship. The fact that the assignments or recommendations made by the therapist have contributed to some improvement in the patient's condition is another indication of the therapist's interest and competence. Such perceptions on the part of the client along with the accompanying positive feelings about the therapist would tend to strengthen the therapeutic alliance, increase the client's involvement in therapy, and also increase the probability of a successful therapeutic outcome. Some recent studies of in-therapy process, for example, have shown a definite and positive relationship between measures of patient involvement and outcome (Gomes-Schwartz, 1978; O'Malley, Suh, & Strupp, 1983).

Another aspect of RET that would influence the relationship in therapy in a positive way is the general problem focus. Ellis clearly emphasizes that neither past events nor early childhood experiences are the causes of the individual's difficulties. Rather, it is the individual's evaluation of and dwelling on these experiences that produce the discordant feelings of anxiety and hostility. As a consequence, the focus is on the present situation and what the patient is currently doing that tends to prolong the discomfort. The concern with the here and now is, of course, not limited solely to RET, but is an emphasis in many other forms of psychotherapy. However, it is an important feature of RET and can be viewed as reflecting the interest and concern of the therapist in how the patient currently functions.

The matter of having a particular focus in psychotherapy has been emphasized by a number of individuals conducting brief psychodynamic psychotherapy. Although all seem to emphasize the basic importance of having a focus, in this instance specifically a psychodynamic focus, there is considerable variability as to what this dynamic focus should be. Sifneos (1981), for example, in discussing the delineation of a psychodynamic focus which underlies the patient's current psychological difficulties, refers particularly to unresolved Oedipal difficulties and separation problems. In Malan's description of his approach to brief psychodynamic therapy, the emphasis is on one focal conflict with particular attention to the interpretation of the transference reaction (1963, 1976). Parent transference links are considered especially significant for positive outcome with this approach. On the other hand, Silberschatz and Curtis (1986) do not find interpretations of the transference to be universally helpful. Instead, they believe that interpretations offered by the therapist that are in line with the patient's unconscious plan for therapy are the critical factors in terms of patient progress.

We can see, therefore, that other approaches to psychotherapy may also lay claim to having a specific focus, particularly when they are forms of brief therapy. Nevertheless, it is obvious that these therapeutic foci differ noticeably, one from the other, even when they are all variants of psychodynamic therapy. The focus of RET, however, clearly differs from these other psychotherapies in emphasizing current problems of the client and not being primarily concerned with unconscious conflicts and transference issues.

The emphasis on the current functioning of the patient along with the emphasis on what is maintaining the client's current discomfort thus provides a reasonably clear focus for the ongoing psychotherapy. This also provides a basis for possible recommendations for homework and other activities to be carried out by the client. Thus, the therapy is highly focused on matters that are currently meaningful to the client. They are not diffuse and they do not center around events in the distant past. I would hypothesize that to most clients this creates a favorable impression and a positive climate for psychotherapeutic work. As compared with some psychodynamic orientations, the focus is not on such hypothetical constructs as the interpretation of the transference, but instead on something that can be perceived by most patients as being personally meaningful.

There are, as hypothesized and described here, a number of different features of RET that have potentially positive implications for the therapeutic relationship. Their potential impact very likely is increased when Albert Ellis is the therapist, for the reasons already cited. Certainly one should usually anticipate some degree of interaction between the type of therapy and the specific therapist involved. However, before saying anything more about the differential impact of those psychotherapists who attempt to follow and use the procedures developed by Ellis, I offer some views and speculations about the type of client that may be most responsive to this type of psychotherapy.

The statements made in the preceding pages should not be taken as implying that all patients will respond favorably to RET and develop very positive therapeutic relationships with the therapist, nor does Ellis make such a claim. Patients' expectations can be quite varied and will influence how the therapist and the therapy are perceived. As mentioned previously, some patients may react negatively to the directive and forceful tone of the therapist and to his emphasis on the patient's role in maintaining his difficulties. Some may resist the efforts to facilitate change and some may even have anticipated an interesting and restful period on the couch. The forceful challenging of the patients' irrational beliefs very early in therapy may also jar or frighten some patients away from therapy before an adequate relationship has been established. Without some empirical data upon which to base judgments of this matter, one can only offer personal conjectures. Although some traditional forms of psychotherapy have appeared to emphasize that the formation of a positive therapeutic relationship or transference requires a fair amount of time, this obviously is not congruent with the briefer forms of therapy popular today. In fact, in both dynamic and behavioral forms of psychotherapy, positive features evident in the third session of therapy are predictive of positive outcome (Garfield, 1986). Thus, despite such possible negative occurrences as have been described here, it is still quite likely that a large number of patients will respond favorably to the way the therapy is structured and that a positive therapeutic relationship will develop.

On the basis of tapes and other material describing clients that have been seen by Ellis, it appears as if many, if not most, are reasonably well educated. Both general comments in the writings on RET and remarks offered to patients by Ellis frequently refer to the intelligence level and sophistication of clients. Whether such cases are used more frequently than others for illustrative purposes I cannot say. However, such references were mentioned frequently enough to impress me. Since the type of patient or client is of some importance in the kind of outcomes secured in psychotherapy, I believe it is worth raising this point here, even though I do not know of any actual data on this matter.

It may well be, and this is stated as an hypothesis, that RET is most attractive to and works best with an educated and articulate clientele. The emphasis is clearly on ideas and thoughts, even when behavioral tasks are assigned. Such procedures and mental activities are viewed more positively and are more likely to be accepted by educated and relatively more intelligent individuals. Individuals with more limited education and intellectual resources might not be as responsive to such an approach. Although other aspects of the therapeutic relationship would of course be part of the therapy situation, the communication process would not proceed as effectively with such clients as it would with the more verbally sophisticated. Unfortunately, as far as I know, no systematic studies of this aspect of the therapy have been conducted. However, knowledge of this type would be useful in attempts to select the most appropriate type of therapy for particular kinds of clients.

Besides client variability, we must also recognize possible therapist variability. Although the general features of RET can be expected to be evident in the therapeutic behavior of those who adhere to this form of psychotherapy, differences in performance and effectiveness among these therapists would also be anticipated. As is true in any endeavor that requires skill and application, some will perform extremely well, some moderately well, and some rather poorly. As mentioned earlier, those who have faith in the basic validity of RET therapy and the necessary personal qualities that seemingly provide maximum results are likely to be successful therapists. From all that has been described thus far, Albert Ellis in particular fits this pattern quite well.

Student therapists and others who are in the process of learning psychotherapy generally seek some form of security by trying to adhere as closely as possible to the prescribed procedures of the specific form of therapy being taught. This sometimes interferes with the spontaneity of the therapist and leads to a somewhat mechanical and rigid pattern of therapist behavior. With time and experience, most of us gain more confidence in what we do and become more flexible and assured in the therapy situation. Ellis, as the founder and leader of an important school of cognitive therapy, has chosen to gradually make modifications in the therapeutic procedures of his form of psychotherapy. He has in several ways broadened his approach by using behavioral techniques and being sensitive to the patient's perception of the therapist and the relationship in therapy. This is clearly to his credit and may in part be responsible for the viability of RET. However, new learners and adherents of the approach may be less confident about modifying or deviating from the established rules and procedures.

A COMPARISON OF RELATIONSHIPS

In the last few years, several scales have been developed to appraise the therapeutic alliance or specific features of the therapeutic relationship (Gomes-Schwartz, 1978; Luborsky, Crits-Christoph, Alexander, Margolis, & Cohen, 1983; O'Malley et al., 1983; Sachs, 1983). This work has come primarily from psychodynamically oriented psychotherapists and attests to the central place they accord the therapeutic relationship in the process and outcome of psychotherapy. I refer to some of these scales shortly. However, I first refer to three earlier published studies. In one of these, a number of initial sessions of Ellis were analyzed (Becker & Rosenfeld, 1976). In the other two, the interviews of Carl Rogers, Fritz Perls, and Albert Ellis with the same client were evaluated and compared (Zimmer & Cowles, 1972; Zimmer & Pepyne, 1971). Let us examine the Zimmer and Cowles study first.

In this investigation, a content analysis using the computer language FORTRAN IV was applied to the typescripts of the interviews of Rogers, Perls, and Ellis. Unfortunately, the analysis is limited to counts and ratios of the words emitted by the participants and does not evaluate other characteristics of the interaction during the interview. Nevertheless, some of the findings do reflect differences in how the different therapists function and thus are of some interest.

In partial support of some of the assertions made earlier of Ellis's style, it can be noted that he is the only one of the three therapists who emits more words than the client. He also produces more words than either of the other therapists. In the interactions with Rogers and Perls, the client verbalizes more frequently than is the case with Ellis, and this is particularly evident in the Rogers interview. This finding reflects the more active verbal stance of Ellis and probably of RET therapists generally. Whereas the client in her session with Rogers verbalized (in terms of number of words) twice as much as Rogers, in the interaction with Ellis this ratio was reversed. Whether this is good or bad is not at issue here since this comparison was not based on ongoing psychotherapy but on a demonstration session, and no appraisals of outcome were performed. The study, however, does point out some differences among therapists in their verbal output and provides evidence of the verbal activity and the generally active–directive role that Ellis exhibits in his psychotherapeutic work with clients.

In the other study of the therapeutic styles of these three well-known therapists, they were compared on six therapist factors based on a factor analysis of a much larger number of therapist actions or variables (Zimmer & Pepyne, 1971). In this instance, the ratings were based on videotapes of the three therapy sessions. Ellis appeared to differ from the other two mainly on a factor labeled "Rational Analyzing." This, again, is congruent with what we might expect, even though we should remember that the analysis is based on just one client and the sessions were conducted for demonstration purposes.

The study by Becker and Rosenfeld (1976) is based on 20 taped initial psychotherapy sessions conducted by Ellis. These were selected randomly from 70 recorded sessions and typescripts made of each one. Two raters were then trained to place each of Ellis's statements into 1 of 17 categories representing a specific technique. The objective of the study was to see "whether his numerous theoretical writings led to specific techniques that Ellis used in his own therapy practice, so that other psychologists would be able to see how one major theorist translates his theory into everyday practice" (Becker & Rosenfeld, 1976, pp. 872–873). The list of categories used included techniques that differentiate RET from client-centered, psychoanalytic, and behavior therapies as well as some that Ellis has stated he does not use.

The results obtained from the study are quite interesting. In general, they appear to lend support to the proposition that Ellis practices the kind of psychotherapy that he preaches. Across the 20 patients, the most frequently engaged-in behavior was didactic teaching. This behavior or technique was utilized at a rate of slightly over 36%. The next most frequently occurring activity was the use of rhetorical questions (16%). Such questions were used almost three times as frequently as factual ones. Concrete examples were used as a teaching aid at a rate of approximately 13%.

In addition, and in line with basic emphases of RET, Ellis often pointed out what specific beliefs the client held (8%) and also argued logically against irrational beliefs (6%). With one exception, these were the most frequently used techniques manifested in these initial interviews. The exception was the use of forceful language, frequently associated with Ellis's personal style of therapy and communication. Such language occurred at a rate of 16%. Surprisingly, homework assignments constituted a very small percentage of Ellis's comments. This was due apparently to the fact that assignment of homework frequently consisted of just one statement. Nevertheless, approximately three-fourths of the clients did receive some type of homework assignment.

The use of these techniques "strongly indicated that Ellis was active and directive, did take the role of a teacher, and was forceful in an attempt to change the philosophy of the client" (Becker & Rosenfeld, 1976, p. 872). It was also noted that he gave advice and usually praised the client a number of times. At the same time, however, Ellis rarely used reflection of feeling or content, and such psychoanalytic emphases as the transference relationship or the discussion and interpretation of dreams did not appear in the transcripts. Ellis thus was found to adhere quite closely to his theoretical description of his therapy, and what we have described as the type of therapeutic relationship typical of Ellis seems to be supported.

However, there is one other observation pertaining to this study that needs to be made. Ellis's behavior was not exactly the same with every patient. He did vary the use of techniques with each client, and in some instances the extent of the variability was quite noticeable. The reasons for such variation are not given. The most obvious explanation, of course, is that clients do differ in a number of ways and the therapist cannot, and should not, respond in exactly the same way to each and every client. In this regard, Ellis and most competent therapists do attempt to select and adapt procedures for the individual case.

Another appraisal of Ellis's relationship to his therapy clients can be offered by referring briefly to two of the therapeutic alliance scales referred to earlier. In the Helping Alliance Counting Signs method developed by Luborsky and his coworkers (1983) at the University of Pennsylvania, two broad types of patients' helping alliances are evaluated. In the first type, "the patient experiences the therapist as providing, or being capable of providing, the help which is needed" (Luborsky et al., 1983, p. 181). In the second type, "the patient experiences treatment as a process of working together with the therapist toward the goals of treatment" (p. 481). Although this scale actually has not been applied to therapy sessions conducted by Ellis, on the basis of the general descriptions already made I would conjecture that Ellis would secure a favorable score.

Another evaluation can be made using the first three items from the Vanderbilt Allliance Scale developed by Hans Strupp and his research collaborators.[1] The current revised version of this scale contains 32 items that are to be rated on a 6-point scale based on listening to segments from five therapy sessions covering the first and last sessions as well as three in between. I want to make clear that I have not listened to five tapes of Ellis's taken over the course of therapy with one client, and I have not attempted any formal rating. However, a reference to some of the items on the scale seems desirable to illustrate further the kind of therapeutic relationship that Ellis may foster in his therapeutic work.

All of the items are evaluated in terms of the basic stem "To what extent did the therapist. . . ." The first item is "convey the idea that he is competent to help with the patients' problems?" We have already emphasized Ellis's potentially high rating in this area. The second item is "express hope and encouragement, a belief that the patient is making (or can make) progress?" The third item is "commit himself and his skills to help the patient to the fullest extent possible?" On these two items, I also believe Ellis would come across quite favorably.

Although the above is a very small sample of items from therapeutic alliance scales, I believe it does provide the reader with at least some idea of how Ellis might be rated, even on scales developed by psychodynamic therapists.

PSYCHOANALYTIC THERAPY AND RET

From what has been described and discussed thus far, it should be apparent that the therapeutic relationship in RET differs in certain ways from that of psychoanalytically oriented therapies. The contrast is particularly marked when RET is compared with psychoanalysis. The RET therapist does not sit back and expect the patient to free associate or to explore earlier repressed thoughts and memories. Instead, the therapist takes on a more active and directive role and focuses more specifically on ferreting out the irrational thoughts of the patient. Also, attention to these thoughts is emphasized repeatedly throughout the therapy session. This is certainly evident in the way Ellis operates in his therapeutic work with clients.

Ellis's experience with his own personal analysis and his earlier therapeutic work with clients has manifestly sensitized him to problems

---

[1] I express my thanks and appreciation to Hans Strupp for sending me a copy of this scale and for allowing me to use it in the preparation of this chapter.

and deficiencies in psychoanalytic therapy. The main features of such an approach, having been found wanting, are to be avoided. In discussing the Freudian view of the unconscious as the main motivation behind one's desires and behaviors with the resultant repression of earlier events such as the Oedipal conflict, Ellis points out the usual conclusion that they "must now be painstakingly brought to light by a longwinded psychoanalytic process of free association, dream analysis, and working through the transference relationship with a trained analyst" (Ellis, 1962, p. 174). In contrast, Ellis states the following as his view:

> I contend, instead, that what is importantly hidden in most instances when the individual is emotionally disturbed is not the facts of his problems, nor the whys and wherefores of his originally acquiring these problems. Rather, it is the *present* causation of his difficulties that is truly unknown to him; and this causation is not deeply hidden but can, in almost all instances, be quickly brought to consciousness. Therefore, I hold, even the most unconscious thoughts can be forthrightly understood, tackled, and the emotional problems that they create solved—providing that the disturbed person and his therapist are not so dogmatically afflicted with so-called depth-centered prejudices that they steadfastly refuse to see the unconscious thinking process (which Freud early in his writings called the preconscious processes) that are practically right under their noses. (Ellis, 1962, p. 174)

Furthermore, Ellis does view his approach to therapy as being more of an educational approach than do most of the psychoanalytically oriented therapists. Consequently, although both approaches may actually attempt to provide greater or more correct understanding on the part of the patient, how they go about this task differs. Ellis's is clearly more direct, current, and I believe potentially easier to comprehend for most clients. It does not deal with earlier repressed conflicts, Oedipal problems, transference neuroses, and the like. Also, to the extent that the focus is on conscious material, it is more closely compared with more formal educational efforts. Ellis does not phrase questions or interpretations in a cautiously tentative manner; he is quite positive about what is wrong and needs to be unlearned as well as what new ideas need to be learned.

Ellis's use of tasks and homework assignments also emphasizes a major difference between RET and most dynamically oriented therapies. Some psychodynamic therapists might be inclined to equate or compare RET with so called supportive therapy, since there is no search for unconscious motivations and conflicts. However, although such a possible comparison would not be very meaningful, it does indicate that RET and the therapeutic relationship involved would be viewed as different from a more psychodynamic approach. To a great extent, also, Ellis's more confrontational approach differs significantly from what might be seen as a purely supportive role.

Although the emphasis in many of Ellis's publications is the important differences between RET and psychoanalytically oriented psychotherapy, it is interesting that his *Overcoming Resistance* (1985d) deals with a topic emphasized by analytically oriented therapists. Ellis points out that ancient philosophers as well as nineteenth-century therapists were aware that individual's seeking positive change in themselves frequently seemed to resist such efforts in their behalf. However, it was psychoanalysis that really gave a prominent emphasis to resistance in psychotherapy. Ellis (1985d) states that ''Following Freud, psychoanalysts (and many other kinds of therapists) have also often been obsessed with problems of resistance'' (p. 6), and he provides support for his statement by writing a whole book on the subject.

Although Ellis treats the problem of resistance in a different manner and with different theoretical constructs than are to be found in the writings of Freud and other psychoanalysts, nevertheless there are some similarities. The basic one, of course, is that the process of change is not simple or magical and self-scrutiny is not always pleasant. Thus, therapeutic approaches that acknowledge the problem of resistance may attempt to deal with it in different ways. Other approaches, particularly behavioral ones, may give it relatively little formal attention. To this extent, RET would actually resemble analytically oriented psychotherapy more than it would behavior therapy. However, many of the procedures used by Ellis are distinct from the psychoanalytic ones; we note some of them briefly.

Ellis does use a variety of cognitive and behavioral techniques, as well as some emotive ones, to overcome resistance in difficult patients. Since irrational beliefs are considered to be at the base of the patients' resistance to change, attempts to modify such beliefs play an important part in this process. Thus, the irrational beliefs are disputed and attacked directly. All clients are encouraged to actively dispute their irrational beliefs and to arrive at a new and effective philosophy. Clients are also taught ''to repetitively say to themselves rational or coping statements and to keep actively autosuggesting these statements until they truly believe them and feel their effects'' (Ellis, 1985d, pp. 44–45). Ellis also uses a number of other techniques that are not unique to RET. Included are such procedures as suggestion and hypnosis, distractions, humor, bibliotherapy, and working with clients' expectancies.

Besides the cognitive techniques mentioned, Ellis also has described his use of behavioral techniques in overcoming resistance: ''Resistant individuals especially require active–directive and usually *in vivo* homework assignments'' (Ellis, 1985d, p. 101). However, his use of behavioral techniques may differ considerably from how techniques designated in this way are used by other behavioral and cognitive therapists. The explanation for this, as pointed out earlier in this chapter, is that techniques do not exist in a vacuum, except when described in books. Rather, techniques are implemented by individual therapists, and since the latter vary in a number of ways, particularly in skill and personality, techniques are implemented in different ways and with different results. The following example is one that Ellis describes in working with a 50-year-old client who wanted to change his occupation and go into a new field because it was too difficult to keep up with the other workers. The technique is called ''courting discomfort.'' The following apparently is what Ellis said to his client:

> You want to know what ''inner sickness'' keeps you from being satisfied at work. Well, I'll tell you what it is. It's called ''two-year-oldism''—your demand that the world treat you like a two year old and do everything for you and let you easily get what you want. Technically, it's called low frustration tolerance. But it's really two-year-oldism— that is, childish demandingness. And as long as you have it and keep watering it, you'll whine and scream, as you are now doing, about working on your new job. But when you admit that that's the real diagnosis—two-year-oldism—you'll then stop your whining and push your ass to do the best you can on this job. And you'll finally do quite well, because you are bright and competent enough to do so. But not at first! At first, you'll be very uncomfortable—because it is hard learning this new job. But if you push and push and push yourself, as you would have to do at playing the piano or at any sport you want to excel at, you'll finally find it easy and enjoyable. (Ellis, 1985d, p. 102)

There are several comments that can be offered concerning this particular segment that are particularly relevant for our discussion of the therapeutic relationship. First, this example is typical, or should I say vintage, Ellis. It typifies the kind of interaction that Ellis has with his clients. He is verbally active, directive, authoritative, and also critically confrontative. There is a small bit of forceful language as well. However, Ellis combines all this with a positive compliment about the client's brightness and competence and his confidence that the client will do quite well. The bitter is mixed with the sweet, but more than that is involved. Despite the critical statements made, and they undoubtedly have to be made a number of times, the therapist's interest, confidence, and desire to help also come through.

It is my hypothesis that these latter elements are fully as important as any purely rational or cognitive elements and that they constitute significant features of whatever positive therapeutic relationships are actually established by Ellis with his clients. At the same time, it should be stressed, all of the different elements mentioned combine to make up what is essentially Ellis's approach to psychotherapy. However, as I have emphasized throughout this chapter, much of the style and emphasis is to a large extent idiosyncratic; it reflects the personality as well as the views of Albert Ellis. Although Ellis presents a real live model for his disciples and followers, not everyone can duplicate his performance or feel at ease with it. I know that I, for one, could not perform as does Ellis in therapy. His style fits him, but I would not feel authentic in trying to imitate him precisely. Thus, once again, we must be aware of possible interactions not only between patient and therapist, but also among theories, techniques, and therapists.

In addition to the techniques already mentioned, Ellis does state that he uses a number of other behavioral techniques, which are discussed briefly in the next section. We can conclude the present section by noting that although Ellis, like the analysts, stresses the importance of resistance as a factor impeding collaboration and progress in psychotherapy, his behaviors and techniques for overcoming resistances differ quite markedly from theirs.

RET AND BEHAVIORAL TECHNIQUES

Although RET has not been derived formally from learning theory, use is made of a number of behavioral procedures. Many of these have been developed or used by behavior therapists, but some have not. Among the methods used are reinforcement, modeling, *in vivo* desensitization, implosive desensitization, skill training, systematic desensitization, homework assignments, and behavioral rehearsal. If these techniques were used exclusively or even primarily, one might be inclined to equate RET with behavior therapy. However, this does not appear to be the reality. Behavioral techniques are used as deemed appropriate by the therapist in individual cases, but the basic procedure or emphasis is cognitive. Since irrational thoughts and beliefs are judged to be the causes and maintaining variables with reference to the clients' difficulties, the major focus is on changing these beliefs and replacing them with rational ones.

As a consequence, we reasonably can view RET as a cognitive–behavioral form of psychotherapy. The basic theoretical formulation is a cognitive one but use is made of behavioral techniques. Indeed, Ellis is inclined to refer to RET as a cognitive–behavioral psychotherapy and even to utilize research on cognitive–behavioral therapies as evidence in support of the efficacy of RET (Ellis, 1977b). Although such an assertion cannot validly be made, and in fact has been criticized (Ewart & Thoresen, 1977; Mahoney, 1977a; Meichenbaum, 1977b), most people in the field would be inclined to include RET among the cognitive–behavioral therapies. At the same time, however, they would also point out differences between RET and other forms of cognitive–behavioral therapy.

For our purposes here we need not be overly concerned about how RET compares with other cognitive–behavioral approaches and how much specific systematic appraisal of efficacy has been conducted. It is clear that although Ellis may emphasize "unconditional acceptance" (1985d, p. 18), which may make people think of Carl Rogers's approach, and although Ellis has written a book on overcoming client resistance in therapy, which may remind them of psychoanalytic approaches, RET is different. It is more like the cognitive–behavioral approaches. Furthermore, as I have tried to point out, the difference is in how Ellis and the RET therapist relate and function in the therapeutic situation and what aspects may be important in facilitating a positive therapeutic relationship.

BRIEF VERSUS LONG THERAPIES

Since Ellis (1957b, 1958a, 1962) found RET to be more efficient in terms of requiring fewer sessions than traditional forms of psychodynamic psychotherapy, one might want to include RET among the briefer forms of therapy. In their review of research on brief psychotherapy, for example, Koss and Butcher (1986) note that several cognitive–behavior therapies fit the brief therapy mode. Among those specifically mentioned is rational–emotive therapy. This categorization is based in part on the observation that these forms of psychotherapy "assume an active role on the part of the therapist and employ techniques to encourage cognitive mediation and early therapeutic change" (Koss & Butcher, 1986, p. 631).

As we have already emphasized, the stance of the RET therapist is indeed an active and directive one and is exemplified by the practice and writings of Ellis. Nevertheless, RET has usually not been referred to specifically as a brief therapy in books describing various forms of brief therapy (Budman, 1981). Furthermore, when analyses of brief therapies have been made as to time limits, patient selection, and related technical factors among the brief psychotherapies, they have not included RET (Koss & Butcher, 1986).

Thus, although Ellis has reported that he found RET to require fewer sessions and more effective than either psychoanalysis or psychoanalytically oriented psychotherapy, and although the nature of RET contains some features emphasized in well-known forms of brief therapy, RET cannot be considered as strictly a brief form of psychotherapy. In the first place, I am not aware of any studies or reports that provide actual systematic data on the length of psychotherapy as practiced by RET therapists. Such data would be of interest and certainly could be secured for different categories of patients or problems. Ellis (1957b) stated that his therapy averaged 26 sessions compared to 35 and 93 for analytically oriented psychotherapy and psychoanalysis, respectively. However, a few years later, he wrote that patients are perhaps "seen for about 75 to 100 times for individual sessions and about 150 times for group sessions" (Ellis, 1962, p. 315). Although 26 sessions of therapy would be considered as relatively brief psychotherapy, the estimate of 75 to 100 sessions no longer would be viewed as falling into this classification.

Second, in the accounts provided by Ellis (1957b, 1973, 1985d) it appears that the length of therapy can be quite variable, from a few weeks or months to several years, depending upon the patient. And third, RET does not have a time-limited focus or any specific selection criteria as frequently specified for patients for brief therapy. According to Ellis, RET can be used with a diverse population of patients including schizophrenics and psychopaths (sociopaths) as well as with less-disturbed clients. Although the same active, directive therapist role and focus on irrational thoughts would remain central features of the therapy and the therapeutic relationship, the therapy would not necessarily be brief. Consequently, although some of the features of RET would be similar to those deemed characteristic of existing brief forms of psychotherapy, the number of therapy sessions used may not actually fit this mode of therapy.

CONCLUDING COMMENTS

In the preceding pages, I have attempted an analysis of rational–emotive therapy with particular attention to the client–therapist relationship. Although acknowledging that there is variability among therapists, even within one school or orientation, the focus of analysis has been on Albert Ellis, the school's founder and best-known practitioner. Thus, all potential conclusions and inferences must be tempered by this fact.

In addition, reflecting the present author's own views of the psychotherapeutic process, some attention was given to possible commonalities that are shared by most forms of psychotherapy, including RET. Most obvious, of course, is the therapeutic relationship which seems to be an essential component in all forms of psychotherapy. Certain features of Ellis's personality and how he relates to patients in therapy were stressed particularly. Included here were such aspects as the therapist's authority and confidence in his approach and the absolute certainty displayed concerning the cause of the client's problems and the means for overcoming them. Pronouncements are handed down from on high and are not to be taken lightly! For example, Ellis has clients read his books and also attend his group sessions or his famous Friday audience-participation sessions. At the same time, Ellis uses encouragement, frequently compliments clients on their attractiveness and intelligence, and employs an expressive tone. Despite the emphasis on rationality, warmth and emotions are also manifested in therapy. Empathy and down-to-earth language also may facilitate a workable relationship in therapy for many patients, e.g., "Your wife sounds like a royal pain in the ass." Ellis also seems to have a very good memory for past events relating to the patient. This is bound to be viewed by patients as a reflection of the therapist's interest in them.

All of the aspects noted above may contribute to the fostering of a positive relationship in therapy and be influential in producing positive outcomes in therapy. A similar view also has been expressed recently by Patterson:

> I would suspect that Ellis's results are more influenced by the relationship he has with his clients than he is willing to admit. His genuine interest in and concern for his clients are apparent and must be important factors. In fact, if there are any necessary and sufficient conditions for personality change resulting from a personal relationship, they are probably these characteristics of the relationship. Ellis himself cites a case in which a paranoid client insisted that Ellis did not understand her, yet she accepted and adopted some of his attitudes and values. Ellis feels that it was the force of his logic that influenced her. It is also possible that it was the relationship itself. Of course, it might possibly have been Ellis's authority and prestige, and these undoubtedly enter into other of his cases, for regardless of how logical and persuasive Ellis is, it is unlikely that he succeeds by logic and persuasion alone. (Patterson, 1986, p. 28)

At the same time, it is certainly likely that Ellis and RET may not be everybody's cup of tea. It is possible or probable that religious individuals might react negatively to Ellis's style and approach. His relatively open or liberal attitudes toward sex, his use of strong language, and his own views about religious beliefs could offend some patients, whereas these same views might be responded to quite positively by other types of patients (Bergin, 1980a, b; Ellis, 1980c). For example, in a case where a female client was lamenting her lack of heterosexual relationships, she was encouraged by Ellis to seek what she wants by picking men up. Some clients may perceive this in a positive manner; others would receive it in a very negative way. This may reflect Ellis's own personality and values rather than RET per se.

Although RET has a particular set of theoretical beliefs that distinguish it from other forms of psychotherapy, the emphasis in this chapter has been on the therapeutic relationship, an aspect of therapy shared by all forms of psychotherapy. Moreover, reference has also been made to other possible common factors that can be found in most forms of psychotherapy, including RET. The latter may conceivably focus more on rational analysis and persuasion than most other forms of therapy. However, RET does share many therapeutic features with other orientations in psychotherapy, particularly other cognitive and behavioral approaches. Ellis is quite open about this and this is to his credit. Such openness may facilitate the movement for rapprochment and integration in psychotherapy, and I for one see this as a very positive development.

8

Assessment in Rational–Emotive Therapy: Empirical Access to the ABCD Model

Timothy W. Smith

INTRODUCTION

Over a period of about 30 years, the rational–emotive model has become popular in both professional and lay circles (D. Smith, 1982). In comparison to the seemingly countless models of emotional dysfunction and psychotherapy that have come and gone during this period, RET occupies a central position in the general cognitive perspective currently dominating much of clinical and counseling psychology. One important reason for the growth and endurance of RET is its openness to empirical study. From his earliest (Ellis, 1962) to his most recent (Ellis, 1985d) major works, Albert Ellis has argued that RET is open to and based in scientific research. Indeed, a vast amount of research on RET has accumulated (for reviews, see Ellis, 1979h; T. W. Smith & Allred, 1986).

Prerequisites for such scientific endeavors are reliable and valid measures of the main constructs in the RET approach: activating events (A), beliefs (B), emotional and behavioral consequences (C), and therapeutic disputing of beliefs (D). The purpose of the present chapter is to review and critique the methods currently available for assessing the main constructs of RET. In reviewing the strengths and weaknesses of these assessment methods, I hope to identify avenues for the further refinement of the empirical foundations of the model.

Although RET has always included consideration of emotional and behavioral processes, it is perhaps most widely recognized for its emphasis on cognition. Any cognitive model of maladaptive functioning and therapeutic change must have available reliable and valid measures of the hypothesized cognitions if it is to be open to empirical evaluation (Kendall & Korgeski, 1979). In previous reviews of RET research, the assessment of irrational beliefs has loomed as perhaps the most central problem (T. W. Smith, 1982; T. W. Smith & Allred, 1986). Limitations in the assessment of irrational beliefs produce constraints on the interpretation of much of the research on the model and threaten to impede additional advances. Not surprisingly then, most of this chapter focuses on this central issue: assessing the B in the ABCD model.

DEFINING THE CONSTRUCT TO BE ASSESSED

In all areas of psychological research, assessment optimally follows clear conceptual definitions. The definition of rational and irrational beliefs has been criticized as being vague and changing by a number of authors (e.g., Ewart & Thoresen, 1977; Eschenroeder, 1982; Mahoney, 1977a; Meichenbaum, 1977b; T. W. Smith, 1982; Sutton-Simon, 1980). This problem is not caused by limited attention to the subject; Ellis's writings about these definitions have been vast (see Ellis, 1984a, 1985d, for recent bibliographies). In this section I hope to delineate some current sources of ambiguity.

Evolving Definitions of Irrationality

One reason the precise RET definition of irrational beliefs sometimes seems elusive is that Ellis's views on rationality are still to some degree developing (A. Ellis, personal communication, 1986). Occasionally irrational beliefs are defined in terms of the dysfunctional emotions and behaviors they are hypothesized to cause. Obviously, this tautological approach is unacceptable as a starting place for assessment devices. We cannot operationalize beliefs in terms of the problems we are attempting to explain. Interestingly, the existing research on RET contains an empirical analogue to this conceptual circularity (see the section on the problem of discriminant validity below).

An often-cited approach to the definition of irrational beliefs involves the content of these beliefs. Early lists of the central beliefs included 10 or 11 rather specific beliefs (e.g., Ellis, 1962; Ellis & Harper, 1975). In more recent treatments, a shorter list of three or four more general beliefs is presented (Ellis, 1979g, 1980b, 1984c; Ellis & Bernard, 1983b, 1985b). While some authors have viewed these changing lists and the distinctions within them as insufficiently explained or lacking in empirical justification (e.g., Arnkoff & Glass, 1982; Sutton-Simon, 1980), the course in the writing of Ellis and other RET theorists is clearly in the direction of the shorter list. It is true, however, that the grouping implies a distillation of higher order, more general beliefs from the earlier, more specific ones, and that there is no apparent empirical justification for this grouping. Factor analyses of irrational belief inventories could potentially provide such justification (Tosi, Forman, Rudy, & Murphy, 1986; Zurawski & Smith, 1987), but the belief inventories available for such analyses have other limitations, as is discussed below.

The definition of irrationality in terms of the content of the shorter list of basic beliefs presents an additional approach to the concept: the style of irrational thinking. As noted by others (Sutton-Simon, 1980), Ellis has always described irrational beliefs as absolutistic and dogmatic, and has indicated that these qualities of the beliefs are responsible for dysfunctional emotions and behaviors (Ellis, 1962, 1979g, 1980b, 1984c). The stylistic approach to defining irrationality is more clearly emphasized in the discussions of irrationality that include the shorter list of beliefs. Some support for this notion is found in correlations between the measures of specific irrational belief content and independent measures of dogmatism (Tobacyk & Milford, 1982).

Relationship of Irrational Beliefs to Other Constructs in the Cognitive–Behavioral Paradigm

Occasionally, RET is described as synonymous with cognitive–behavioral therapy, while at other times it is described as a very specific type of cognitively oriented therapy. Ellis (1984a) resolves this apparent contradiction by drawing a distinction between general and preferential (or inelegant and elegant) RET, the latter version including the very specific, unique elements of the model. Such comparisons raise the question of the conceptual definition of irrational beliefs relative to other constructs in the cognitive–behavioral paradigm. It is beyond the scope of the present chapter to examine all such parallels and comparisons, but some are obviously important.

For example, negative self-statements (Kendall & Hollon, 1980) are often viewed as related to irrational beliefs, and research findings involving these more specific, transitory cognitions are often cited as supporting the RET model (Ellis, 1979h). There is clearly a large conceptual difference between self-statements and the enduring, general cognitive construct implied in Ellis's various definitions of irrational beliefs. Some authors have suggested that dysfunctional self-statements represent the activation and conscious awareness of irrational beliefs in specific situations (Bernard, 1981; Ellis, 1973; Kendall & Hollon, 1980). Empirical studies of this relationship, however, are mixed. Some studies find an association between measures of these two types of cognitive phenomenon (e.g., Harrell, Chambless, & Calhoun, 1981; T. W. Smith, Houston, & Zurawski, 1984), but others do not (Davison, Feldman, & Osborn, 1984).

Cognitive distortions (Beck, 1976a) include a variety of specific information-processing errors (e.g., catastrophizing, selective abstraction, overgeneralization). These cognitions are often described as similar to irrational beliefs, and evidence of their relationship to emotional distress has been cited as consistent with the RET model (Ellis, 1979h). Ellis (1984a; Ellis & Bernard, 1985b), however, has argued that illogical or distorted cognitive processes such as these only cause serious distress when the unrealistic views they produce are evaluated in the context of underlying absolutistic, dogmatic irrational beliefs. For example, the individual whose overgeneralizing and catastrophizing leads him or her to view a failed examination as indicating a likely course failure for the entire academic year becomes seriously distraught only if he or she also believes that it is absolutely essential to succeed. Again, although cognitive distortions are viewed as possibly related to irrational beliefs, the latter construct is the more basic and necessary in explaining dysfunction.

Although these distinctions among cognitive constructs are made in theory, empirical evaluations have been less frequent. It remains to be seen if the operational definitions contain as much specificity as can be gleaned from a careful reading of the relevant RET papers.

The Question of Awareness

There is considerable debate regarding the extent to which individuals can accurately self-report on their cognitive processes (Nisbett & Wilson, 1977). This general issue has been raised concerning the availability of irrational beliefs in conscious awareness. Bernard (1981), for example, has argued that basic irrational beliefs may not be conscious, and Ellis (1973) has similarly argued that irrational beliefs "are just below the top level of consciousness" (p. 244). This conceptual issue is critical, given the fact that virtually all of the available instruments for assessing irrational beliefs employ the self-report method.

If these beliefs, by definition, are not easily available for self-report, then the interpretation of data acquired with the available measures presents a problem. Kendall (1982), for example, has indicated that studies of therapeutic process could be invalid if they used self-report methods to assess beliefs. Changes in scores on such self-report measures over the course of therapy would reflect both the initially increasing awareness of, and as a result reporting of, previously unarticulated beliefs and, if the therapy is successful, decreasing actual endorsement of the beliefs. This process could produce the misleading result of a curvilinear pattern in irrationality during therapy if assessments are made before, during, and after RET, or the completely erroneous finding of no net change in irrationality if assessments were taken simply before and after treatment. At the very least, changes in self-reports would not accurately reflect the timing and degree of changes in beliefs.

Are Beliefs Distinct from Affect?

The relative primacy of affect and cognition is the source of a lively current debate (R.S. Lazarus, 1984; Zajonc, 1984). RET is often cited as a member of the cognitive primacy camp. Although the rather explicit and intentional emphasis on beliefs as the cause of affect contributes to this perception, RET actually is based on an interactional model (Ellis, 1984a). From its inception the RET model has held that cognition, emotions, overt behaviors, and situational factors are reciprocally related. Ellis (1962) has gone as far as to say that cognition and affect ''significantly overlap and are in some respects, for all practical purposes, essentially the same thing'' (p. 39). This significant overlap of affect and cognition is not obvious given the emphasis placed on the importance of irrational beliefs in RET accounts of the origin and remediation of emotional disturbance. Ellis (1984a) has recently indicated that this emphasis represented an attempt ''to highlight [RET's] differences from the popular theories of that day'' (p. 19), but goes on to suggest that RET has always been emotive, behavioral, and rational.

Support for this general interactive view is found in a variety of studies on the effect of emotion on cognition (e.g., Isen, Shalker, Clark, & Karp, 1978). More specific support is found in a study of the effect of mood on the endorsement of irrational beliefs. Madigan and Bollenbach (1986) found that the induction of negative affect (Velten, 1968) produced an increased endorsement of several of the specific beliefs included in Ellis's (1962) original list. Thus, there may be some support for the assertion that affect and irrational beliefs are reciprocally related.

The further assertion that affect and irrational beliefs are ''essentially the same thing,'' however, presents a conceptual dilemma that complicates the assessment of irrational beliefs. Although RET theory clearly holds that beliefs and affect are reciprocally, not simply linearly, related, it also clearly indicates that irrational beliefs are quite distinct from affect. At a theoretical level, the RET model explains two persons' differing emotional reactions to a single activating event by appealing to differing beliefs about the event as the cause of the affect. Further, lasting and significant therapeutic changes in emotional distress are caused by the alteration of irrational beliefs. If belief and affect are synonymous, then RET is based on a tautology, not an elegant, scientifically testable hypothesis. At the empirical level, correlations between measures of affect and measures of beliefs are widely cited as consistent with the RET account of the cause of emotional distress (Ellis, 1979h). Such correlations do nothing of the sort if affect and beliefs are synonymous. These findings would instead reflect correlations between two measures of a single construct.

This seemingly "straw man" argument is important in that it clarifies the breadth of construct to be assessed. Although affect and belief are interrelated in the RET model, tests of the basic RET hypotheses require that the constructs can be assessed independently. As I describe later, this is a major problem with the available assessment devices.

Summary of Conceptual Issues in Assessing Beliefs

It is obvious that clarification of several conceptual ambiguities will facilitate the assessment of irrational beliefs. Although conceptual definitions of the construct to be assessed are currently somewhat less precise than might be desired, there is a trend toward increasing specification. A shorter, more general list of irrational beliefs has been posited, and the stylistic aspects of beliefs are receiving somewhat more emphasis. Further clarification of the relationship of irrational beliefs to other constructs in the cognitive–behavioral paradigm would be useful. Important initial steps in this direction are available in recent works, but a more definitive statement is necessary. These trends should facilitate the development of a second generation of irrational belief assessment devices, because they help to define the construct more specifically. Additional conceptual refinements—clearly articulated by RET theorists—could, however, increase the likelihood of even more useful and compelling tests of the model.

The issue of awareness, though at least partially an empirical question, requires additional attention in order to insure that the method of assessment chosen is consistent with theory. Finally, recent reemphasis of the interactional nature of the ABCD model must avoid dissolving the distinctions among the constructs. Such decreasing distinction makes the task of assessment far more difficult. Development of assessment tools is nearly impossible without conceptual specificity regarding phenomena within and outside the construct to be assessed. The slide into wholism (i.e., the view of beliefs and affect as synonymous) is more than a problem for assessment; it seriously weakens the explanatory power of the theory. The elements of an interactional, reciprocal system can be separated, albeit somewhat artificially perhaps, for experimental validation, but only if conceptual distinctions among those elements are retained.

CRITIQUE OF EXISTING MEASURES OF IRRATIONAL BELIEFS

The foregoing discussion on conceptual issues is most relevant to the development of new assessment devices, although aspects of the discussion may be useful in the interpretation of research conducted with existing measures. Most of the existing measures are based on older, content definitions of irrational beliefs and have their origin in the longer list of specific beliefs. Careful examination of the existing measures produces concerns over interpreting much of the apparent support for the RET model that has accumulated and raises the question of our ability to conduct additional useful tests of the model with these devices.

Overview of the Most Widely Used Instruments

Literally dozens of irrational belief assessment devices exist. The majority generate scores for the specific beliefs in the older list, as well as a score for general or total irrationality. They invariably use the self-report format, but differ quite widely in their psychometric refinement (for a review, see Sutton-Simon, 1980). Of these devices, the most carefully developed and widely used are the Jones (1968) Irrational Beliefs Test (IBT), the Shorkey and Whiteman (1977) Rational Behavior Inventory (RBI), and the Kassinove, Crisci, and Tiegerman (1977) Idea Inventory (II).

The IBT is a 100-item Likert-type inventory. It generates 10 scores for specific irrational beliefs, as well as a total irrationality score. The scale has been found to have satisfactory levels of internal consistency and temporal stability (Jones, 1968), although a factorially derived alternative scoring system that enhances the reliability of some subscales has been suggested (Lohr & Bonge, 1982a). Evidence of the validity of the test is provided by numerous predicted correlations with measures of emotional distress (for a review, see T. W. Smith & Allred, 1986), correlations with other measures of irrational beliefs (Ray & Bak, 1980; T. W. Smith & Zurawski, 1983; Zurawski & Smith, 1987), and sensitivity to the effects of RET (Trexler & Karst, 1972).

The RBI is a 37-item inventory. It also provides scores for specific irrational beliefs and total irrationality, although the specific beliefs are not completely parallel with the list generated by Ellis (1962). As with the IBT, there is considerable evidence of the reliability of the RBI (Shorkey & Sutton-Simon, 1983; Shorkey & Whiteman, 1977). Evidence of its validity consists of correlations with measures of emotional distress (T. W. Smith & Allred, 1986), moderation of the effects of stressful life events (T. W. Smith, Boaz, & Denney, 1984), correlations with other measures of irrational beliefs (Ray & Bak, 1980; T. W. Smith & Zurawski, 1983; Zurawski & Smith, 1987), and sensitivity to the effects of RET procedures (Shorkey & Sutton-Simon, 1983).

Finally, the II consists of 33 items, and as with the IBT and RBI it produces specific belief and general irrationality scores. The test appears to be reliable (Kassinove et al., 1977; Vestre, 1984b), and evidence of validity consists of predicted correlations with measures of adjustment (Kassinove et al., 1977; Vestre, 1984a, Vestre & Burnis, in press) and sensitivity to the effects of RET (Lipsky, Kassinove, & Miller, 1980).

Thus, these three measures demonstrate adequate reliability, and substantial evidence of validity through their correlations with each other and with distress and through their sensitivity to reational–emotive interventions. Not surprisingly, they have been employed in many studies, the results of which are often cited as providing a substantial empirical base for RET.

The Problem of Discriminant Validity

Although including a variety of information related to validity, evaluations of discriminant validity (Campbell & Fiske, 1959) are missing from the kinds of studies on the IBT, RBI, and II reviewed above (T. W. Smith, 1982). Although it is important to demonstrate expected correlations, thorough evaluations of construct validity should demonstrate the absence of unexpected correlations or larger correlations with measures of the same construct than with measures of different constructs. Self-report measures are often evaluated for discriminant validity relative to measures of response sets such as social desirability, and measures of irrational beliefs have fared relatively well in such evaluations (Barnes & Vulcano, 1982; Joubert, 1984; Lohr, Bonge, & Jones, 1983).

An additional evaluation of the discriminant validity of measures of beliefs, missing until recently, involves emotional distress. Obviously, the RET model predicts significant, large correlations between measures of irrational beliefs and measures of distress. Presumably such correlations would reflect the expected relationship between cognition and affect. Such an interpretation is appropriate, however, only if it can be demonstrated that the measures of cognition and affect are not actually two measures of a single construct. Put simply, although "measures of irrational beliefs should correlate with measures of distress, they should not correlate so highly with them as to be indistinguishable" (T. W. Smith & Allred, 1986, p. 66). Recall that in the earlier discussion of conceptual issues in assessing irrational beliefs it was argued that not even a reciprocal, interactional version of the ABC model can tolerate indistinguishable constructs. Large cross-construct correlations (Campbell & Fiske, 1959) would be predicted by the model, but our ability to test the assumptions of this model require that the correlation between two measures of the same construct be even larger. Otherwise the operational definitions of belief and emotion become synonymous, and the predicted correlation represents a "thinly veiled tautology" (Coyne & Gotlib, 1983, p. 496) rather than a relationship between belief and emotion.

To evaluate this issue, T. W. Smith and Zurawski (1983) compared the convergent correlation of the IBT and RBI to the correlation of these scales with several measures of trait anxiety—the trait from of the State-Trait Anxiety Inventory (STAI-T; Spielberger, Gorsuch, & Lushene, 1970), the Test Anxiety Inventory (TAI; Spielberger, 1980), the Fear of Negative Evaluation Scale (FNE; D. Watson & Friend, 1969), and the Cognitive–Somatic Anxiety Scale (CTAS, STAS; G. E. Schwartz, Davison, & Coleman, 1978). The subjects were 142 students.

Pearson correlation coefficients among the scales are presented in Table 8.1. Tests of the significance of the differences between correlations indicated that the correlation between the RBI and the IBT was larger than the correlation of the RBI with each measure of anxiety, even though all of the correlations were highly significant. Thus, the RBI demonstrated at least some evidence of both convergent and discriminant validity.

The discriminant validity of the IBT, however, was questionable. The convergent correlation between the IBT and RBI was significantly larger than only IBT's correlation with test anxiety and somatic anxiety. The discriminant correlations provided no basis on which to distinguish

TABLE 8.1
Correlations between Measures of Irrational Beliefs and Measures of Trait Anxiety[a]

	RBI[b,c]	STAI-T	TAI	FNE	CTAS	STAS
IBT[c]	66	68	51	57	60	38
RBI		49	51	54	50	36

[a] From T. W. Smith and Zurawski (1983).
[b] All $p < .001$; $n = 142$; decimals deleted.
[c] Scoring for the RBI is reversed so that higher scores equal more irrationality.

irrationality as measured by the IBT from general anxiety, evaluative anxiety, or cognitive anxiety. Again, although the RET model, especially when its reciprocal features are emphasized, would predict large correlations between anxiety and irrationality, inability to distinguish between the B and C of the model precludes evaluation of its tenets.

To attempt a replication of these convergent and discriminant validity analyses in a sample of more immediate clinical interest, Zurawski and Smith (1987) administered the IBT and RBI, along with multiple measures of trait anxiety, depression, and anger, to 73 community mental health center outpatients. The affect measures included the J. A. Taylor (1953) Manifest Anxiety Scale (TMAS), the IPAT Total Anxiety Scale (Krug, Scheier, & Cattell, 1976), the trait form of the State–Trait Anxiety Inventory (STAI-T; Spielberger et al., 1970), the Beck (1967) Depression Inventory (BDI), the Dempsey (1964) D30 depression scale (D30), the trait form of the State-Trait Anger Scale (STAS-T; Spielberger, Jacobs, Russell, & Crane, 1983), and the Novaco (1975) Anger Inventory (AI).

Correlations among the scales are presented in Table 8.2. As in the T. W. Smith and Zurawski (1983) results, the convergent correlation between the RBI and IBT was very high. These two measures of beliefs were equally highly correlated, however, with the three measures of anxiety, the two measures of depression, and one of the two measures of anger. That is, the discriminant correlations were just as large as the convergent ones. Further, the measures of the separate affects correlated as highly with measures of other affects as they did with other measures of the same affect. Therefore, it appears that all of these inventories,

TABLE 8.2

Correlations among Irrational Belief Measures, Anxiety, Depression, and Anger[a]

	2[b]	3	4	5	6	7	8	9
1. IBT	71	66	66	70	59	61	55	38
2. RBI[c]		69	73	77	70	70	50	43
3. TMAS			87	86	77	89	63	44
4. IPAT				77	73	81	70	46
5. STAI-T					81	85	57	38
6. BDI						80	51	40
7. D30							55	39
8. STAS-T								38
9. AI								

[a] From Zurawski and Smith (1987).
[b] n = 73; all ps < .001; decimals deleted.
[c] Scoring on the RBI is reversed so that higher scores equal greater irrationality.

including the IBT and RBI, actually assess a more general dimension, previously labeled general dysphoria (Gotlib, 1984) or negative affectivity (D. Watson & Clark, 1984). Most important for the present discussion, however, is the fact that the measures of beliefs could not be distinguished from measures of distress. Thus, when using these operational definitions of the B and C in the RET model, the constructs cannot be distinguished. Any correlations between these measures, therefore, are essentially tautological rather than indicative of the hypothesized relationship between cognition and affect.

Very similar results are evident in a study by Lohr and Bonge (1981) that found the correlation between the IBT total score and a measure of dysfunctional attitudes (Weissman, 1978) was nearly identical to that between the IBT and a measure of trait anxiety (i.e., $r = .50$ vs. .49). Given that the construct of dysfunctional attitudes is conceptually quite similar to descriptions of irrational beliefs, these results can be viewed as an additional indication of the limited discriminant validity of the IBT.

A close examination of the item content of the irrational belief scales reveals a probable cause of the poor discriminant validity. Many items contain references to dysfunctional behaviors and affects. On some, irrational beliefs are only implied by the described maladaptive affective response to a potentially upsetting situation. For example, an item on the IBT reads, "I often worry about how much people approve of and accept me." Thus, the poor discriminant validity may be due to very similar item wording on measures of beliefs and measures of distress. This is a common problem in research using questionnaires to study personality processes, and certainly is not unique to RET research (Nicholls, Licht, & Pearl, 1982).

Implications of Limited Discriminant Validity

The implications of the discriminant validity analyses become clear when one examines the typical methodologies in RET research. The prototypic study of the relationship between irrationality and emotional dysfunction is a simple one: Measures of beliefs are correlated with measures of distress. The results are quite consistent. Significant correlations are invariably found. Obviously, such tests are by their nature not very compelling. Very little theoretical risk accrues when the researcher must only guess the direction of a correlation, and as a result such evidence is a weak test of the theory (Meehl, 1978). Numerous such correlations exist in the literature (for reviews, see Ellis, 1979h; T. W. Smith, 1982; T. W. Smith & Allred, 1986). Findings among studies using this methodology include expected correlations with psychiatric diagnoses (Newmark & Whitt, 1983), assertiveness deficits (Lohr & Bonge, 1982b), anxiety (Deffenbacher,

Zwemer, Whisman, Hill, & Sloan, 1986; Himle, Thyer, & Papsdorf, 1982; Rohsenow & Smith, 1982; Zwemer & Deffenbacher, 1984), depression (Cash, 1984; Vestre, 1984a), anger (Hogg & Deffenbacher, 1986; Zwemer & Deffenbacher, 1984), low self-esteem (Daly & Burton, 1983), suicidal ideation and intent (Ellis & Ratliff, 1986), and bulimic symptoms (Ruderman, 1986). Indeed, if one simply counts "tabular asterisks" (i.e., significant effects, Meehl, 1978), such findings perhaps represent the majority of the support for the hypothesis that irrational beliefs mediate the arousal of distress.

Obviously, the inability to easily distinguish the most widely used measures of irrational beliefs from measures of emotional distress on an empirical basis places such correlations in a different light. Rather than provide evidence of an association between cognition and affect, the results of such studies may reflect the hardly surprising intercorrelation of various measures of distress and maladaptive behavior.

As a direct test of this alternative explanation, Zurawski and Smith (1987) subjected their data to additional analyses. First, they attempted to replicate previous studies demonstrating correlations of IBT specific belief and total irrationality scales with measures of depression (Cash, 1984; Nelson, 1977) and anger (Zwemer & Deffenbacher, 1984). These zero-order correlations are presented in Table 8.3. As can be seen, the correlations largely replicate the earlier findings. The correlations were then recalculated, removing variance shared with general dysphoria or negative affectivity through partial correlation. D. Watson and Clark (1984) have previously demonstrated that the Taylor (1953) Manifest Anxiety Scale (TMAS) is a satisfactory measure of negative affectivity, so this variable was selected. The partial correlations controlling for TMAS scores are also presented in Table 8.3. As can be seen, the otherwise highly significant correlations between IBT total scores and both depression and anger are eliminated when negative affectivity is controlled, as are 11 of 16 correlations involving the specific belief scales. Thus, a plausible alternative interpretation of correlations between beliefs and distress is that such relationships largely reflect variance shared with general dysphoria. An already limited methodology appears still more limited.

Zurawski and Smith (1987) conducted similar analyses using the RBI. The results can be seen in Table 8.4. The RBI total irrationality score was significantly correlated with depression and anger. When the variance attributable to negative affectivity is removed, these associations are attenuated but not eliminated. Further, several correlations of affect with specific belief subscales remain significant when negative affectivity is controlled. Thus, the expected correlations between the RBI and measures of affect are clearly contaminated by negative affectivity, but perhaps to

TABLE 8.3

Correlations of IBT Scales with Depression and Anger, with and without Controlling for Neuroticism[a,b]

IBT Scales	Beck Depression Inventory		Anger Inventory	
	Zero-order	Partial	Zero-order	Partial
Demand for approval	31[d]	−14	33[d]	14
High self-expectations	49[e]	6	50[e]	34[d]
Blame proneness	49[e]	42[e]	14	1
Frustration reactivity	52[e]	15	20[c]	7
Emotional irresponsibility	27[d]	9	25[c]	15
Anxious overconcern	60[e]	20[c]	29[d]	1
Problem avoidance	31[d]	14	32[d]	13
Dependency	−28[d]	−30[d]	−9	4
Helplessness	61[e]	40[e]	27[d]	6
Perfectionism	−15	0	−10	−2
Total	59[e]	18	38[e]	13

[a] From Zurawski and Smith (1987).
[b] $n = 73$; decimals deleted.
[c] $p < .05$.
[d] $p < .01$.
[e] $p < .001$.

a lesser extent than the corresponding correlations involving the IBT (see Table 8.3).

While demonstrating the interpretive problems produced by limited discriminant validity, the Zurawski and Smith (1987) results also provided some evidence of correlations between irrational beliefs and negative affect that could not be attributed to poor discriminant validity. That is, several of the partial correlations remained significant. This provides some support for the RET perspective, and perhaps points to the possibility that improved assessment devices may produce more compelling evidence of correlations between beliefs and emotions.

Other methods exist for testing the hypothesis that beliefs mediate the arousal of distress. A common one, for example, involves the presentation of an experimental stressor to persons differing in their previously determined endorsement of irrational beliefs. The RET model would predict that irrational persons will become more upset following the stressor than will rational subjects.

The problem with discriminant validity complicates the interpretation

TABLE 8.4

Correlations of RBI Scales[a] with Depression and Anger, with and without Controlling for Neuroticism[b,c]

RBI Scales	Beck Depression Inventory		Anger Inventory	
	Zero-order	Partial	Zero-order	Partial
Catastrophizing	57[f]	3	32[e]	0
Guilt	36[f]	21[d]	28[e]	17
Perfectionism	33[e]	38[f]	14	11
Need for approval	31[e]	9	14	1
Caring and helping	8	11	8	10
Blame and punishment	47[f]	32[e]	19	3
Inertia and avoidance	43	19	23[d]	6
Independence	20[d]	5	34[e]	28[e]
Self-downing	52[f]	30[e]	28[e]	10
Projected misfortune	56[f]	17	38[f]	15
Control of emotions	40[f]	10	30[e]	13
Total	68[f]	33[e]	43[f]	20[d]

[a] Scoring reversed.
[b] From Zurawski and Smith (1987).
[c] $n = 73$.
[d] $p < .05$.
[e] $p < .01$.
[f] $p < .001$.

of these findings as well, as illustrated by a study by Cash, Rimm, and MacKinnon (1986), who selected high and low irrationality groups on the basis of IBT total scores. They then exposed these subjects to a positive, neutral, or negative Velten (1968) mood induction, and recorded pre–post changes in reported mood. As would be predicted by the RET model, irrationals responded to the negative induction with more negative mood, and to the positive induction with less positive mood, than did rational subjects. This otherwise interesting and specific test of the RET model is rendered of questionable relevance, however, given that the individual difference classification is likely to reflect general dysphoria rather than irrationality.

The same interpretive problems complicate studies of RET process. For example, T. W. Smith (1983) found that changes in self-reported emotional distress over the course of RET were correlated with changes in self-reported irrational beliefs as measured by the II. Unfortunately, with the discriminant validity of the II in doubt, it cannot be determined if these findings reflect the expected therapeutic process or the simple and much less interesting covariation among measures of distress over the course of therapy. Thus, many basic tests of the RET model are complicated by the fact that measures of beliefs may actually be additional measures of distress.

New Directions in Assessing Beliefs

Several new irrational belief inventories have been developed. Some of these are intended for use with very specific populations or presenting problems, including children (Bernard & Laws, 1985), marital relationships (Eidelson & Epstein, 1982), and families (Roehling & Robin, 1986). Based on previous speculations and data regarding beliefs underlying the Type A pattern (T. W. Smith & Brehm, 1981), Thurman (1985a) has developed a measure of irrational beliefs relevant to that hard-driving, aggressive style. Although each of these measures brings with it the possibility of useful contributions, the conceptual and empirical issues in assessing irrationality described above are obviously relevant. That is, these new, specific inventories need to be evaluated for discriminant as well as convergent validity. Expected effects or relationships are much more meaningful if they occur in the context of other effects that are predicted to be significantly smaller.

Kassinove (1986) has recently developed a new inventory which may be less vulnerable to problems with discriminant validity. He has attempted to eliminate the references to affect in the test items that may underly the problem with other scales. Although the inventory is in the early stages of development and evaluation, initial convergent correlations appear promising. Similarly, a new inventory by Malouff and Schutte (1986) appears to be more highly correlated with the RBI than with measures of anxiety (Malouff, Valdenegro, & Schutte, in press). This work not only promises to produce a useful measure, but reflects the critical construct evaluation strategy.

These newer inventories still rely on the traditional self-report format, and as a result are open to the question of whether the core irrational constructs are accessible through such reports. Recent developments in the application of the information-processing paradigm to clinical psychology (Ingram, 1986) have the potential to provide non-self-report methods of assessment. For example, Goldfried, Padawer, and Robins (1984) and T. W. Smith, Ingram, and Brehm (1983), using very different information-processing approaches, both found evidence of preoccupation with evaluations by others as a central cognitive theme in social anxiety. Obviously, these findings are quite consistent with the RET approach. Thus, the variety of information-processing tasks could serve as cognitive assessment devices (Kihlstrom & Nasby, 1980; Merluzzi, Rudy, & Glass, 1981).

Summary of Issues in Existing Assessment Procedures

Obviously the existing approaches to assessing irrational beliefs contain several serious problems. First and foremost, limited discriminant validity leaves too many previous and future studies open to alternative interpretations. Although not contradicting the RET model, these alternative interpretations weaken the support for the model that was derived with the existing measures. Further, existing measures do not provide the interested researcher with the opportunity to generate new, unambiguous tests of the model. Refinement of the self-report format or the development of alternative formats seem to be important tasks for the near future.

A second major problem is the fact that the existing devices have their origin in older definitions of irrational beliefs. They are almost all based on the long list of irrational beliefs, and all emphasize the content definition approach. Measures based on the shorter list of beliefs and measures emphasizing the element of irrational style in cognition are needed if assessment is to keep pace with RET theory (see Burgess, 1986).

ASSESSING THE REST OF THE ABCD MODEL

Although the most crucial issues of assessment in RET involve irrational beliefs, three other critical constructs must also be assessed. In what follows, I briefly comment on specific problems in these areas.

First, in tests of the complete ABC model, it is important to examine the way in which activating events are operationalized. In many cases, these are manipulated (Craigheard, Kimball, & Rehak, 1979; Goldfried & Sobocinski, 1975; T. W. Smith, Houston, & Zurawski, 1984). Such studies provide experimental control over the A in the ABC hypothesis, but can be faulted for the possible artificiality of laboratory stressors. In studies of nonlaboratory stressors, subjects are asked to identify or rate the A in the ABC process. This raises the question of whether or not irrational persons can be expected to generate accurate descriptions. Most current methods for assessing minor daily stresses (Kanner, Coyne, Schaefer, & Lazarus, 1981) and major life changes (I. G. Sarason, Johnson, & Seigel, 1978) require subjective ratings of impact of the stressors. Not surprisingly, Vestre and Burnis (in press) found that persons scoring higher on the II measure of irrationality rated given life events more negatively than did more rational subjects. Although this finding is consistent with the RET model, it raises some concern about the confounding of A and B in the assessment process. Such confounding may be inevitable outside of the laboratory, especially since many theoretical models, including RET, view environmental events, appraisals of those events, and reactions to them as closely interrelated (R. S. Lazarus & Folkman, 1984). Nonetheless, researchers should at least be aware of the problem. One possible solution to this dilemma would involve assessing high and low irrational subjects' responses to a predictable, naturally occurring stressor that is objectively fairly equivalent for all subjects (e.g., elective surgery, relocation). Such prospective studies could provide a fairly compelling test of the ABC hypothesis.

Second, many measures of dysphoric emotions include cognitive items (e.g., Beck [1957] Depression Inventory). While the reader may be painfully versed in the pitfalls of including affective content in purported measures of cognition, the other direction of contamination is no less important. Again, given the interrelationships inherent in the dynamic thinking–feeling process, contamination may not be completely avoidable. Conclusions about either half of the reciprocal causal relationship between affect and cognition, however, require separation of the constructs and the associated assessment operations.

Finally, little has been said about assessing the therapy process in RET. Several studies have demonstrated that RET produces decreased endorsement of irrational beliefs along with decreased emotional distress (e.g., Kanter & Goldfried, 1979; Lipsky et al., 1980; Trexler & Karst, 1972), and at least one study has indicated that changes in beliefs and affect during therapy are correlated (T. W. Smith, 1983). As noted above, the usual interpretation of these findings as supportive of the RET model of change is challenged by the problem with discriminant validity: These findings may simply reflect parallel changes in multiple measures of distress. Obviously, effective assessment of the changes in the beliefs hypothesized to produce therapeutic progress will require attention to the problems with measures of beliefs discussed previously.

In addition, the RET model is fairly specific about the ways in which those changes are brought about. Irrationalities are ferreted out and actively disputed through a variety of methods. Other schools of therapy have developed reliable and valid means of assessing therapist behaviors (e.g., Vallis, Shaw, & Dobson, 1986). The availability of such measures not only allows an independent check on the quality of therapy and therapist competence, such instruments would also permit examination of the relationships among various therapeutic activities, changes in beliefs, and changes in target problems. Elsewhere (T. W. Smith, 1986) I have criticized some RET writings for incomplete specification of the rationale for the variety of techniques employed in RET, many of which do not require cognitive constructs to explain their effectiveness. Others (Eschenroeder, 1982) have criticized Ellis for discrepancies between the descriptions of RET procedures and the content of actual RET sessions. The development of devices for assessing RET procedures and their implementation could allow empirically based responses to such complaints. Cognitive and emotional responses to specific therapeutic techniques could be tested in the context of ongoing RET.

CONCLUSIONS AND FUTURE DIRECTIONS

There are both benefits and burdens resulting from RET's openness to empirical scrutiny. The obvious benefits include its important place in our discipline after three decades of development and dissemination. The burdens involve the ongoing criticism inherent in the scientific method. Application of this critical stance to the problem of assessment in RET produces much cause for concern, but useful guidance as well.

The refinement of methods for assessing irrationality is essential for the continuing empirical study of the basic tenets of RET. In an earlier review of that support, Ellis (1979h) called it "immense—indeed; almost awesome" (p. 103). If the number of predicted relationships is the index, there is cause for celebration. If the limited theoretical risks taken by these studies (Meehl, 1978) and the parsimonious alternative explanations for many of the findings are considered, I believe the conclusion should be far more modest. Issues of assessment lie at the heart of these limitations. Attention to conceptual clarity in the continuing evolution of RET theory will facilitate the essential task of development and evaluation of new methods of assessing irrational beliefs.

Perhaps somewhat surprisingly, I have not included a discussion of assessment in the strictly clinical enterprise of RET. I have emphasized research almost exclusively. This undoubtedly reflects my personal opinions regarding where the attention is needed most. It may also reflect the relative importance of assessment in RET theory or research as opposed to practice. Ellis (1984a) views most traditional psychological assessment as ranging from useless to inefficient. Instead, he advocates the use of therapeutic process and interviews as a means of diagnosis and identification of relevant irrationalities (see Sutton-Simon, 1980, for a discussion of interview assessments of irrationality). Eschenroeder (1982) has suggested that reviews of therapy transcripts reveal that Ellis frequently engages in little or no assessment of irrational beliefs. He infers the particular belief from the complaint and proceeds to attack the hypothesized irrationality. This raises the question of whether or not assessment is useful at all in the clinical practice of RET. Perhaps the theory is so accurate as to render assessment of beliefs unnecessary. Irrational beliefs can, perhaps, be inferred from the kind of emotional distress and the situational variables which elicit it. Alternatively, perhaps the theory concerning beliefs and distress is inaccurate, but serves as a very useful metaphor in explaining and changing maladaptive behavior. That is, emotional problems may not be caused by irrational beliefs, but construing them in this framework and participating in RET techniques may be quite useful anyway. This too would render assessment of beliefs unnecessary.

As is the case in the RET explanation of the arousal of distress, additional research is obviously required in order to demonstrate, more convincingly, the accuracy of the RET model of therapeutic process. Again, issues of assessment are critical in making such advances. Continued development of the assessment of all four components of the ABCD model could provide important opportunities for such work. A focus on RET process also would allow the return of the study of RET to its birthplace— the offices of therapists who subscribe to the scientific method and search for more effective and efficient means of helping those in need. Given additional refinement of the assessment of the elements of the ABCD model, the vast amount of RET conducted in this country and others could yield a rich harvest of empirical studies on therapy process.

It is quite likely that RET will remain popular and important without such research efforts. Albert Ellis's well deserved award for Distinguished Professional Contributions to Knowledge from the American Psychological Association (1986) is as much a commentary on the probable future of RET as its past. Nonetheless, without critical attention to the status and limitations of RET research and our ability to advance it, much of the vital promise and potential of this model will be lost. I hope that the critical review presented here is useful in guiding some of these efforts.

9

Outcome Studies of Rational–Emotive Therapy

David A. F. Haaga
Gerald C. Davison

INTRODUCTION

This chapter provides a qualitative review of treatment outcome studies of rational–emotive therapy (RET; Ellis, 1962) and a variant of RET, systematic rational restructuring (SRR; Goldfried, Decenteceo, & Weinberg, 1974). We have organized studies according to the type of problem or disorder being treated. This should maximize the utility of the information for clinical decision-making. Confronted with a client of Type X, what can existing data say about the likely utility of a rational–emotive treatment?

Although communication might be best served by fitting problems into DSM-III (American Psychiatric Association, 1980) categories (Kazdin, 1986b), many outcome studies of RET and SRR resist such classification, either because the subjects were subclinical or because the target problem is not a DSM-III category.

A Caveat

Unlike systematic desensitization and even the more complex cognitive therapy of Beck, Ellis's rational–emotive therapy is less clearly operationally specified than one might hope for in making in-depth outcome comparisons as we do in this chapter. Another way to formulate the problem is that the independent variable of RET is very variable indeed. Clinical supervisors have long been aware of this, and Ellis himself is certainly not unaware. The consequence for this review chapter is that the comparison of results from Study A and Study B will necessarily suffer from the strong possibility that Ellis's principles were not implemented in the same or even closely similar fashion. What we do know and understand is that RET is much more than just telling the client that she or he is thinking irrationally and would be better off thinking differently. Assuming that Ellis is correct in his theory of personality and personality change, we would expect that anyone who could change his or her thoughts (and therefore emotions and behavior) only upon being explained the theory and told what changes to make is a person who does not have the kind of psychological problem that brings people to see a mental health professional.

Wherever possible we specify aspects of the therapy conducted. But we are more often unable to go much beyond statements of how many sessions of RET clients had. Indeed, most of the published articles themselves contain little operational information.

QUALITATIVE REVIEW OF OUTCOME RESEARCH

General Problems (Children)

Nonclinical Subjects

RET has been adapted to a psychoeducational format for children and adolescents in the form of rational–emotive education (REE; Knaus, 1974). REE tries to teach the general cognitive rationale that thoughts influence feelings, the distinctions between rational and irrational thinking, some common irrational beliefs, and ways to handle difficult situations such as being teased by peers or making mistakes. Class discussions, lectures, and stories help to convey concepts such as that situations evoke different feelings in different people (and therefore cannot be the only cause of our reactions), and that to make mistakes is human and does not justify global negative self-evaluations.

First we consider REE studies involving unselected samples but using clinically relevant dependent measures such as anxiety and self-concept. Cangelosi, Gressard, and Mines (1980) found a 24-session "rational thinking group" treatment superior to a placebo treatment (loosely structured group discussions) and no treatment in improving self-reported self-concept among high school student volunteers (n = 36, 33 girls). There were no assessments to ensure that the placebo treatment (which, along with the rational–emotive group, was run by the first author) actually matched the rational thinking group on nonspecific factors. As in other studies of REE with nonclinical samples, there was no longitudinal follow-up to document a preventive impact, the ultimate goal of such programs.

Knaus and Bokor (1975) evaluated REE as a treatment for test anxiety and self-concept among sixth grade students (n = 54). REE and a self-concept enhancement program were conducted in 85 sessions of 10–30 min each, 3 days a week, and a no-treatment control was also included. One month after the end of treatment, REE students had significantly higher self-esteem scores than did those in either of the other groups, and both treated groups were lower in test anxiety than were controls. This result, if replicable, would be especially encouraging, in that the treatment programs were administered by classroom teachers after only 3 hours of formal training, suggesting excellent disseminability of the treatment. The finding is somewhat dubious, however, in view of a high attrition rate (26 of original 80 subjects) and, especially, nonrandom assignment of classes to treatment conditions (REE was assigned to a particularly enthusiastic teacher).

Grade level affected the impact of REE on self-reports of neuroticism and trait anxiety in one study (DiGiuseppe & Kassinove, 1976). A 15-session REE program was compared to a human relations course involving psychodynamic principles, as well as a no-treatment control. At posttreatment, REE was significantly superior to the other groups in terms of irrationality, neuroticism, and trait anxiety among fourth-grade students. REE seemed less effective for eighth-grade students, though, showing significant superiority only on irrationality.

An unusual feature of this study was the omission of pretesting on the dependent measures. Although this has been criticized (Seeman, 1976), it does eliminate possible demand characteristics of repeated testing (Mahoney, 1978). The most serious methodological weakness affecting interpretability of the impact of REE for the fourth graders is that the two active treatments were both conducted by the first author, leaving open the possibility of differential leader enthusiasm and competence favoring REE.

Following up these encouraging results among fourth graders, N. Miller and Kassinove (1978) conducted a components analysis of REE with fourth graders, using the same dependent measures. REE in a strictly lecture and discussion format was compared to REE with behavior rehearsal and REE with behavior rehearsal and formal homework (written ABC [activating events–beliefs–emotional consequences] analyses of situations). All treatments were 12 weekly sessions. The no-treatment control was selected from another school, and the first author was therapist for all three treatments, so results should probably be considered tentative. All three REE groups exceeded controls on rationality measures, with some indication of added benefit from the full-treatment package. All treated groups did better than controls in terms of neuroticism, the full treatment being superior to REE alone. Finally, trait anxiety was reduced significantly more by the full package than by REE or no treatment; REE with behavior rehearsal also exceeded control on this measure. Thus, there was some suggestion that the full program was superior to the lecture–discussion format alone, though neither additional component alone seemed to add much. Intelligence did not interact with treatment outcome. The lower-IQ group ($M = 102$) was in the average range, though, making this a fairly conservative test of the prediction that more intelligent subjects would respond better to RET.

Finally, Jasnow (1982) treated sixth graders with 15 semiweekly 30-min sessions of relaxation training ($n = 36$) or RET with rational–emotive imagery (REI; Maultsby, 1977) ($n = 37$), compared to no treatment ($n = 22$). RET exceeded no treatment in reducing self-reported neuroticism and trait anxiety; relaxation training was superior to control on these measures as well as parent ratings of the child's anxiety. RET was significantly better than relaxation training for reducing neuroticism.

Summary. Rational–emotive psychoeducational programs for nonclinical children seem to be effective in reducing self-reported irrationality, neuroticism, test anxiety, and trait anxiety, as well as improving self-concept. These results may hold especially for elementary school students (DiGiuseppe & Kassinove, 1976), though Cangelosi et al. (1980) reported improved self-concept among high school students. Most of the data base seems flawed by possible biases such as having the author conduct both REE and comparison treatments or having a placebo control without ensuring its credibility. There is little evidence of REE's superiority to other credible treatments such as relaxation training or of its impact on non-self-report measures (Jasnow, 1982).

Besides attending to methodological refinements such as fully random assignment of interventions to classrooms and the use of multiple therapists equally enthusiastic and competent for each treatment condition, we see two most important next steps for REE research with nonclinical populations: (1) Conceptual/methodological analysis of the treatment target of "self-concept" or "self-esteem." This tends to get measured by scales (e.g., Piers Harris Children's Self-Concept Scale; Piers & Harris, 1969) on which high scores apparently reflect positive self-rating (e.g., "I am good in my school work," "I have a pleasant face"). The treatment philosophy embedded in RET, on the other hand, seems directed much more toward lack of self-rating (Ellis, 1977a; A. A. Lazarus, 1977), so it is not clear to us that traditional self-concept measures are appropriate. (2) Above all, there is a need for longitudinal studies documenting that REE prevents subsequent emotional/behavioral disorders to some degree. This would appear to be the most critical test of a psychological intervention for nondisturbed children.

Clinical Subjects

REE has also been applied to clinical child samples. Von Pohl (1982) studied REE, in a residential and day treatment facility, for six emotionally disturbed children (aged 6 to 12, mostly with acting-out problems). Subjects were selected on the basis of the experimenter's informal impression that they exhibited irrational thinking, which was not assessed. Neither inferential statistical analysis nor a controlled experimental design could be implemented due to small sample size, and behavioral trends were less than clear. However, three of four off-task behavior categories (talking out of turn, complaining, wasting time, being out of seat) appeared to decline during the 4-week treatment phase, though follow-up assessments during the 3 weeks after treatment suggested some return toward pretreatment levels of problematic behaviors.

Rose (1982) compared REE to REE with REI and to a control (human relations course) with emotionally disturbed ($n = 35$, not formally diagnosed but reported to be mostly conduct or attention-deficit disorder cases) and nonclinical ($n = 71$) students aged 8 to 12. Treatments were conducted in 15 weekly 30-min sessions. Although the nonclinical students in the REE and REI group seemed to learn the concepts of the treatment (significantly greater improvement in rationality scores than in control group), there were no group differences, nor any interactions with clinical status of subjects, on measures of self-concept, trait anxiety, or classroom behavior ratings made by teachers.

With learning disabled children aged 8 to 11 ($n = 60$), on the other hand, a 24-session REE class outperformed an attentional control condition in increasing internal locus of control and three of five scales of a self-concept measure (Dimensions of Self-Concept: level of aspiration, leadership and initiative, anxiety; Omizo, Cubberly, & Omizo, 1985). It may be that this REE study with a clinical sample looked more favorable for the program because it was longer than in Rose (1982) (24 vs. 7.5 hr of treatment). Less favorably, it could be because differential attrition was ignored in calculating group differences (the 6, of 30, REE subjects missing at least

4 of 24 sessions were not included in data analyses) or because the control condition was less formidable (small group meetings to listen to short stories).

Summary. Outcome data do not support REE as a treatment for the core disorder of any clinical group, and only weak evidence indicates its possible utility as an adjunctive treatment to bolster self-concept and the like.

General Problems (Adults)

In the first report on RET outcome, Ellis (1957b) indicated his own differential effectiveness using RET, analytically oriented psychotherapy, or orthodox psychoanalysis, each of which he had embraced in turn as a mode of practice. Clients were a mixed group, diagnosed as neurotic or borderline psychotic, each of whom had remained in treatment for at least 10 sessions ($M = 26$ sessions for RET, many more than in most systematic outcome studies to follow). Ellis's global rating of "little or no," "some distinct," or "considerable" improvement, made when each case was closed, suggested significantly more favorable results with RET than with other treatments. Nearly half (44%) of the RET ($n = 78$) cases showed considerable improvement, compared to 18% for analytically oriented therapy ($n = 78$) and 13% for analysis ($n = 16$).

In the light of current standards of outcome research, this study is obviously flawed evidence favoring RET (e.g., type of treatment is confounded with the therapist's professional development, RET being his eventual choice; criteria for judging improvement are unspecified, and ratings were not corroborated by independent judges blind to group membership; we do not know how many clients failed to complete at least 10 sessions of each treatment and why; comparison treatments are poorly specified; assignment was not random).

Still, this report stands as an historically significant clinical announcement of the potential viability of a new treatment approach, analogous to Wolpe's (1958) book, *Psychotherapy by Reciprocal Inhibition*, and provided interesting leads amenable to subsequent formal evaluation. Ellis's impression was that neurotic clients who showed at least some distinct improvement during RET changed many but not all of their irrational beliefs, with excessive needs for competence and achievement being perhaps the most difficult to give up. Decline in irrational beliefs appeared to be associated with greater treatment effectiveness (see T. W. Smith, 1983, discussed below), in accord with Ellis's theory of therapy.

An employee assistance program based on RET was offered to 600 oil company employees (60% self-referred, 40% other-referred), over a 3-year period (Klarriech, DiGiuseppe, & DiMattia, 1987). About one-eighth (13%) refused treatment. Presenting problems involved personal–emotional troubles in a slight majority of cases, others being marital–family, alcohol–drug, and job-related problems. After treatment (M = 4.1 sessions), most (75%) employees rated the program as "very helpful" and their problems as "totally improved." For a subsample of completers (n = 295) for whom all relevant data were available, absenteeism was substantially lower (M = 3.0 days) the year after participation in the program than the year before (M = 10.3 days). The high level of consumer satisfaction and impact on absenteeism suggest that it would be very worthwhile to conduct controlled evaluations of RET in such settings, including more thorough psychological assessments of the employee-clients.

Gombatz (1983) reported generally similar effectiveness of brief (three individual sessions) programs of RET, client-centered therapy, and paradoxical directives for student volunteers. Subjects were not very distressed (e.g., not currently in therapy, not judged by experimenter to need professional attention). Each subject selected a focal problem to address (e.g., weight loss, career decisions) and then rated after treatment to what extent improvement had been made in this area. All three treatment groups achieved average ratings somewhere between "moderate" and "great" improvement, significantly exceeding a no-treatment control condition. Anxiety, depression, and hostility scales of the Brief Symptom Inventory revealed nonsignificant posttreatment differences between RET and no-treatment or client-centered therapy subjects, paradoxical directives being superior only on the anxiety scale.

Two common adjunctive components of RET, bibliotherapy and audiotherapy, were tested in the context of a Community Mental Health Center waiting list (Kassinove, Miller, & Kalin, 1980). Subjects (n = 34) were described as "neurotic." During 8 weeks of waiting for a therapy assignment, subjects received either (1) no contact from the center; (2) rational–emotive bibliotherapy, 16 sessions of coming to the center to read materials on RET; or (3) rational–emotive audiotherapy, 16 sessions of listening to audiotapes describing rational–emotive philosophies and approaches to dealing with problems. Both treated groups exceeded the no-treatment group in increasing rational thinking, but only bibliotherapy was superior to no treatment in lowering self-reported trait anxiety and neuroticism. Bibliotherapy is not typically used alone, but it seems to be a promising option for clinics faced with the practical problem of maintaining interest among, and providing some benefit to, clients who cannot be seen immediately for treatment.

Fifty CMHC clients with mixed symptoms, such as marital distress, depression, anxiety, and guilt, were assigned to either (1) no treatment;

(2) supportive therapy plus Jacobsonian muscle-relaxation training; or one of three variants of RET (3) orthodox RET, including behavioral homework assignments and bibliotherapy as appropriate; (4) RET and rational role reversal (RRR)—including a 15-min period in each of the last 10 (of 12) sessions in which the client leads the therapist through an ABC analysis of a problem; or (5) RET and REI (Lipsky *et al.*, 1980).

All three RET groups improved on self-reported rationality, neuroticism, and depression more than did relaxation or no-treatment groups. RET groups significantly bettered no treatment on one anxiety scale, the Multiple Affect Adjective Check List (MAACL; Zuckerman, Lubin, & Robins, 1965) and were nonsignificantly superior to both controls on another, the trait scale of State-Trait Anxiety Inventory (STAI-T; Spielberger *et al.*, 1970). Adding RRR significantly improved standard RET in terms of neuroticism, trait anxiety, and depression, while including REI added to the effectiveness of RET for both anxiety measures.

A major focus of this study concerned the relationship of client intelligence, measured with a short form of the WAIS, and treatment effectiveness. The lower-IQ group ($M = 94$) reduced depression scores more than did the higher-IQ group ($M = 110$), and for trait anxiety intelligence interacted with group status, higher IQ subjects doing better in RET + REI and lower IQ subjects doing better with relaxation training. Thus, there was relatively little evidence of a rational–emotive approach being more appropriate for more intelligent clients, though a wider range of IQ scores and a greater number of subjects (median splits left five higher-IQ and five lower-IQ subjects in each treatment condition) might have altered this conclusion.

T. W. Smith (1983) reanalyzed the Lipsky *et al.* data to see if, as predicted by RET theory, change in irrational beliefs related to change on the primary clinical dependent measures. After adjustment for pretreatment levels and group membership, change scores on irrational beliefs (Idea Inventory, II; Kassinove *et al.*, 1977) correlated significantly with change on each of the dependent measures, ranging from − .41 (MAACL anxiety scale) to − .63 (neuroticism). These correlations were at least as great, though, in control as in RET groups. This might mean that increasing rationality, no matter how achieved, is associated with decreased negative affect. However, it could just as well mean that the II measure of irrationality is confounded with distress; before treatment, II scores correlated significantly with each of the other measures but MAACL-A scale, and there is no convincing evidence of the IIs convergent and discriminant validity (T. W. Smith, 1982).

Summary.   The set of studies discussed above is unusual among those we review. All concerned individual therapy; samples were heterogeneous with respect to target problems, and four of the five samples consisted of clients who had sought treatment.

Lack of follow-up assessments or multisource dependent measures tempers confidence in the changes observed in most of these studies, but the following conclusions seem defensible: (1) even a brief RET program can lead to some change on target problems, though this benefit does not generalize to mood measures or exceed that of alternative counseling methods (client-centered, paradoxical) for nonclinical subjects (Gombatz, 1983); (2) for mixed clinical samples, (a) preliminary evidence suggests that an employee assistance program based on RET could help to address personal problems and reduce employee absenteeism (Klarriech et al., 1986); (b) bibliotherapy may be a useful adjunct (Kassinove et al., 1980); (c) RET appears to be more helpful than is relaxation or no treatment, with rational role reversal and rational–emotive imagery seemingly useful techniques (Lipsky et al., 1980); (d) no tailoring information based on client–treatment interactions is available; and (e) reduction in irrational beliefs is associated with reductions in self-reported negative affect (Ellis, 1957b; T. W. Smith, 1983), but this may represent confounding of irrationality and distress measures (T. W. Smith, 1983).

Stress Reduction

RET has been adapted in two studies to the form of psychoeducational workshops designed, in a primary prevention effort, to help currently well people manage stress effectively and thereby avoid becoming distressed. Wakefield (1982) evaluated a three-session course for undergraduates in which the RET group ($n = 23$) learned a rational–emotive conceptualization of stress, how to analyze personal problems in an ABCDE framework (D, disputation; E, effects of the disputation), and how to use REI in generating rational responses to potentially stressful situations. Comparison groups included a wait-list control ($n = 22$) and a health counseling group ($n = 23$) which utilized Bensonian relaxation training (Benson, 1975) along with nutritional and exercise advice; the RET class also received some of the same information about health habits.

At posttreatment and 2-month follow-up, RET subjects showed the greatest improvements in rationality. They also indicated reductions in global severity of symptoms on the BSI, significantly more so than did the waiting-list group, nonsignificantly more so than the health-counseling group. RET significantly bettered both comparison groups in effecting improvement (through posttreatment and follow-up) on a novel self-report measure of how distressing subjects would find a list of events. Both active treatments were associated with reports of fewer undesirable events in the 2 months between posttreatment and follow-up. Paralleling T. W.

Smith's (1983) analysis, change in II scores from pretreatment to follow-up were strongly related to changes in distress as measured by the BSI (.56 for total sample, .69 for RET subjects).

One concern in evaluating the stress-reducing impact of this RET course is that nearly one-fourth (5 of 23) of the subjects dropped out of their groups prior to completing the three sessions, and follow-up data were based on 17 of the original 23 randomly assigned subjects, compared to 21 of 23 in the health counseling group.

McGee (1984) assigned volunteer subjects (n = 61) who considered themselves stress-prone to no treatment or to a 4-week Cognitive Behavioral Stress Management (CBSM) program. The CBSM program included education about the physiology and psychology of stress, irra-tional beliefs, and ABC analyses of situations. On the self-report Derogatis Stress Profile, CBSM groups showed significant advantages over no treat-ment on subscales measuring sense of time pressure and relaxation poten-tial, as well as a combined category of stress in one's personal domain, and a total stress score. No follow-up data were available to confirm the preventive impact of reductions in perceived stress. Some attempt to control the experiment-wise Type I error rate would also have been helpful in interpreting the significant findings, given that 16 analyses of covariance on posttreatment scores were conducted.

Summary.   There is preliminary evidence that RET can effect reductions in perceived stress among well people. Evidence of a preventive effect is weak, though. Only one study conducted a follow-up, and (1) the advan-tage of RET over relaxation training for reducing self-reported global symp-toms was nonsignificant; (2) attrition, higher in RET, was ignored in evaluating the results; and (3) no attention was given to issues of treat-ment compliance (e.g., did relaxation subjects actually practice twice a day?).

Anxiety

Generalized Anxiety

Undergraduates (n = 51) wanting to participate in anxiety-reduction workshops were randomly assigned to the following groups for seven ses-sions: (1) RET; (2) progressive relaxation training (Bernstein & Borkovec, 1973); (3) an attention placebo group, who were told that they could reduce anxiety by learning about different "learning styles"; and (4) no treat-ment (Walsh, 1982). Interestingly, subjects' pretreatment levels of self-reported trait anxiety were only average for a college sample.

At posttreatment, RET was superior to the other groups in reducing trait anxiety (STAI-T), as well as informant reports of how anxious the subject had seemed recently. Another self-report anxiety measure (MAACL-A) showed no significant effects of group status on an analysis of variance, so no multiple comparisons of group means were conducted. Making multiple comparisons contingent on a significant F test is a common practice, but it restrains the type I error rate below the nominal alpha level (Wilcox, 1985) and should probably be reconsidered. The experimenter led all groups, potentially a source of bias, though a rater who monitored two sessions of each type reported observing equal enthusiasm across conditions.

Stewart (1983) recruited undergraduates (n = 30) for four sessions of individual treatment to reduce anxiety, randomly assigning them to systematic desensitization (SD; Wolpe, 1958) or RET. RET was less effective than SD in lowering self-reported state anxiety by the end of the first session, but the two were equivalent thereafter.

A 4-week study/discussion group RET program for well older adults (>60 years old) was compared to no treatment (n = 15 per group) (Keller, Croake, & Brooking, 1975). The treated group lowered self-reported trait anxiety from pre- to posttreatment significantly but modestly (STAI-T, M = 47.4 pretreatment, 44.1 posttreatment) and lowered irrational belief scores. They were not directly compared to the untreated controls, but the latter group did not change significantly on either dependent variable.

Summary. The meaning of this set of studies is somewhat difficult to evaluate. RET does seem helpful in reducing self-reported general anxiety. Subjects in these studies do not appear to have been very distressed, however, and the only indication of RET's superiority to another active treatment, relaxation training, derived from a study in which the author conducted all treatments and in which subjects began treatment at normative levels of anxiety.

None of these studies measured anxiety through overt behavioral or physiological channels, which could have provided a more thorough picture of the efficacy of therapy (Bernstein, Borkovec, & Coles, 1986) and allowed identification of synchronous and desynchronous responders (Turner & Michelson, 1984).

Social Phobia

Speech Anxiety. Undergraduates (n = 22) reporting "more-than-minimal level of anxiety" (Karst & Trexler, 1970, p. 361) but not phobically avoidant of public speaking were assigned to RET, fixed-role therapy (FRT) based on the theory of George Kelly (1955), or no treatment. Treatments took place in three small-group sessions led by the authors as cotherapists.

Immediately after treatment, improvement scores favored fixed-role therapy, relative to RET, which in turn exceeded no treatment, on a single-item anxiety measure taken just before the subject gave a speech. Speech anxiety and general anxiety self-reports indicated equality of the treatment groups, with both superior to no treatment. The behavioral observation measure of speech anxiety could not be coded reliably.

Six months after treatment, treated subjects were contacted by mail and asked some general questions about their progress, none of which indicated significant between-groups differences: Overall, 80% reported being at least somewhat less anxious than before the study, and 60% reported receiving at least some benefit by way of generalization to anxiety in other interpersonal situations.

All self-report measures in this study favored fixed-role therapy, at least in nonsignificant trends, but the authors acknowledged that this could have stemmed from the FRT subjects being slightly worse off to begin with and therefore having more room for improvement. Also, FRT apparently involved more direct behavioral practice than did RET.

Trexler and Karst (1972) compared RET (four sessions) to an "attention-placebo" treatment (relaxation training) and no treatment in the small-group treatment of undergraduates ($n = 33$) with greater than average speech anxiety. Both treatments were conducted by the first author. At posttreatment, change scores favored RET over the other groups on self-reports of irrationality (Irrational Beliefs Test, IBT; Jones, 1968) and speech anxiety (modified Personal Report of Confidence as a Speaker, PRCS; Paul, 1966). Relaxation training exceeded the other groups in improving state anxiety just before a speech, and blind raters' behavioral observations of speech anxiety indicated no significant group differences. Treatment expectancies measured at the first session and ratings of the therapy and therapist after treatment did not differ significantly across groups.

All subjects eventually received the RET treatment, and with all subjects combined RET effected significant improvement on all dependent measures. Follow-up (6 to 7 months) self-reports suggested a trend toward continued reduction of speech anxiety.

Systematic rational restructuring (SRR; Goldfried et al., 1974) is a variation of RET which involves teaching a client to use rational self-statements to reduce emotional arousal while imagining a graded hierarchy of upsetting situations. Lent, Russell, and Zamostny (1981) compared SRR to cue-controlled desensitization, a placebo treatment (presentation of nonsense syllables at high speed through tachistoscope, billed as "subconscious reconditioning"), and no treatment, for undergraduates scoring above the 80th percentile on the PRCS ($n = 53$). Groups met for five weekly sessions. Credibility ratings were made after sessions 1, 3, and 5, and with the exception of SRR being more credible than the placebo after the first session, differences across groups were nonsignificant throughout, suggesting good control for this factor.

SRR led to significant improvement on total duration of a practice speech (shorter duration assumed to indicate greater anxiety) and the Anxiety Differential, a measure of state anxiety before the test speech. It failed to significantly influence behavioral ratings of anxiety in the test speech or several other speech anxiety and general social anxiety self-reports. Desensitization and even placebo showed positive outcomes on more measures. Desensitization was significantly superior to SRR on self-report speech anxiety measures. By 8-week follow-up, though, SRR subjects were showing greater continued improvement on self-reported speech anxiety, exceeded no-treatment controls and caught up to desensitization subjects on the PRCS.

Thorpe, Amatu, Blakey, and Burns (1976) studied RET for speech anxiety by way of conducting a components analysis of self-instructional training. Secondary school students ($n = 32$) who had volunteered for an anxiety reduction program were assigned to the following treatment groups: (1) In General Insight (GI, considered the RET representative), subjects learned about common irrational beliefs without specific reference to public-speaking anxiety. (2) Students in the Specific Insight (SI) group discussed a few irrational beliefs thought to relate to speech anxiety. (3) In the Instructional Rehearsal (IR) group, four putatively adaptive rational beliefs were presented and rehearsed while imagining a speaking situation. (4) Specific Insight and Rehearsal was a combination of SI and IR components.

Therapists were rated as equally competent and likable, and treatments did not differ in credibility to subjects. Behavioral speech-anxiety measures showed no differences across groups. General insight into irrational beliefs was more helpful than the rehearsal treatments with regard to self-reported perceived benefit. Treatments excluding rehearsal of RB's (general or specific insight) were superior on several self-report measures of anxiety.

Summary. SRR did not appear at posttreatment to be a useful treatment for speech anxiety, being inferior to desensitization and failing to reduce behavioral and general self-report indices of speech anxiety (Lent *et al.*, 1981), though follow-up self-reports were more favorable. RET has yet to show superiority to no treatment on observational measures of speech anxiety, and it appears to be less effective than alternatives (relaxation, fixed-role therapy) for reducing state anxiety before a speech. It does seem to improve general self-reports of speech anxiety, and this effect is maintained. It probably achieves results more from insight into irrational beliefs rather than practice of adaptive, rational beliefs (Thorpe *et al.*, 1976).

Test Anxiety. Undergraduates scoring above the 75th percentile on a self-report measure of test anxiety ($n = 61$) were assigned to a placebo treatment (which entailed a classical conditioning rationale and a practice test under nonevaluative conditions to extinguish test anxiety), study skills information, progressive muscle relaxation training, or RET (Ricketts & Galloway, 1984). Each treatment consisted of one session, just after the middle of the semester, and postassessments were conducted just before final exams.

The self-report measure indicated significantly superior improvement among relaxation subjects than among placebo subjects. Otherwise there were no significant differences on test anxiety or exam scores.

Warren, Deffenbacher, and Brading (1976) compared RET groups (seven sessions) to no treatment for fifth and sixth graders ($n = 36$) scoring over 15 (highest 28%) on the Test Anxiety Scale for Children (TASC; S. Sarason, Davidson, Lighthall, Waite, & Ruebush, 1960). RET subjects reduced their TASC scores from pretreatment to posttreatment significantly more than did controls ($M = 18.9$ to 11.4, vs. 18.3 to 15.0). The groups did not differ, however, at posttreatment on a general anxiety scale or on performance on an arithmetic exam.

A six-session RET program for test anxiety was compared to the same program with 10 min of each of the last three sessions devoted to REI with test-anxious undergraduates ($n = 11$) (Hymen & Warren, 1978). Both groups were co-led by the authors.

Dependent measures included assessments of irrationality (IBT), social anxiety, state and trait test anxiety, and test performance (Digit Symbols test), and grade point average. Between-group differences were nonsignificant on all measures, perhaps because there were too few subjects to detect small-to-moderate effects. The combined groups showed significant improvement on all measures (including GPA, from $M = 2.60$ to 2.86) from pre- to posttreatment, nonsignificant change from posttreatment to 1-month follow-up on those that were retested (IBT, test anxiety, test performance). Self-monitoring records indicated that neither group spent the instructed amount of time on homework assignments, reducing the integrity of treatments (Primakoff, Epstein, & Covi, 1986).

Barabasz and Barabasz (1981) noted that many test-anxiety studies fail to measure psychophysiological aspects of anxiety. Test-anxious students ($n = 54$) were assigned randomly to RET (four sessions), an attention placebo condition (study skills information, judged by subjects to have been highly plausible), or no treatment. Both treatments were presented on audiotape. RET was significantly more successful than the other conditions in reducing test anxiety as measured by self report and by skin conductance responses to one of two test anxiety scenes (anticipatory anxiety, not actual bad performance).

The authors noted that they administered the test anxiety self-report only after treatment because pilot data involving a Solomon four-group design revealed significant pretesting effects (see above discussion of DiGiuseppe & Kassinove, 1976).

Wise and Haynes (1983) compared SRR to attentional training and a wait-list control for undergraduates (n = 38) who volunteered for test anxiety treatment and reported at least moderate text anxiety. Treatment groups were conducted in five weekly sessions using imaginal exposure to test scenes and then coping either with rational restructuring or focusing one's attention on task-relevant features. SRR and attentional training did not differ significantly in results, though SRR was marginally superior in lowering social anxiety (SAD, FNE). The combined pool of treated subjects did better than wait-list subjects in reducing self-reported test anxiety and test performance (WAIS subscales), not on social anxiety or state test anxiety prior to completing the performance tests. Test anxiety and social anxiety scores were nonsignificantly different for each group at 8-month follow-up from posttreatment, suggesting maintenance of gains, although only 60% of the subjects could be followed.

Some interesting results emerged from attempts to predict outcome in this project. Success expectancies at the end of the first session did not predict outcome, contrary to what one would expect from arguments that such ratings constitute a necessary control for the separation of placebo from specific factors in treatment.

A process measure did predict outcome on the test anxiety scales, beyond what could be accounted for by pretreatment scores. Subjects' ratings of the anxiety reduction experienced as a function of their coping response for the first scene presented in the fourth session significantly predicted final outcome.

Goldfried, Linehan, and Smith (1978) compared SRR, prolonged imaginal exposure (to test anxiety hierarchy, with client's focus on his/her emotional reaction, which should then extinguish, as opposed to focus on irrational beliefs and rational reevaluations), and a wait-list control. Subjects were adults (n = 36) who responded to advertisements and who were not in treatment at the time.

SRR was significantly superior to the other groups on several measures of test anxiety (Suinn Test Anxiety Behavior Scale, STABS; Suinn [1969], Achievement Anxiety Test debilitating scale; Alpert & Haber [1960], SR Inventory of Anxiousness "exam;" SRIA, Endler, Hunt, & Rosenstein, 1962) and social anxiety (Fear of Negative Evaluation and Social Avoidance and Distress scales, FNE, SAD; D. Watson & Friend, 1969). By 6-week follow-up of the treated groups, SRR was superior to exposure on the STABS, SAD, and SR Inventory situation only.

Finally, Arnkoff (1986) evaluated a coping component of cognitive restructuring, a restructuring component, and a wait-list control for test-anxious students ($n = 49$). The coping treatment, derived from Meichenbaum (1972), focused on what students could do to cope with stress in an exam situation (e.g., direct attention to the test itself rather than oneself, reduce worrying). Restructuring, which we take to be the RET proxy in this study, involved helping students rethink the proper role of achievement in life, the need to perform competently at all times, and the like, the hope being that exams would come to be less stress-inducing in the first place. Both treatments were conducted in groups, in four weekly sessions. In between sessions, subjects were instructed to practice their techniques via imaginal rehearsal of test situations.

On the main test anxiety measure there were no significant differences across groups after treatment, though both treated groups showed trends toward superiority over wait-list controls, and both treated groups improved from posttreatment to 10-week follow-up. An analogue test performance measure, evaluation of the treatments at follow-up, credibility ratings after one session, and a state anxiety measure filled out just before one of the subject's final exams all showed no between-group differences. Coping subjects got better grades during the term of treatment than did restructuring subjects (controls being in the middle, nonsignificantly different from either), but this difference did not continue through the next semester.

Although the overall results of treatment were disappointing in this study, several methodological niceties made it an especially interesting study. First, a counterdemand manipulation was employed to try to isolate "specific" from placebo effects of treatment. Subjects heard that test anxiety would likely decline only the semester after treatment, when they had had sufficient time to practice the techniques they had learned. Sure enough, both treatment groups showed significant declines in test anxiety scores only from posttreatment to follow-up the next term.

Second, two types of treatment-relevant cognitive assessment were employed, the IBT (tailored to content of the restructuring treatment) and a thought listing of 3 min of subjects' cognitions shortly before a final exam (coinciding more with the material dealt with in the coping treatment). Surprisingly, only the coping group was significantly superior to controls on the IBT at posttreatment, though the two treatment groups did not differ significantly. On the thought-listing measure, the coping group reported proportionately more positive and fewer negative thoughts than did controls, the restructuring group fewer negative thoughts than did controls. Thus, the cognitive impact of treatment was not entirely predictable from the theoretical focus of the treatments.

Finally, 1-minute videotaped segments from treatment sessions were shown in random order to coders who had not seen treatment manuals or descriptions. Over 80% of the segments from each condition were rated as containing only the intended type of content (discussion of self-statements in the coping groups, beliefs in the restructuring groups), and no segments contained only the type of content relevant to the other treatment. This sort of information helps to satisfy some logical prerequisites for interpretation of comparative outcome studies (Kazdin, 1986a). That is, the treatments differed in the intended ways, enough that differences could be detected in brief out-of-context segments by nonexperts.

Summary. SRR appears to be useful for treating test anxiety, possibly improving more general social anxiety and test performance as well, and being at least equal to alternative treatments, possibly superior to imaginal exposure alone.

RET was useless as a one-session educational intervention (Ricketts & Galloway, 1984), relatively so in the form of its cognitive restructuring component alone (Arnkoff, 1986). Superiority to no treatment and a credible placebo was established on self-report and psychophysiological measures in one study (Barabasz & Barabasz, 1981), and within-group improvement on self-report and behavioral measures in another (Hymen & Warren, 1978).

Interpersonal/Social Anxiety. Numerous studies have examined the effectiveness of RET and SRR for reducing social anxiety. We detail four studies of SRR for social anxiety; in general they seem to suggest that it is at least as effective as desensitization and more effective than no treatment.

Doppelt (1984) compared SRR to self-control desensitization (SCD; Goldfried, 1971) and no treatment for socially anxious (>16 on SAD) adults (*n* = 60) who responded to advertisements. Treatments consisted of six weekly 90-minute group sessions. SCD resembles SRR except that subjects try to cope with anxiety-arousing imagery through relaxation rather than through rational reevaluation of the beliefs that upset them.

In terms of the SAD, SCD and SRR were equivalent at both posttreatment and a 3-week follow-up, both superior to no treatment. The same pattern held on the other social anxiety measure (FNE) for high-rational subjects only. Among low-rational subjects (above median on IBT before treatment), SRR fared worse than the other groups at posttreatment, and all were equivalent at follow-up. Both SCD and SRR lowered trait anxiety (STAI-T) as well and were equivalent to one another. Only SRR was significantly superior to the wait-list control in reducing IBT scores.

For the most part, then, the treated groups were equivalently successful overall (there were no significant overall differences between SCD and SRR at posttreatment or follow-up), and there was little evidence of an interaction of client rationality with type of treatment. In fact, one might have expected low-rational subjects to do better with SRR rather than worse.

Likewise, Shahar and Merbaum (1981) found nonsignificant differences between SRR and SCD for subjects (n = 54) reporting high social anxiety, with both improving subjects' self-rated interpersonal activity through 4-month follow-up. Both groups also improved self-reported anxiety after a role play interaction, as well as several overt behavioral dimensions, but not pulse rate after the role play. Interaction of treatment type with subject's physiological reactivity (SRR expected to be most effective for low physiological reactors) was nonsignificant on most measures.

Malkiewich and Merluzzi (1980) compared SRR to systematic desensitization (SD) and a wait-list control group in the brief (five weekly sessions) group treatment of socially anxious male undergraduates (n = 59). Dependent measures included the SAD and FNE, a behavioral rating of social anxiety derived from the subject's conversation with two other subjects, and the subject's positive and negative thoughts after this conversation, collected via thought listing (Cacioppo & Petty, 1981).

Multivariate analysis of treatment effects on all these measures showed SRR to be significantly superior to no treatment, whereas SD was marginally superior to no treatment, and the two active treatments did not differ significantly from one another. SRR significantly exceeded SD on the self-report social anxiety measures combined and was the only treatment to better the control group on behaviorally rated social anxiety (only when the first 4 min were extracted from the 8-min conversation). Interestingly, the three groups did not differ on positive or neutral thought categories, and SD equaled SRR (both doing better than no treatment) in reducing negative thoughts during the behavioral test, so cognitive modification was not the special province of the "cognitive" treatment condition.

Fewer than half (27 of 59) of the subjects provided 4-week follow-up data, which were limited to the FNE and SAD and revealed maintenance of treatment gains.

Although SRR exceeded SD in reducing scores on the combined self-report social anxiety measures, confidence in its superiority to SD for social anxiety is tempered by the lack of differential effects on overt behavioral measures and the possibly subclinical nature of both subjects (who were accepted if they scored above the pretreatment median on SAD and FNE combined) and therapists (undergraduates trained for the project).

Kanter and Goldfried (1979) recruited subjects (n = 68) responding to advertisements and reporting interpersonal anxiety as a primary problem, but not currently in treatment, for a comparison of SRR, SCD, SCD and SRR, and a wait-list control. Treatment groups met for seven sessions, using a standard hierarchy of 12 social situations.

All groups resulted in equivalent expectations for success, as rated after the first treatment session, and in equivalent consumer satisfaction ratings after treatment and at 9-week follow-up. There were no significant group differences in behaviorally assessed social anxiety, nor in pulse rate reactivity to the behavioral test. Self-report indices of social anxiety (FNE, SAD, SRIA social subscales), general anxiety (STAI-T, SRIA nonsocial subscales), and irrational beliefs (IBT) suggested more consistent effects of SRR and SRR and SCD than of SCD, relative to controls. SRR was significantly superior to SCD on only a few of the variables, however (STAI-T, IBT, STAI-S after the behavioral test on pre–post change scores; STAI-T, FNE, IBT on pre-follow-up change scores). The combination treatment was no more effective than SRR alone.

The authors concluded that SRR seems preferable to SCD for social anxiety. There are several problems to be noted, however: (1) Much of the authors' conviction is based on the number of dependent measures altered to a statistically significant degree, as though each subscale of the SRIA were as important as the entire overt behavioral rating of social anxiety. (2) Few statistically significant (let alone large) differences between active treatments emerged, relative to how many tests were conducted. (3) The first author was the sole therapist for all treatments and may have been more competent in conducting SRR than SCD.

Six individual sessions of RET directed at excessive approval needs proved to be more helpful in alleviating social anxiety/sensitivity than an attention placebo treatment in which the therapists limited themselves to reflective statements and to no treatment (Yu & Schill, 1976). The superiority of RET held for posttreatment and 3-week follow-up on a homemade scale for Fear of Disapproval, a rating of the anxiety felt when in the presence of a person nominated before treatment by each subject as especially difficult, and a measure of irrational self-talk derived from coding subjects' responses to 10 hypothetical situations. No standard measures of social anxiety or irrational beliefs were included.

In this study there was no operational description of the RET treatment, no measure of the adequacy of the attention placebo treatment for equalizing any of the variables sometimes considered under the rubric of "placebo" factors, and no way of knowing how anxious or sensitive the subjects initially were.

Junior high school students ($n = 59$) scoring 30 or above before treatment on the combined SAD and FNE were assigned to seven group sessions of either RET with part of each session devoted to REI, RET without REI, "relationship-oriented counseling" (group interactions focused primarily on the communication of feelings), or no treatment (Warren, Smith & Velten, 1984). Both RET treatments involved in-session role plays of how to handle difficult social situations, as well as homework assignments involving confrontation with fearful social situations.

Both RET groups were significantly better than the other conditions in reducing irrationality, and RET without REI significantly reduced social anxiety (FNE and SAD combined) from pretreatment to 3-week follow-up. There were no significant between-group differences in social anxiety at posttreatment or follow-up, though. Both RET groups improved upon the no-treatment control in terms of a sociometric measure, peer and teacher ratings of social anxiety.

DiLoreto (1971) conducted the only study reviewed here that showed RET to be inferior to another therapy for social anxiety, as well as the only one to find a strong interaction of a subject characteristic with type of treatment in determining outcome. Undergraduate volunteers (n = 100) scoring above 50 on a homemade interpersonal anxiety scale and above 15 either way (introversion–extroversion) on the Myer-Briggs Type Indicator (Myers, 1962) (this eliminates one-fourth of Ss, so generalizability is somewhat reduced [Goldstein & Wolpe, 1971]) were assigned to nine weekly group meetings of (1) RET; (2) client-centered therapy; (3) SD; (4) a placebo treatment involving meetings with the author to discuss general concerns such as study skills; or (5) no treatment. Therapists were advocates of their respective approaches and were instructed to do what they normally would do with such clients; there was no detailed treatment manual as in some later studies. Dependent measures at posttreatment and 3-month follow-up included self-reports of interpersonal anxiety and generalized anxiety, as well as unobtrusive behavioral ratings of anxiety during an interaction in a group of subjects unfamiliar with each other and a self-monitored record of interpersonal contacts.

Posttreatment and follow-up results were equivalent. RET subjects did significantly better than all other groups as far as interpersonal contacts, but SD exceeded CCT and RET, which in turn did better than either control group, on all anxiety measures. SD had consistently good results across client personality type, whereas CCT equaled it and exceeded RET for extroverts, the converse for introverts. Before treatment, self-reported anxiety was higher among introverts, behaviorally rated anxiety higher among extroverts, implying that research using self-reported anxiety as the sole screening criterion (most common practice) overrepresents introverts among the socially anxious sample. Given the outcome data, this suggests that RET effectiveness would be overstated by most outcome studies if this personality-by-treatment interaction proved to be robust (e.g., in clinical samples).

The report of this study was in many ways exemplary and included some of the types of data not often reported: (1) Process measures of CCT and RET showed that depth of client self-exploration mirrored outcome data (e.g., RET prompted deeper exploration among introverts). (2) One RET therapist was significantly more effective than the other. This seemed to be associated with greater experience, which is noteworthy given that most outcome studies use very inexperienced therapists (Parloff, 1984). (3) Ratings of session tapes confirmed numerous differences between RET and CCT therapist behaviors (e.g., RET involved more confrontation, information, advice, and homework, CCT more reflection, clarification, and self-disclosure).

There was no measure of client expectancies or the like, and the placebo may well have been uninspiring, but at least RET's superiority to no treatment, albeit comparative ineffectiveness, seems to be evident in these results.

Emmelkamp and his associates completed two studies testing *in vivo* exposure, self-instructional training, and RET for social anxiety (Emmelkamp, Mersch, & Vissia, 1985; Emmelkamp, Mersch, Vissia, & Van der Helm, 1985). The first (Emmelkamp, Mersch, Vissia, & Van der Helm, 1985) involved 34 subjects meeting DSM-III criteria for social phobia. Treatments were six 2½ hr group sessions. SIT and RET did not involve behavioral exposure tasks. Exposure treatment included in-session (e.g., speaking to the group) as well as *in vivo* (e.g., talking to a stranger) assignments.

All treatments improved self-reports of social anxiety, general symptoms (SCL-90), and phobic anxiety in five relevant situations. Only the cognitive treatments lowered IBT scores, while exposure exceeded the cognitive treatments at lowering pulse rate prior to and following an interaction with a confederate. At 1-month follow-up, the combined cognitive treatments were significantly superior to exposure on the IBT, and at both posttreatment and follow-up RET was superior to SIT on self-reported phobic anxiety. Otherwise the treatment conditions were equivalent. A strength of this study was the use of a fully clinical sample, though it is not clear how the diagnoses were made. Also, no overt behavioral assessment data were reported.

Emmelkamp, Mersch, and Vissia (1985) applied the same treatments and dependent measures with socially anxious "analogue" subjects recruited either via newspaper ads ($n = 17$) or for scoring more than one standard deviation above the mean on the social anxiety scale of the Fear Survey Schedule ($n = 18$). Again, all treatments were generally effective, albeit on fewer of the measures in the case of SIT. Exposure was nonsignificantly different on all measures from the combined cognitive therapies at posttreatment and follow-up. RET exceeded SIT on reduction of irrational beliefs at posttreatment and phobic anxiety self-reports at posttreatment and follow-up.

The two recruitment methods were not associated with differential results, nor did results differ significantly from those with social phobics in the first study. However, the analogue samples were more severely anxious than in many studies, so it is not certain that generalization across studies is safe in social anxiety RET outcome research.

Finally, DiGiuseppe, Sutton-Simon, McGowen, and Gardner (in press) completed a study of social anxiety treatment with RET, cognitive therapy, SIT, interpersonal cognitive problem solving, behavioral assertion training, or a wait-list control group. Groups met weekly for ten 90-min sessions. All active treatment groups lowered self-reported social anxiety (SAD, FNE) and behaviorally rated social anxiety in an interaction with an opposite-sex person, more so than did no treatment, but there were not significant differences across active treatment groups. None of the treatments affected pulse rates during the social interaction. In general, the same pattern (all treatments superior to control, nonsignificant between-treatment differences) held for self-report generalization measures of anxiety (SRIA, MAACL-A) and depression (MAACL-D).

Some limitations to the conclusion of equivalent effectiveness across cognitive therapies and behavioral assertion training for social anxiety include no formal data indicating differences among the treatments, which are in some ways similar, as implemented. Nor was there any indication that the treatments as implemented conformed to expert stipulations for each type of treatment (Beck *et al.*'s [1979] depression treatment manual, for instance, is the reference on the CT condition, so it is not obvious how CT was adapted to social anxiety). The nature of homework assignments is unclear; no follow-up data were reported, and substantial dropout (22 of 79 overall) was ignored in data analyses.

Summary.   SRR seems to be superior to no treatment in reducing self-reported social anxiety and general anxiety, as well as self-rated state anxiety and negative thoughts during interactions. One study found that it led to increased interpersonal activity as well (Shahar & Merbaum, 1981). For reducing self-reported social anxiety, it seems to be at least as effective as self-control desensitization, perhaps more so than standard systematic desensitization. SRR seems to have less impact on overt behavioral and physiological indices of social anxiety. Attempts to enhance its effectiveness by adding SCD or to predict differential response to SRR and SCD have been fairly unsuccessful.

RET seems better than no treatment for self-reported and behaviorally rated social anxiety, less useful for physiologically measured anxiety. RET has exceeded groups called "placebo" on self-report and behavioral measures (DiLoreto, 1971; Yu & Schill, 1976), but it is not certain that the placebo treatments were effective controls. Relative to comparison treatments, RET seemed less effective than systematic desensitization in one study but generally equivalent to client-centered therapy, exposure, and several cognitive–behavioral treatments. Exceptions include one finding of less effectiveness than exposure on pulse rate, a replicated finding of superiority to SIT on self-rated phobic anxiety, and superiority to SD and CCT in increasing interpersonal activity. DiLoreto (1971) found RET more helpful for introverts, a potentially useful piece of information that has not been followed up in subsequent studies using more fully clinical samples (e.g., Emmelkamp, Mersch, Vissia, & Van der Helm, 1985).

Agoraphobia

The cognitive techniques associated with RET, stripped of behavioral homework assignments often used clinically, have fared relatively poorly in the treatment of agoraphobia in a series of studies conducted by Emmelkamp and his co-workers.

Emmelkamp *et al.* (1978) compared *in vivo* exposure to difficult situations with a cognitive package including SIT and disputation of irrational beliefs considered relevant to agoraphobia. Treatments were conducted in five 2-hour group sessions in the course of just a week, and a crossover design was used such that each subject received both treatments. Combining across first and second treatments, exposure was superior at increasing the amount of time the average client could stay out alone walking a standardized test route and at reducing anxiety and avoidance (as rated by both the client and an observer) in agoraphobic situations. One-month follow-up suggested that overall treatment effects were maintained; differential effects of treatments could not be evaluated at followup, as all subjects had received both treatments.

Emmelkamp *et al.* (1978) noted several possible interpretations of the above results, which were much less favorable to a cognitive approach than most subclinical anxiety studies: (1) Relative to student analogues, agoraphobic patients may have a greater component of physiological reactivity, which might not be ameliorated by the verbal cognitive treatment. (2) A combined cognitive treatment (RET and SIT) may need more time than one week to take effect. (3) Even if the cognitive component alone is inferior to *in vivo* exposure, a cognitive–behavioral package might be preferable to exposure alone.

Some of these possibilities were tested by a study ($n = 27$) of the cognitive treatment noted above, exposure (as above), and a cognitive–behavioral treatment featuring *in vivo* exposure and SIT (Emmelkamp & Mersch, 1982). Treatment involved eight 2-hour group sessions. At posttreatment the RET and SIT condition appeared to have less impact on behavioral measures than did the groups receiving *in vivo* exposure.

By 1-month follow-up, though, the cognitive group had continued to improve while the exposure-only group relapsed somewhat. No between-group differences were significant, except that the cognitive treatment exceeded exposure alone in improving self-reported assertiveness.

The cognitive treatment in Emmelkamp and Mersch (1982) had focused more on insight into irrational beliefs than on rehearsal of adaptive self-instructions. That this seemed more successful than the more equal combination of the two in the 1978 study, as well as the finding that SIT added nothing to the effectiveness of exposure in the 1982 study, prompted a direct comparison of SIT and RET as separate treatments (Emmelkamp, Brilman, Kuiper, & Mersch, 1986). Exposure was again included as the third treatment, this time with explicit instruction to practice *in vivo* exposure as homework between sessions. Treatments consisted of six 2½-hour group sessions in 3 weeks, and subjects were 43 agoraphobics by DSM-III criteria.

Although all treatments showed significant within-group improvement on target symptom and generalization (SCL-90) measures, only RET achieved significant reduction of irrational thinking as measured by the IBT. Exposure was significantly better than the cognitive treatments at increasing the number of steps along a standardized walk which subjects could complete, as well as therapist and observer-rated anxiety and avoidance behavior. Anxiety and avoidance differences were maintained through 1-month follow-up. Subsequent exposure treatment effected further improvement on self-reported and behaviorally assessed agoraphobia measures among subjects who had received RET as a first treatment.

A clinical rating scale based on the extent to which subjects lowered their average (9-point scales) ratings for phobic anxiety and avoidance in difficult situations showed that RET failed (less than 2 points change) for 11 of 15 subjects as a first treatment, with only 1 subject being much improved (over 4 points average change). By comparison, SIT was a failure for 6 of 14 and exposure for 4 of 14. Five of 14 exposure subjects were much improved.

Summary.   As a cognitive-only treatment, RET appears to be inferior to *in vivo* exposure in reducing anxiety and avoidance behavior among people with agoraphobia, especially when the exposure treatment includes self-directed exposure as homework. An integrated cognitive–behavioral (simultaneously) version of RET remains to be tested, but as yet there is no evidence that rational–emotive analyses add anything to *in vivo* exposure. This may be because live confrontation with feared situations is the optimal way to change cognitions about them, rather than using office discussions for this purpose (Emmelkamp *et al.*, 1978). Whether adding RET to exposure treatment leads to better maintenance of gains remains to be studied.

Simple Phobia

SRR has fared poorly as a treatment for simple phobias. In a single-case experimental design (multiple baseline across subjects), SRR was tested against therapist-assisted *in vivo* exposure for scriptophobics (n = 3; Biran, Augusto, & Wilson, 1981). Each phase of treatment consisted of five individual 90-minute sessions, two subjects receiving SRR before exposure, the third exposure only. On a 13-task Behavioral Approach Test (highest item on hierarchy being to open a new savings account at a bank), baseline phases and SRR phases had no impact, whereas exposure sessions effected maximal performance, which was maintained by all three subjects through 9-month follow-up assessment and seemed to generalize to naturalistic settings; for instance, two of the subjects obtained full-time employment, the other volunteer work. Subjective fear during behavioral performance, though, tended to return after treatment to prior levels, and more general emotional adjustment measures (e.g., of social anxiety, depression, marital satisfaction, assertiveness) were for the most part not altered by treatment. Thus, *in vivo* exposure had a strong and lasting effect on behavioral performance, less impact on subjective fear or more general measures than the target phobia, and preceding it with SRR did not help. The authors speculated that the SRR sessions may have been too brief to generate cognitive change (not measured here) or may have focused too narrowly on the phobia, rather than a general overconcern about social evaluation that might underlie fear of writing in public.

Guided exposure treatment proved more effective than SRR combined with some elements of Meichenbaum's self-instructional training for clients (n = 22) suffering from various simple phobias (DSM-III diagnoses—fears of heights, elevators, or darkness) (Biran & Wilson, 1981). Exposure was more effective in improving Behavioral Approach Test performance; 9 of 11 clients achieved maximal performance on their hierarchies, compared to 1 of 11 in the SRR group. Exposure also improved subjective fear during the behavioral test, self-efficacy expectations for completing the test, maximum heart rate, and skin potential amplitude during phobic imagery, more so than did SRR. SRR subjects showed significant improvement in irrational thinking (IBT), depressive symptoms (Beck Depression Inventory, BDI; Beck, Ward, Mendelson, Mock, & Erbaugh, 1961), and social anxiety (FNE), unlike exposure subjects, suggesting the possible utility of combining treatment of the focal phobia with *in vivo* exposure and treatment of more general social concerns with cognitive methods.

Effects of exposure treatment were maintained through 6-month follow-up. SRR subjects were offered exposure treatment after 1-month follow-up if they had not achieved maximal BAT performance, and of the seven who accepted, six achieved maximal performance after the exposure sessions.

Confidence in the meaning of these comparative results was strengthened by (1) nonsignificant differences between exposure and SRR in treatment credibility and client expectations of success after the first session, and (2) indications from clients' homework sheets that all exposure subjects practiced confronting the feared stimuli in real life whereas only 2 of 11 SRR subjects did, the latter practicing (per instructions) rational reevaluation of anxiety reactions they noted.

Summary. SRR appears to be less effective than *in vivo* exposure in treating subjective, behavioral, and physiological indices of fear associated with simple phobia. It may have a place as a supplementary treatment to address general social anxiety.

Obsessions

Neuman (1985) reported on therapy for six clients who sought treatment at an outpatient clinic for intrusive unpleasant obsessive thoughts, regardless of whether they had full Obsessive–Compulsive Disorder. Clients received weekly individual sessions of RET (focusing largely on obsessive tendency to get upset about having obsessions, think that one must not have them, etc.), thought stopping, and exposure in imagery. Each phase of treatment lasted at least 4 weeks, until either termination due to successful resolution (elimination of obsessions, or at least 90% reduction in the duration of obsessions from previous week, maintained for 2 consecutive weeks) or a phase switch due to reaching a plateau (<20% reduction from one week to the next in duration of obsessions).

Response to treatment varied. The two clients who received RET first improved sufficiently that no other treatment was needed. It would be misleading to conclude superiority of RET to the other treatments on this basis, though; one of the clients had relatively mild symptoms to begin with, and the other showed a substantial decrease in obsessions during baseline, just before the introduction of treatment, so that improvement could not be clearly attributed to the intervention (Kazdin, 1982). Three other clients were helped very little by any of the treatments. Finally, one improved some with exposure in imagery and then continued to improve with RET until being considered a treatment success.

Overall, change scores from the previous phase suggested slight increase in frequency, decrease in duration and intensity of obsessions with RET, slightly better results on each dimension with exposure, and worsening of duration and intensity, reduction in frequency during thought stopping. RET was more helpful than the other phases in terms of improving self and collateral-reported social adjustment (interference of obsessions in daily functioning), social anxiety (SAD), and especially depression (BDI and therapist-rated Hamilton scale).

It should be noted that 9 of 15 subjects were not included in data analyses, having either dropped out or been eliminated (e.g., for excessive noncompliance), so generalizability is uncertain.

Summary.   Effectiveness of RET (relative to no treatment) for treating obsessions could not be established by this study, given its design. But it would seem that for relatively less severe obsessions RET may be an appropriate treatment. It may be especially useful as an adjunctive treatment in that it seemed to reduce depression and functional problems around the obsessions, more so than the obsessions themselves.

Assertiveness

Rational–emotive approaches have shown effectiveness in the treatment of unassertiveness, but it is not clear that they add anything to standard behavioral approaches to assertion training.

Alden, Safran, and Weideman (1978) compared a six-session behavioral skills training program, involving modeling and rehearsal of assertive responses and self-monitoring of *in vivo* practice as homework, a cognitive–behavioral treatment incorporating both RET and SIT techniques, and no treatment with subjects ($n = 27$) seeking assertion training. The two active treatments were equivalent on all measures, both significantly exceeding the control group at posttreatment on irrational beliefs (homemade measure), a self-report measure of assertion, global behavioral ratings of assertiveness and anxiety from role plays, as well as two of five (facial expression, body expression) specific assertiveness dimensions.

Likewise, Hammen, Jacobs, Mayol, and Cochran (1980) found that incorporation of rational–emotive and self-instructional techniques did not improve upon the results of an 8-week skill-training program for assertion, though both conditions exceeded no treatment. Subjects ($n = 55$) scored below zero on the Rathus Assertiveness Schedule (RAS) before treatment and were screened in interviews for having significant assertion problems. At posttreatment (and through 4-week follow-up on self-report measures and Goal Attainment Scaling) the active treatments equaled each other and outperformed no treatment on self-reports of assertion, social anxiety (FNE, nonsignificant trend on SAD), and dysfunctional attitudes (DAS), as well as global behaviorally rated assertive content; nonverbal assertion dimensions were less clearly responsive to treatment.

A median split on pretreatment DAS scores, creating groups with high-versus-low levels of dysfunctional attitudes, predicted response to treatment, with low-DAS subjects generally doing better, but there were no significant interactions of DAS status with type of treatment. Outcome also did not significantly differ for subjects who were in therapy at the start of the study, suggesting that the common practice of excluding such subjects may not affect conclusions about the efficacy of treatments for unassertiveness.

Cognitive aspects of RET, behavioral assertion training, and the combination of the two were compared to no treatment or an unstructured discussion group with nondistressed college student subjects ($n = 51$) (Tiegerman & Kassinove, 1977). The RET alone group did not reduce social anxiety (FNE, SAD) significantly more than did the control groups; treatments including behavioral assertion training did so only on the SAD. All active treatments increased self-reported assertiveness (College Self-Expression Scale) more than did controls.

Thus, there was no advantage of combining cognitive and behavioral components of assertion training here. As in most components studies, the number of sessions and amount of time in treatment was the same in the combined conditions as in the component treatments, rather than increasing the time to allow for equal treatment of each element as in the other groups. This prevents finding superior effectiveness of combined treatments solely because of additional therapist time, but it may result in inferior application of each component and therefore not exploit the full potential of an integrated treatment (Kendall & Norton-Ford, 1982). Process measures (behavioral skill, cognitions targeted by the cognitive-only condition) could have provided a check on this possibility.

A very similar study (LeVine-Welsh, 1982) found no significant impact at posttreatment or 5-week follow-up on self-reported assertiveness of RET, behavioral assertion training, or a combination, relative to no treatment. Posttreatment behavioral observations, however, suggested significantly improved assertion on the part of the behavioral and combined treatment groups, not the RET group. Subjects were women who had signed up for noncredit community college assertion workshops. The treatment was only 5 weekly group sessions, which may have contributed to the failure of RET alone to show some benefits.

An even briefer program (two sessions) combining disputation of irrational beliefs with behavioral assertion training failed to add to the effectiveness of the behavioral treatment alone (Wolfe & Fodor, 1977) on any measure with women ($n = 64$) who had responded to assertion training notices at an outpatient clinic. Both were superior to a consciousness-raising discussion group and to no treatment for improving assertive content on a role play assessment. Paralinguistic assertiveness cues in the role play were improved more by the behavioral treatment than by consciousness raising, with all three active treatments superior to no treatment. Self-reports of assertiveness and social anxiety did not significantly differ across groups, though the combined treatment reduced state anxiety during assertion role plays.

Linehan, Goldfried, and Goldfried (1979) compared SRR with behavior rehearsal, a combination of the two, a nondirective control, or no treatment for women ($n = 79$) scoring below zero on the RAS before treatment. Treatment was conducted individually over eight weekly sessions. All treatments significantly increased self-reported assertion (RAS; homemade Assertion Difficulty Inventory, ADI) and reduced anxiety (SRIA) through posttreatment and 8–10 week follow-up. The combined BR/SRR group exceeded the nondirective group on the ADI and the no-treatment control on all self-reports, while SRR exceeded no treatment on all but the RAS, BR only on the ADI. There were no significant between-group differences among the cognitive and behavioral treatments on self-reports. Behavioral role-play tests showed no significant advantage of adding SRR to BR; both were superior to the other three groups on assertive content. An *in vivo* test showed both BR groups to be superior to both control groups.

All three cognitive and behavioral groups exceeded both controls on peer informant reports that the subject was easier to get along with (44% [11% said she was harder to get along with] vs. 17% [14% said harder]). This sort of information seems valuable in ensuring that assertion principles are carrying over into real life and are being implemented in a nonabrasive, rights-respecting fashion by the subject.

Finally, Carmody (1978) reported the only comparison of RET to another cognitive treatment, SIT, for unassertiveness. Both treatments included behavior rehearsal, and a behavioral-assertion training group and no-treatment controls were also included. Subjects ($n = 56$ completers) were not in treatment and had responded to recruiting advertisements. The active treatments outdid controls only on improvement of Self-Assertion Scale scores, not RAS, SAD, FNE, or behaviorally assessed role plays, though only the active treatments showed within-group improvement. RET exceeded SIT and control at posttreatment on an *in vivo* refusal test. There were no significant group differences at 3-month follow-up.

Summary.   The cognitive aspects of RET alone may improve self-reported assertion, though this did not generalize to reduction of social anxiety

(Tiegerman & Kassinove, 1977). SRR as a cognitive-only treatment led to improvement on self-reported assertion, social anxiety, and informant reports of ease of getting along with the subject, though behaviorally assessed assertion increased more if specific behavioral training was added (Linehan et al., 1979). When behavioral assertion-training components are incorporated (e.g., behavior rehearsal, modeling), both RET and SRR usually appear to be helpful. Evidence from community and clinical samples suggests that this impact is greater than that of nondirective or consciousness-raising discussion groups (Linehan et al., 1979; Wolfe & Fodor, 1977). Behavioral tests respond more consistently than do self-reports.

Across varying follow-up intervals (0 to 3 months), recruitment methods (students to fully clinical samples), dependent measures (self-reports, behavioral observations, peer reports), and treatment formats (individual or group, 2 to 12 sessions), there seems consistently to be no significant advantage to adding RET or SRR cognitive techniques to standard behavioral-assertion training therapies. The possibility that adding cognitive components would be especially helpful for a subset of clients has been tested only once, with a negative result (Hammen et al., 1980).

Headaches

RET did not add to the utility of a 10-session program of digit temperature biofeedback for treatment of migraine headaches (Lake, Rainey, & Papsdorf, 1979). Reduction in daily average headache activity from baseline to 3-month follow-up showed no significant differences among EMG biofeedback, a self-monitoring control group, and digit temperature biofeedback with or without RET. Small samples ($n = 6$ per group) limited the power of this study to detect group differences, however.

Considering 33% reduction from baseline to be a clinically significant response, the EMG biofeedback group (6/6 responding) was significantly superior to control (1/6), with digit temperature biofeedback with (2/6) or without (4/6) RET nonsignificantly different from control. As the authors acknowledged, three 30–40 min sessions of RET-oriented discussion added on to biofeedback sessions do not provide an adequate test of the utility of RET for this population. Perhaps the most notable finding, then, was that IBT scores declined significantly after treatment and equally across groups; irrational beliefs were not preferentially affected by RET.

RET showed better results, evaluated as a sole treatment, with muscle contraction or "tension" headache (Finn & DiGiuseppe, in press). A group RET program incorporating REI and rational role reversal was compared to progressive muscle relaxation training (Bernstein & Borkovec, 1973), an insight-oriented headache discussion group, and a control self-monitoring group.

RET and relaxation training had similar effects: Both failed to significantly reduce average duration of headaches; both reduced average headache severity, but these improvements did not last through 2-month follow-up; both reduced headache frequency and increased the proportion of headache-free days, significantly outperforming the other groups on these measures. Collateral reports of the subjects' improvement corroborated self-ratings. Resting frontalis EMG, on the other hand, showed no treatment effects for any group.

The above results concerned completers of the program; 13 of 48 original subjects dropped out. Considering all subjects, for both RET and progressive relaxation, one-third dropped out, about one-third showed clinically significant reduction in headache measures from pretreatment to follow-up (defined here as 50% reduction), and one-third completed but did not respond successfully. No information on prediction of response to either treatment was available, which would facilitate decision-making regarding when to prefer RET to a standard treatment such as relaxation or biofeedback training.

Summary. RET showed no effectiveness in the treatment of migraine headaches (Lake *et al.*, 1979), but it has been tested only as a brief adjunct to biofeedback training. By itself, it appeared to be about as effective as progressive muscle relaxation training in reducing frequency of tension headaches, achieving substantial benefits for about one-third of subjects (Finn & DiGiuseppe, in press).

Stuttering

Stuttering patients ($n = 20$) from a speech and hearing department were assigned to one of five conditions: (1) RET with *in vivo* tasks (telephone calls to significant acquaintances and conversations with relative strangers), (2) RET without *in vivo* tasks, (3) systematic desensitization with *in vivo* tasks, (4) Systematic desensitization without *in vivo* tasks, or (5) no treatment (Moleski & Tosi, 1976). Treatments involved eight individual sessions. Expert raters deemed each therapist to be adhering to the intended treatments, based on session audiotapes.

Dependent variables included self-reports of anxiety and attitudes toward stuttering, as well as both the rate of speaking and proportion of disfluencies on two speaking tasks. Analyses of variance on pre–post change scores for each dependent variable suggested that RET was superior (nonsignificant trends) to SD in reducing disfluencies on both behavioral tasks. On one measure of disfluencies, *in vivo* assignments were significantly beneficial. From posttreatment to 1-month follow-up, RET was significantly superior to SD in reducing anxiety and marginally superior in improving attitudes toward stuttering. Presence of *in vivo* tasks had a marginally significant positive impact on improving attitudes, Considering the entire time from pretreatment to follow-up, RET was significantly superior to SD in improving attitudes, marginally superior in reducing disfluencies on one task. Absence of *in vivo* assignments was marginally more useful for reducing disfluencies on one measure.

The authors concluded from these findings that RET had generally outperformed SD for treatment of stuttering. Atkinson (1983), however, reviewed this study from a statistical point of view and showed that the above findings, as well as some significant findings from multiple comparisons of individual group means not cited above, could well be Type I errors, given the extremely liberal approach to hypothesis testing taken in analyzing the data.

Summary. One study suggested that RET might be valuable in the treatment of stuttering, though its standing compared to systematic desensitization was obscured by the statistical methods used.

Psychosexual Dysfunctions

A 12-session group RET treatment did not appear to be very helpful for secondary erectile failure relative to no treatment (Munjack *et al.*, 1984). Subjects were heterosexual men ($n = 16$) who for at least 6 months had been achieving satisfactory erections no more than 25% of the time but who did not have any organic pathology accounting for the problem.

RET subjects reported more successful attempts at intercourse during treatment ($M = 7.6$ vs. 0.25), but there appeared to be considerable relapse after therapy ended. All seven treated subjects who were followed up by telephone 6 to 9 months later had declined from posttreatment in success rates, three of them to 0%, the others to 25 to 66%. These percentages were still higher than at pretreatment; without knowing absolute rates of attempts and successes it is not obvious whether subjects were having intercourse more often, unsuccessfully trying less often, or both. Neither group significantly lowered irrational beliefs, so perhaps RET could help with this problem but was delivered ineffectively here.

Everaerd and associates evaluated a small-group (about five each, with two therapists) treatment beginning with six sessions of RET, followed by nine sessions of sensate focus and masturbation training and about three sessions of social skills training (Everaerd *et al.*, 1982). The group ($n = 21$ completers, 6 others having dropped out during treatment) was mixed with regard to sexual orientation and sexual dysfunction. Most subjects (18 of 21) had no regular partner, and all were men.

There was no control group included, the idea being that long-standing problems (M = 6 years, range 1.5 to 20 years) probably would not remit without treatment. Subjects showed increased self-reported sexual motivation (heterosexual subjects only), lowered social anxiety, and nearly complete elimination of masturbatory dysfunctions (15 of 18 clients with such problems rated as cured by clients' overall evaluations). The impact on sexual performance with a partner was weaker: 8 of 21 were rated as cured, 5 as unchanged, and the remaining 8 had had no new experience with a partner and so could not report on changes in behavior. Two-month follow-ups indicated virtually the same results on sexual performance.

Lack of a control group, process measures (e.g., irrational beliefs), data on frequency of satisfactory intercourse, assessments at the end of each treatment phase, or extended follow-up make it impossible to say if the more favorable results reported here contradict the data of Munjack *et al.* (1984). If they do, then various explanatory hypotheses (need for more extended treatment or more directive behavioral components such as masturbatory training, greater appropriateness of RET for the types of clients included in this study but not in Munjack *et al.*, e.g., primary erectile dysfunctions, ejaculatory dysfunctions) could be explored.

Dekker, Dronkers, and Staffeleu (1985) reported on a new sample of 40 men going through their multicomponent treatment and replicated the findings of increased self-reported sexual motivation and decreased social anxiety. Again, the clients who experienced masturbatory dysfunction (n = 20) fared quite well as evaluated by their therapists (none got worse, 1 unchanged, 8 improved, and 11 cured). With respect to performance with a partner, 8 had had no new experiences to evaluate by the posttreatment report, while none seemed worse, 2 unchanged, 14 improved and 16 cured. There was again no control group and in this study no follow-up either.

A major emphasis in this report concerned prediction of response to treatment. As far as sexual motivation was concerned, those subjects with inhibited sexual desire before treatment seemed to fare worse. Reduction of social anxiety was greater among those who had been in a longer relationship with a partner and had had problems for a shorter period of time. Type of sexual dysfunction did not make any difference.

Finally, Everaerd and Dekker (1985) conducted the only comparative study of RET (M = 18 sessions) for sexual dysfunctions, evaluating it against an outpatient version of Masters and Johnson's treatment, in a couples format. Fully half of the 32 couples in the study dropped out of treatment; they may have been less motivated, as these couples had reported better male sexual functioning and a shorter history of problems.

Results for the RET group must be considered of questionable generalizability, given that only six couples finished treatment, and only three of these were available for follow-up interviews 6 to 12 months later. Sexual motivation increased at posttreatment and follow-up only among men, while both men and women reported improved relationship satisfaction immediately after treatment but not at follow-up. At posttreatment, four of the six RET couples were judged as cured, one other as improved. There were no significant group differences in outcome, though of course larger samples might alter this conclusion.

Summary. RET seems best regarded as unproven in the treatment of sexual dysfunctions. Uncontrolled studies have suggested some effectiveness, especially for masturbatory dysfunctions, of a treatment package including RET but also other sex therapy components (Dekker *et al.*, 1985; Everaerd *et al.*, 1982). RET alone has shown only short-lived effects for men with secondary erectile dysfunction (Munjack *et al.*, 1984) and a very high attrition rate in couples treatment (Everaerd & Dekker, 1985).

Type A Behavior Pattern[1]

The Type A Behavior Pattern (TABP; Friedman & Rosenman, 1974) includes excessive competitiveness, aggressiveness, and a chronic sense of time urgency. Although recent data have been equivocal (McLellarn, Bornstein, & Carmody, 1986), TABP has generally been accepted as an independent risk factor for coronary heart disease (CHD; The Review Panel on Coronary-Prone Behavior and Coronary Heart Disease, 1981).

Jenni and Wollersheim (1979) designed an RET program for TABP. Like the Anxiety Management Training (Suinn, 1974) package to which it was compared, RET lowered trait anxiety through 6-week follow-up but did not reduce cholesterol or resting blood pressure. Bortner Type A scores were reduced, but the clinical significance of this reduction was obscured by the use of a different scoring system from the one used in developing the measure (Bortner, 1969) and in validating it as a predictor of CHD (French–Belgian Collaborative Group, 1982).

Thurman (1983) found RET significantly superior to no treatment in reducing TABP and irrationality among college student Type A's (10 or higher on Jenkins Activity Survey [JAS; Jenkins, Zyzanski, & Rosenman, 1971]). Two-month follow-up evaluations of the treated group revealed maintenance of gains. Thurman (1984) subsequently developed a Type A-specific irrational beliefs questionnaire to measure beliefs (e.g., "faster is always better," p. 360) that may be more specific to TABP and hence even more sensitive to TABP change than are general measures such as the IBT. The complexity of cognitive assessment is illustrated by Thurman's

[1] This section is based on Haaga (1987).

(1984) acknowledgment that "Although many Type A's might not assent verbally to holding these (irrational) beliefs, they clearly seem to be acting on them in their day-to-day lives" (p. 360).

Later, Thurman (1985a) added to RET some features of Novaco's (1979) anger control treatment for university faculty scoring above the 60th percentile on the JAS. One comparison treatment added two sessions of assertiveness training as described by Lange and Jakubowski (1976). A third, minimal treatment group received information regarding TABP in one session. On the composite JAS Type A score, Type A (but not general) irrational beliefs, the Bortner A scale, trait anger, and hostility self-reports, both cognitive–behavioral groups improved more than did the minimal treatment group, equaling each other. Collateral reports for both treatment groups showed effects on TABP but not on trait anger. Treatments failed to lower blood pressure reactivity. Assertiveness training did not improve the cognitive–behavioral intervention.

Follow-up assessments showed that equality of RET groups and their superiority to minimal treatment were maintained one year after treatment on the JAS Type A composite score, Type A irrational beliefs, and manifest hostility (Thurman, 1985b). JAS speed and impatience factor scores also showed significant group differences favoring RET groups at follow-up.

Summary. RET appears to reduce self-reported TABP and irrational beliefs, perhaps especially Type A-specific beliefs. Collateral reports confirmed TABP reduction in one study (Thurman, 1985a), and the impact exceeded that of a minimal educational intervention. No effects of RET on physiological measures have been documented, though the conceptual status of physiological reactivity as a dependent measure in TABP treatment research has been questioned recently (Roskies *et al.*, 1986). Neither is there yet any convincing evidence of superiority to other psychotherapies for TABP nor any evidence of effectiveness of RET for postcardiac Type A patients. In terms of healthy Type A people, the most important next steps for RET research would seem to be (1) documenting treatment effects on Structured Interview assessments of TABP, the measure most strongly associated with CHD (Rosenman *et al.*, 1975); and (2) showing prevention of CHD by way of TABP reduction, which has not yet been documented for any psychological intervention (Haaga, 1987).

Anger

Thurman's (1985a) finding of posttreatment reductions in self-reported anger could not be unambiguously attributed to RET, as elements of

Novaco's anger-control treatment had been incorporated. However, Conoley, Conoley, McConnell, and Kimzey (1983) conducted an analogue study of RET for anger reduction. Undergraduate women ($n = 61$) wrote down five recent anger-arousing events and recalled them, as a way to induce anger in the laboratory. They then discussed the situation they considered the worst for 20 minutes with a counselor, this discussion including either (1) a gestalt empty-chair exercise; (2) an ABC analysis as might be employed in RET; or (3) a control condition involving reflective listening by the therapist. The two active treatments were equally effective, significantly more so than was the control condition, in terms of self-reported anger after the discussion as well as reduction of systolic blood pressure.

Repression-sensitization, measured with a subscale of the MMPI, did not interact with treatment effectiveness in reducing anger. It had been hypothesized that the ABC analysis would be more helpful to repressors, who are thought to use cognitive control of emotions more frequently.

Future process studies of this type might do well to include at least a crude measure of the degree to which the subject reduces his or her faith in whatever irrational belief is attacked in the ABC analysis (Teasdale & Fennell, 1982). A high correlation between reduction in agreement with the IB and reduction in anger would be consistent with the notion that the RET intervention worked in accordance with RET theory.

Summary.   Conoley *et al.*'s (1983) analogue experiment suggested that RET may contribute to reduction of excessive anger.

Obesity

Block (1980) compared RET to relaxation training with discussion of weight problems and to no treatment for overweight clients ($n = 40$). Treatment groups met for 10 weekly sessions and were led by one of two eclectic therapists who were told to expect that both therapies would be effective; therapists were monitored via audiotapes to ensure fidelity to each type of treatment.

RET was significantly more effective, based on reduction in number of pounds overweight (according to standard tables), than the relaxation/ discussion group or no treatment. RET subjects were an average of 25 pounds overweight before treatment, 16 after treatment, and 6 at 18-week follow-up. Subjects in the other groups remained at least 20 pounds overweight, on average, throughout the study. There were no dropouts, suggesting that the treatment was acceptable to clients, and the efficiency of treatment, though not measured (e.g., as dollars of cost per pound lost), would seem to have been good (10 hours of therapist contact for eight people to lose an average of 19 pounds each from pretreatment to follow-up).

Summary. Block's study would suggest that RET could be very promising as a weight control treatment, particularly in light of the continued weight loss after treatment. Future studies might wish to add more thorough assessments to get a clearer picture of the generality and consistency of RET's effectiveness in this area. Possibilities include (1) reporting a weight reduction index that takes into account initial weight as well as pounds lost and initial overweight; (2) body fat percentage changes; (3) health side effects (e.g., blood pressure); (4) emotional side effects of weight reduction; (5) measures of homework compliance and the relationship of compliance to clinical outcome; (6) an indication of the variability of response, for instance the percentage of clients reaching their weight goals, percentage who gained weight, or who made no improvement (Wilson, 1978); (7) measures of client expectancies, to bolster the conclusion that RET was significantly superior to a placebo treatment.

Depression

RET and social problem solving (D'Zurilla & Goldfried, 1971) equaled each other and were superior to no treatment in reducing depressive symptoms among people ($n = 43$) who had been separated or divorced an average of 10 months previously (Malouff, 1984). Subjects were selected for scoring 10 or above on the BDI, which probably yielded a diagnostically heterogeneous sample rather than a group of subjects with depressive disorders (Carson, 1986; Deardorff & Funabiki, 1985). Nevertheless, the relatively brief (4-week) group treatments seemed to achieve substantial reductions of self-reported depressive symptoms (BDI average declined from 20.1 to 7.3 in the RET group, 6.8 at 1-month follow-up, compared to 21.1, 10.0, and 8.1, respectively, in the SPS group), a change which was paralleled by collateral reports of the subjects' affect.

L. M. Kelly (1982) compared 6-week group treatments of RET, a behavioral treatment based on Lewinsohn's (1975) theory of depression and featuring assertion training and activity scheduling, and a supportive treatment whose discussion topics were left up to group members. Subjects ($n = 20$ completers) were nonsuicidal, nonpsychotic, unipolar depressed patients (DSM-III diagnoses) who scored at least 15 on a pretreatment BDI.

Raters (not the clients themselves) considered therapist credibility and empathy and expectancy of success to be uniformly high in each treatment. Raters also attested to the content validity of the treatments, scoring at least 95% of the time from videotapes of sessions as "on task" for that treatment. However, the "specific" treatments did not appear to have differentially affected their target behaviors. None of the groups significantly reduced irrational beliefs or increased pleasant activities, and behavioral assessment based on 2-min role play conversation showed no overall social skill advantage for the behavioral group.

On both depression measures (BDI, checklist based on DSM-III criteria), all groups improved significantly from pre- to posttreatment, with no significant differences among groups. There was a trend toward RET being less effective than the other treatments (e.g., BDI declines from average to 24.3 to 16.0 vs. 24.6 to 10.6 for behavioral treatment and 26.4 to 7.4 for nondirective treatment). Small sample sizes make it difficult to know how much credence to place in the equivalence of results among the treatments represented in this study, and failure to alter the theoretically relevant target behaviors (pleasant activities, irrational beliefs) calls into question the adequacy of the treatments as delivered.

Both RET (entirely cognitive focus) and a behavioral treatment (activity scheduling only) significantly reduced depressive symptoms through 5-week follow-up in another comparison, though there were no significant group differences (P. Gardner & Oei, 1981). Subjects ($n = 16$) had responded to advertisements but were not diagnosed. No control group was included, but the depression measures had been stable during 3 weeks of baseline measurement. Again sample size was small for detecting between-group differences, and in this study there was no assessment of the target behaviors addressed by each treatment.

Finally, adult women diagnosed with major affective disorder (SADS-RDC; Spitzer, Endicott, & Robins, 1978) and scoring at least 70 (scaled score) on the MMPI depression scale and at least 18 on the Depression Adjective Checklist (Lubin, 1967) but not currently in treatment for depression nor seriously suicidal were recruited for a study of RET and social skills training (McKnight, Nelson, Hayes, & Jarrett, 1984). An alternating treatments design with multiple baseline across subjects was used, each subject receiving four individual sessions of social skills training and four of RET.

Overall, treatment appeared to be consistently successful, to a clinically significant degree; eight of the nine subjects were diagnosed as nondepressed after treatment, and the average MMPI-D score was in the nondepressed range. Social skills and irrational beliefs, assessed with both self-report and role play measures, improved. Treatment effects maintained through 1-year follow-up: seven of the eight recontacted subjects were in the nondepressed range on MMPI-D and DACL self-reports, and no subjects met pretreatment criteria for having problems with irrationality or social skills deficits.

The most interesting aspect of this study, though, concerned the role of pretreatment assessments in matching client and treatment, which has rarely been done successfully in RET research. Three subjects each were identified in advance of treatment as having particular difficulties with irrational beliefs, social skills deficits, or both. Session-by-session ratings suggested that for low-social-skill clients, social skills training was superior to RET in improving social skills and in reducing depression, whereas for highly irrational subjects RET was superior in reducing depression and irrational beliefs. For the ''both'' subgroup, RET was superior in reducing irrational beliefs, SST in improving social skills, and the two were equivalent in reducing self-reported depression.

These results indicated the utility of matching type of depression treatment to type of problem shown by the client before treatment, information which would have been obscured in a customary group analysis of the data. The treatments would have looked equivalent overall in reducing depressive symptoms, and no statements regarding rational treatment selection for depressed clients could have been made.

Summary. Fairly brief (4 to 8 week) programs of RET consistently reduce self-reported depressive symptoms, usually to the point that the average subject is in a nondepressed range after treatment. One study used interview-based diagnoses as a dependent measure, and this indicated that a combination of RET and social skills training led most subjects (seven of eight at 1-year follow-up) to no longer meet criteria for major affective disorder (McKnight *et al.*, 1984). No evidence exists to support a general superiority of RET relative to any of the treatments to which it has been compared (social skills training, social problem solving, activity scheduling, nondirective discussions), but within-subject, session-by-session analyses suggested that it may be especially helpful to subjects high in irrational beliefs prior to treatment (McKnight *et al.*, 1984).

Antisocial Behavior

G. S. Solomon and Ray (1984) devised an 8-hour group counseling treatment based on ''RET principles'' (details not spelled out much) for convicted first-time adult shoplifters. Participation was a mandatory condition of probation, so subjects may not have been especially motivated for treatment. The subjects showed normative IBT scores, but the authors' impression was that they did subscribe to a particularized set of shoplifters' irrational beliefs (e.g., the merchants deserve what they get, I must have an item I desire) and that treatment could proceed effectively by disputing these beliefs.

Only one of the 94 subjects shoplifted again within one year, and 97% reported having found the program helpful. Without a control or comparison group, however, it is difficult to evaluate the preventive impact of the treatment. Nonetheless, it seems clearly worthwhile to study further the utility of RET for such a significant social problem.

Block (1978) compared rational–emotive education (REE) to a psychodynamic human relations class and no treatment for underachieving, disruptive tenth and eleventh graders ($n = 40$). The interventions were conducted as daily classes, for course credit, and consisted of 47 sessions (there were no dropouts, and each subject attended at least 85% of classes). REE significantly outperformed the other treatments with respect to teacher-rated disruptive actions, class cuts, and grade point averages during the semester of treatment and the following semester. Grades remained fairly low, however, increasing from an average of 60 before the intervention to 69 during and 68 the following semester.

Summary. RET seems to hold promise in the treatment of antisocial behavior. Through one-semester follow-up, REE reduced disruptive behavior and slightly improved grades among underachieving high school students, more than did no treatment or an alternative psychodynamic intervention (Block, 1978). An uncontrolled pilot study suggested a possible impact of RET on recidivism among adult shoplifters as well (G. S. Solomon & Ray, 1984).

Summary of Evaluations

Rational–emotive education seems to have beneficial effects on clinically relevant self-report measures but has yet to show utility either in treating a core clinical dysfunction or in preventing psychopathology.

Systematic rational restructuring (SRR) has had its best results with test anxiety and self-reported social anxiety, possibly exceeding imaginal exposure-based treatments in these areas, which would imply that its effects derive from processes other than extinction alone. It also appears to be useful in assertiveness training, though there is not yet evidence that it adds to typical behavioral programs. It seems less useful than *in vivo* exposure for simple phobias, though in this area as in test anxiety it may reduce self-reported general social anxiety. Its relatively weaker impact on behavioral and psychophysiological indices of anxiety in most studies would suggest the possible utility of combining SRR with techniques aimed at these modalities, or of targeting a subgroup of subjects for whom

SRR would be especially appropriate, but little progress has been made in these areas.

RET has shown some effectiveness for mixed clinical samples, possibly exceeding relaxation training. It appears to reduce self-reports of perceived stress and general anxiety, though evidence of preventive impact of stress reduction or superiority in either area to alternative therapies is weak. RET seems to help speech anxiety as indexed by self-report, not behavioral observations, and may be inferior to other active treatments for reducing state anxiety prior to a speech. Test-anxiety results are more mixed, but there is at least some suggestion of improvement in all three major channels of anxiety responding. In the treatment of social anxiety, RET seems helpful on self-report and behavioral but not physiological measures, seems equivalent to several cognitive–behavioral and behavioral treatments, as well as client-centered therapy, but possibly worse than desensitization, at least with extroverts. RET appears to be inferior to exposure to agoraphobia and does not add to standard behavioral treatments for assertion or tension headaches. Preliminary evidence supports its utility for treating obsessions, stuttering, excessive anger, and antisocial behavior. It has helped people with sexual dysfunctions only when combined with behavioral sex therapy components in uncontrolled studies. RET has made a very promising start in the treatment of obesity and of the Type A Behavior Pattern, showing maintenance of effects superior to minimal treatments to TABP and relaxation training for obesity. More thorough evaluations of its effects in these areas are needed.

CONCLUDING REMARKS

This chapter has described numerous outcome studies of rational–emotive education, systematic rational restructuring, and rational–emotive therapy. Nevertheless, three decades after the initial empirical report on the effectiveness of RET (Ellis, 1957b), even fairly basic questions remain essentially unanswered. For example: (a) Is there any disorder or problem for which RET is a treatment of choice? (b) What proportion of patients achieve clinically significant improvement in RET? (c) What patient and therapist variables predict response to RET, and what predicts relapse after successful RET? (d) Is reduction in irrationality as defined by Ellis a necessary and sufficient condition for change in RET? Is this sort of cognitive change achieved more rapidly or to a greater degree when therapists adopt the forceful style advocated by Ellis rather than the gentler style characterizing SRR?

Research on cognitive therapy (CT) seems to be progressing more rapidly and in a more cumulative fashion than RET outcome research (Hollon & Beck, 1986). CT for depression appears to be at least as effective as standard pharmacotherapy in the short term (Beck, Hollon, Young, Bedrosian, & Budenz, 1985; Blackburn, Bishop, Glen, Whalley, & Christie, 1981; Murphy, Simons, Wetzel, & Lustman, 1984; Rush, Beck, Kovacs, & Hollon, 1977; Teasdale, Fennell, Hibbert, & Amies, 1984), perhaps superior at preventing relapse (Blackburn, Eunson, & Bishop, 1986; Simons, Murphy, Levine, & Wetzel, 1986). Some information is available on patient variables (Simons, Lustman, Wetzel, & Murphy, 1985) and early process indicators (Fennell & Teasdale, 1987) predictive of favorable response to CT. Moreover, patterns of symptom change in clinical trials, as well as the impact of drug therapy on CT-tailored cognitive assessments (Simons, Garfield, & Murphy, 1984) have prompted new theoretical speculations within the cognitive framework regarding maintenance and treatment of depression (Teasdale, 1985).

We have not seen much evidence that rational–emotive theories of the origin, maintenance, or treatment of various disorders are affected by outcome research. Much of the difficulty in conducting outcome research that would significantly advance the RET field undoubtedly relates to problems in assessing key constructs such as irrational beliefs (see Chapter 8, this volume). Improvements in assessment methodology would facilitate progress in outcome research. Application of recent advances in the general field of psychotherapy outcome research methodology would also enhance the informational yield of future RET studies.

As a result of space limitations for this chapter, we are preparing a separate paper to elaborate and rationalize our suggestions concerning strategies and tactics for RET outcome researchers, but a summary of these suggestions is listed here: (1) test RET as a standard, well-specified technology, using quantitative measures of treatment integrity, (2) use comparative research designs rather than no-treatment control designs, (3) conduct follow-up assessments to test the hypothesis that the philosophical shifts aimed for in RET promote more durable improvements in emotion and behavior than do interventions such as behavioral skill training, (4) study fully clinical samples, (5) report data on the incidence and prediction of attrition and negative outcomes, (6) use placebo controls only if specific questions about therapeutic mechanisms of action so indicate, (7) use cognitive assessment procedures to test RET theory and predict differential treatment response, (8) use additive designs when comparing RET to more strictly behavioral methods (rather than cognitive-alone vs behavioral-alone designs), (9) tailor RET methods and irrational beliefs assessments to the specifics of the target problem, as exemplified by Thurman's (1985a, 1985b) research on treatment of the Type A Behavior Pattern.

The belief and hope are that the incorporation of conceptual and methodological advances will improve both the internal and external validity of RET and contribute to a more cumulative, empirically based discipline of psychotherapy.

Comments on My Critics

Albert Ellis

COMMENTS ON WOOLFOLK AND SASS'S CHAPTER

Woolfolk and Sass make many instructive and valid points about some of the main philosophical foundations of RET, and I tend to agree with most of their analyses. Some of their observations, however, largely refer to my earlier views rather than my current ones, so I comment in such a way as to emphasize my present positions.

First, let me discuss my views on positivism. I have never been a hardline logical positivist, though I was once partly in that camp. Even in my first major book on RET, I went out of my way to abjure either a strictly rationalist or empiricist position. I noted,

> Science is intrinsically empirical; and scientific knowledge must, at least, in principle, be confirmable by some form of human experience. However, theorizing that is limited only to generalizations inducted from empirical evidence is often not the best form of theory making; and the hypothetico-deductive method, including the employment of rational curves, may be more productive for advancing scientific research than a pure adherence to inductive methods of reasoning. (Ellis, 1962, p. 123)

Other RET writers, especially DiGiuseppe (1986) and Rorer (1987), have also criticized a purely empiricist approach and favored the hypothetical-

199

deductive method. In addition, I espoused an existentialist–humanist view that is in some ways quite opposed to logical positivism (Ellis, 1962, pp. 124–125).

I abandoned even more elements of logical positivism when I later read Bartley (1962), Mahoney (1976), and Popper (1962), all of whom hold that to be scientific a hypothesis had better be falsifiable. In recent years I adopted Barley's more open-ended position, which states that no hypothesis can be completely proven (or even disproven) by empirical "evidence." But favoring probability (and neither absolute certainty nor uncertainty), I am quite unenthusiastic about Feyerabend's (1975) nihilistic theory that since we do not have certainty of any kind, "anything goes."

RET especially has favored openness and anticertainty in recent years because it holds that absolute dogmatic "musts" are most probably the core of human disturbance (Ellis, 1985b, 1985d, 1987a, 1987b, 1987c). Other cognitive behavioral therapies—such as those of Beck (1976a), Goldfried and Davison (1976), A. A. Lazarus (1981), R. S. Lazarus (1966), Maultsby (1984), Meichenbaum (1977a), and Raimy (1975)—stress the mistaken, misperceived, and overgeneralized inferences that disturbed people wrongly make from empirical data. Thus, they take your empirical observation, "John refused my dinner invitation" and they show you that it does not prove that (1) John hates you, nor (2) that you did something wrong, nor (3) that John will never accept your future invitations, nor (4) that you are an inadequate, unlovable person. All these are inferences or assumptions that you may make from the fact of John's refusal. So most cognitive-behavioral therapies actively dispute sloppy inferencing.

So does RET. But it also goes deeper philosophically. For it hypothesizes that one of the main (but not the only) reason why most people commonly make self-defeating or disturbed inferences and overgeneralizations is that they often bring and add to their preferences additional grandiose, perfectionistic, dogmatic "musts" and demands.

Thus when you invite John to dinner, you not only want or prefer him to accept your invitation, but you may (consciously or unconsciously) command, "Since I want John to accept, he under all conditions at all times must do as I wish!" With this stated or implied absolutistic premise, you can then "logically" conclude, "Since John has not accepted my invitation, as he must, it therefore means that (1) he hates me, (2) he sees that I've done something wrong, (3) he'll never accept my future invitations, and (4) I'm an inadequate, unlovable person." Thus the incorrect inferences are deduced from the absolutistic must.

RET further assumes that without your grandiose, perfectionistic demands for John's complete acceptance, you would still easily make misleading inferences, misperceptions, and overgeneralizations; but you would do so much less often; and they would seldom lead to distorted, negative perceptions of yourself, others, and the world.

The main point of what I have just said is that RET is philosophically open because it theorizes that closed mindedness, bigotry, dogma, "musturbation," and (secular and theistic) devout religiosity are key ideologies that underlie neurotic disturbance. Not merely unrealistic and antiempirical, but rigid, categorical thinking is the deep layer behind most disturbed emotions and behaviors (Ellis, 1987a, 1987b, 1987c).

Again, RET is not merely based on empiricism (as is science) but also on logico-empiricism and the hypothetico-deductive method. By logico-empiricism, I have meant the use of logical and empirical arguments of disputing. It makes observations of human functioning and malfunctioning; it assumes that the latter is significantly related to musturbatory thinking; it tests this hypothesis in therapy sessions (and in controlled experiments). It does not rigidly stick to inductive or deductive processes as the method of science but open-endedly uses both (DiGiuseppe, 1986; Ellis, 1962, 1973).

Woolfolk and Sass make some interesting points about my humanistic-atheistic philosophy, and I have few quarrels with their analysis. Some points with which I do disagree, however, are these:

1. "He is out to create a personal philosophy of life for a world in which only science has authority." No, science (or anything else) has authority only because we humans give it authority. Science only exists because people created it—and sometimes use it! In my philosophy, nothing is sacred, even science. It is probably the best way, if properly used, to obtain human happiness. But hardly the only way. And human happiness, and nondisturbability, seem to be the best goals humans have yet constructed. But for all people all of the time under all conditions? Not necessarily! Even happiness, says RET, is not sacred. What is? Nothing that I can imagine.

2. "If one is fundamentally and primarily for oneself, it would seem that on assessing long-term prospects for satisfaction, one might just as well resolve to become a very effective psychopath as choose to fashion oneself into an altruistic social democrat." No, psychopaths go for short-term rather than long-term satisfaction, since they normally get caught and penalized. They also sabotage the social group in which they choose to live, and thereby, in the short and long run, tend to live more miserably themselves.

3. "Standards of rationality are no more fixed and eternal than are human values or other social creations." Correct. RET does not have one invariant criterion of rationality, as Woolfolk and Sass imply. It mainly says

that if people in our culture want to have minimal anxiety, depression, hostility, and few behavioral problems, they most probably would be better off giving up their dogmatic, absolutistic thinking and staying with their preferences. But it hardly promises them eternal, rationality-invoked bliss!

4. "The status of rationality itself is a subject of much controversy within contemporary philosophy. The absolute status and epistemological superiority of modern Western thought simply cannot be defended as conclusively as the thinkers of the Enlightenment supposed." The implication here is that I am a rationalist, in the old ideal of that term. But I took pains (Ellis, 1962) to disavow that notion.

Actually, RET for many years has preached against "perfect" rationality and has shown that even that kind of perfection, like any other kind, simply does not exist. It only encourages greater flexibility and antidogmatism.

5. "The tenets of RET require for justification only the proposition that if they are believed and acted upon, the principle of life will be attenuated and happiness will ensue. But within this last assertion may be the rub." No, the tenets of RET say that if they are believed and acted upon, painful disturbance and behavior will often (not always) be attenuated, but they do not say that positive happiness will automatically ensue. RET holds that when people are no longer neurotically miserable they will probably actualize themselves and create many different paths to happiness. RET shows people how to usually avoid misery and despair but it does not prescribe specific or superior kinds of happiness.

Woolfolk and Sass endorse the views of Antonovsky (1979) and Kobasa (1979) that if people acquire a sense of coherence, purpose, and commitment they will probably tolerate stress better and be happier. They imply that this aspect of happiness is absent from RET. But in one of the most popular books on RET (Ellis & Harper, 1975), Robert Harper and I espouse people preferably acquiring a "vital absorbing interest" if they want to be lastingly happy. Meaningful life purposes have always been encouraged in RET.

6. "In Ellis's system, we take account of others' needs because this is the best way to get our own needs met—a means to an end, rather than an end in itself." Not true! RET says that one main reason for acting ethically is to help create a world in which others will also be ethical to you. But it also says that you can well choose to be kind, considerate, friendly, or loving just because you feel like acting that way, merely because you enjoy helping others. In fact, it holds that generosity, altruism, and love are partly innate, human tendencies and are not merely learned or figured out as the result of self-interest.

7. "Ellis has quite rightly emphasized how the development of some degree of skepticism can free one from self-destructive patterns. One wonders, however, whether he has been sensitive enough to its dangers and disadvantages—the way it can foster Nietzsche's homogenized 'weightlessness of all things.' " Yes, RET acknowledges this danger and therefore is not devoutly anything—including devoutly skeptical. As noted above, it favors people acquiring a vital absorbing interest in some long-term goal or purpose. And it disfavors nihilistic brands of skepticism, such as that of Feyerabend (1975). It does not hold that there is any intrinsic or cosmic meaning in the world; but, like many existentialists, it encourages people to create their own meanings.

8. "When Ellis advocates the abolition of irrational beliefs, he cannot be seen as appealing to some transcendental, ultimate standard by which all thought and action can be evaluated. Rather, he is advancing a value position that advocates the most expedient pursuit of happiness—a happiness defined totally in terms of a personal hedonic calculus." Not quite! I do not advocate the abolition of all irrational beliefs, but merely those that usually lead to emotional and behavioral disturbance. Some unrealistic and illogical ideas—such as the dogmatic belief that one absolutely will go to heaven and experience eternal bliss if one prays to God every day—may sometimes lead to little disturbance and to some benefits, so they easily can be tolerated. Only self-defeating shoulds and musts had better be surrendered!

RET, moreover, does not define happiness totally in terms of a personal hedonic calculus. It fully accepts the fact that humans are social creatures and would hardly survive, let alone be happy, completely on their own. They normally enjoy group living and lead a fuller existence within a social framework. RET therefore includes social interest as one of the main aspects of mental health (Ellis & Bernard, 1985b).

COMMENTS ON ZIEGLER'S CHAPTER

I am highly pleased that Ziegler has gone to the trouble of really understanding my theory of personality, and I am delighted to discover that I basically agree with most of the criticisms that he makes. Let me first list my agreements and then disagree somewhat with some finer points he makes. In my view, his valid criticisms are as follows:

1. RET is not a "fully developed, comprehensive personalogical system." It is mainly a theory of personality change, and even in that

respect it could be, and I hope that eventually will be, more fully developed and comprehensive.

2. "Ellis has done a marvelous job of elucidating the contents of beliefs, especially irrational beliefs. Now it is time for a detailed analysis of their properties as well." Indeed it is, and I and some other RETers had better get around to this interesting task.

3. "The details of. . .this original process of indoctrination [of irrational beliefs]. . .are not spelled out. Likewise for whatever cognitive–learning mechanisms that make possible the hypothesized reindoctrination process. And, finally, there is no pointed, cogent explanation of the relationship between original indoctrination and subsequent reindoctrination." True. These details could well be thought about and investigated.

4. "Ellis alludes to a holistic or central 'consciousness' or 'will.' What is this? Elsewhere in his writings this concept does not appear to be spelled out, and a personological construct of this presumed centrality really should be." I agree. In some of my talks and writings I have defined willpower but have somewhat neglected to specifically delineate will. Willpower I see as (1) the perception that change is desirable, (2) the actual wish or desire to change, (3) the firm decision to implement that desire, (4) the action that will probably lead to that implementation, (5) the continuation of that action, (6) the checking back to see if the action works and the desire is fulfilled, and (7) the continuation of these processes. Will itself is probably the first three of these operations.

5. "It is one thing to argue convincingly for the biological basis of human irrationality, it is quite another to hypothesize in scientifically acceptable detail the precise biological underpinnings for the origin, development, and maintenance of irrational (and rational) beliefs." Yes, this aspect of RET theory can well be delineated in much greater detail.

6. "What is missing in RET personality theory is a detailed account of precisely how personality develops and changes throughout the life span without RET intervention." Yes, again. My lifelong emphasis on personality change, and particularly change through therapy, has led me to neglect personality change that indubitably often takes place by itself. This could profitably be explored from an RET perspective. "Given Ellis's strong commitment to the changeability assumption, a detailed theoretical description of personality development and change, in the normal course of events, would greatly strengthen RET theory as a comprehensive personality theory." True; and if I do not get around to making this detailed theoretical description myself, some other followers of RET could fruitfully do this.

7. "What is needed is a more substantive, thorough, detailed, and systematic theoretical description of human motivation within RET

theory." Again, this would seem to be distinctly desirable and would add to RET theory.

8. "RET theory could profit enormously from continued, concerted efforts to expand and specify more precisely the ABC model and its constituent elements. What might be lost in parsimony would be more than made up for in completeness." As Ziegler points out, work along these lines has recently been done by myself and others (DiGiuseppe, 1986; Ellis, 1985b, 1987b, 1987c; Ellis & Bernard, 1986; Ellis & Dryden, 1987; Grieger, 1986; R. A. Wessler & Wessler, 1980; R. L. Wessler, 1986b). But considerable attention can still be given to this important issue.

As can be seen from my foregoing comments, I have many agreements with the deficiencies and lapses in RET personality theory to which Ziegler rightly keeps alluding in his chapter. Some rather minor disagreements which I have with his comments include the following:

1. "An important point here is that a theorist's basic assumptions about human nature (in this case, freedom–determinism) incline him or her to perceive clearly certain aspects of human behavior while simultaneously having theoretical blind (or at least hazy) spots for certain others." This is generally true, but I am not so sure that it specifically applies to my own blind or hazy spots about personality theory. I think that they largely stem from my preoccupation with personality change rather than with personality itself, and from the fact that I devote so much of my time to seeing individual and group therapy clients, to supervising and to giving public and professional talks and workshops that I sometimes neglect important theoretical issues for more practical ones.

2. "Ellis's strong constitutionlist leanings lead him to downplay, relatively speaking, careful attention to potentially important specific environmental influences in personality development." Most probably, there is some truth in this statement. But, once again, my overwhelming interest is in personality change. The fact that I spend so much of my time trying to help people change takes me away from examining how people develop when they are not making a conscious effort to change.

3. "In RET theory, it is clearly the individual's subjective beliefs (rational and irrational), rather than objective, external factors per se, that most influence his or her behavior. Ellis's commitment to the subjectivity assumption could hardly be stronger." This is not true in regard to my view of general but of disturbed behavior. I believe that objective, external factors—such as people's experiences in life and the teaching they imbibe from their families, teachers, and culture—strongly influence their general behavior and give them many standards, values, goals, and purposes which they easily accept because they are born highly teachable

and gullible. Thus, in the United States, boys are largely taught to favor baseball, in England cricket, and in South America soccer. Their healthy desires are therefore largely under "objective" or "external" control. But when they become emotionally disturbed about playing baseball, cricket, or soccer, they mainly do so because they take their preferences for these sports and escalate them into absolutistic commands and demands. So rational–emotive theory does not neglect people's "normal" or "healthy" desires and the enormous influences on these desires which are "external" and "objective." It only points out that when they are emotionally and behaviorally disturbed, they then are very powerfully influenced by their biological tendencies to be profound musturbators.

4. "Personality (and, by implication, human nature) is simply too complex to be captured by any one approach—even that of science." I partly hold this view because I believe that, in keeping with our present scientific knowledge, we do not have enough information to say why an individual performs a given act, especially an important act, such as murder. What we call his or her "personality" is too complex and vague to give us such specific understanding. But we can investigate exactly what this individual tells himself or herself just prior to performing an act and thereby determine some crucial aspects of his or her personality. If this individual is emotionally disturbed, we can again examine certain of his or her ideas and attitudes that significantly contribute to this disturbance. But even here we shall most probably only arrive at limited explanations. So let us shy away from overgeneralized statements, such as "he or she had the type of personality which made him or her resort to murder." In regard to the use of terms like "personality," let us exert, at least for the present, due scientific caution!

Aside from these minor quibbles, I find little to object to in Ziegler's chapter on RET personality theory. I think that he is quite right about seeing RET and the cognitive–behavioral movement as being on the brink of developing a comprehensive theory of personality that will be more valid and more scientific than those presented thus far by other schools of psychotherapy. Some of the suggestions in his chapter can be instrumental in aiding this kind of growth and development in rational–emotive theory.

COMMENTS ON R. LAZARUS'S CHAPTER

Richard Lazarus's chapter is a comprehensive discussion of the psychological theories of cognition and emotion and of the RET view of the circular relationship of thinking and feeling. I disagree with exceptionally little that he says and am highly pleased that our views significantly overlap, although mine mainly derive from clinical therapy while his formulations largely stem from academic teaching and research. It is good to know that our following two different pathways has led to similar theories, though this hardly proves that our convergent theorizing is correct!

The several points in Lazarus's chapter that I have only partially endorsed before but that I would like to more fully discuss now include these:

1. "The coping process generated by the appraisal of harm, threat, or challenge can modify the original appraisal and thus change the subsequent emotional state." A good point! When clients greatly fear failure and they cope by trying harder to succeed, by telling themselves they can still enjoy life even if they fail, or by withdrawing from a task in which they may fail, they then usually decrease their fears.

2. Emotions transact with and have two-way encounters with the environment. "Neither the environmental nor the internal event is sufficient by itself to explain an emotional reaction; an emotion reflects the joint contribution of both." Yes, humans relate, inevitably, to each other and to their surroundings and they almost always disturb themselves about what is going on or what is not going on in the world and with the people around them.

3. "A theory of emotion must be able to handle both stability and flux with equal virtuosity." Lazarus is clearly on the right track. RET emphasizes stability of emotion by pointing out the crucial importance of rigid shoulds and musts in creating and maintaining disturbed feelings. But it also shows that appropriate negative and positive feelings usually vary widely and largely depend on how strongly clients' situations seem to satisfy their goals, wants, and preferences.

4. "From the holistic standpoint, separation of cognition and emotion is not a biological principle nor normative and occurs mainly in ego defense or disease. Models of the mind that depend on separation are therefore distortions of how things usually operate in healthy adults." Yes. Even in ego defense, according to RET, clients are defensive because they evaluate failure or disapproval as awful and think that they have to escape from it by denying their "bad" actions. And in the case of disease, people sometimes evaluate their ailments as horrible, put themselves down for being diseased, and thereby upset themselves about the disease. People with healthy thinking cognize and feel differently.

5. "Thoughts and feelings affect each other." Yes; as Lazarus shows, I pointed this out in my first major paper on RET (Ellis, 1958a). For therapeutic purposes, we emphasize in RET that thoughts usually (not

always) lead to feelings; and that often or usually (not always) feelings lead to (or contribute to) thoughts. We stress (and perhaps somewhat overdo) these "causative" relations in order to increase clients' incentives to uncreate their dysfunctional thoughts and feelings.

6. "In addition to stable beliefs that affect recurrent or characteristic emotional responses, we need a set of principles about how the person goes about judging how things are going at any given moment." Lazarus makes another good point here. RET implies these principles at present but could well spell them out in more detail.

Along with these important agreements with Lazarus, I have a few minor disagreements:

1. He states that I hold that "all human goals are appropriate even when they are not easily fulfilled, but all absolutistic commands, demands, insistences, and musts are inappropriate and self-sabotaging." I dislike his inclusion of all in this statement. A few human goals (such as genocide) may hardly be appropriate even when they are merely desires; and although I hold that absolutistic demands are very likely to be inappropriate and self-sabotaging, I do not believe that they always are. A little later on Lazarus attributes to me the position that some musturbatory beliefs "are inherently irrational." That, again, is not quite true. It may be inherently illogical to say "I must do well and win approval or else I am a rotten person." It cannot be empirically proven that you are entirely "rotten" as a person just because you do not do well or win approval. But *irrational* in RET mainly means self-defeating. Musturbatory statements will usually but not always lead to self-defeating feelings and behaviors.

2. Lazarus states that when I hold that people's absolutistic assumptions are erroneous because they trap them into inappropriate negative and positive emotions, "this is, of course, circular reasoning because irrationality is defined largely by the negative outcome, namely, emotional disturbance and dysfunction, and this negative outcome is explained by the offending assumptions." I do not agree that this is necessarily circular thinking. My reasoning is as follows: (a) Inappropriate negative emotions (e.g., feelings of panic) and inappropriate positive emotions (e.g., feelings of grandiosity) exist and lead to poor results, not merely by RET standards but by general standards of emotional health. (b) Dogmatic musturbatory cognitions also exist and are observable. (c) When the latter exist, there is a significantly higher degree of probability that the former will also exist, and this can be empirically observed and confirmed. (d) It can be logically figured out that when I tell myself "I must do well and am a rotten person when I don't" and when it is likely that, being fallible, I often will not do well, I will frequently feel panicked and worthless;

while when I believe "I prefer to do well but if I don't, I don't; and my worth as a person is not intrinsically related to how well I do," I will rarely feel panicked and worthless. But this logical relationship between needing to do well and feeling panicked and worthless when I do not succeed as I "need" to do can be empirically checked to see if it is merely tautological and definitional (as it logically is) or whether it also is empirically confirmable. My "circular" hypotheses, therefore, can also be falsified or probabilistically (not absolutely) confirmed.

3. "Ellis...does not subscribe to the theory of the positive value of emotion-focused coping (e.g., denial and illusion) by means of which, as I have argued (R. S. Lazarus, 1983) even psychologically sound people regulate their feelings when nothing can be done to change negative conditions of life. More than I, Ellis wants people to be relentlessly realistic in the way they see things as the best guarantee of psychological soundness." True, but in RET we merely prefer an elegant and realistic way for people to see things as the best guarantee of psychological soundness. We do not insist on this best solution; and we can accept, if not get enthusiastic about, unrealistic, defensive, or illusory solutions (Ellis, 1985d).

4. I most disagree with this point in Lazarus's chapter: "Much dysphoric or depressed mood is thoroughly justified by the changing circumstances of a person's life, for example, loss of loved ones, sickness, and the loss of roles and functions in aging which once helped make life attractive.... Surely depression, brought about by severe loss, cannot be considered pathological per se." My disagreement in this respect may be mainly a matter of definition of what depression really is; but I think that RET makes a very important distinction between depression and sadness (Ellis, 1987c) that virtually none of the other cognitive–behavioral therapies (such as those of Beck, Lewinsohn, Rehm, and Seligman) make.

Although feelings of depression usually start with feelings of intense sadness, sorrow, frustration, and regret, and although these latter feelings are usually quite appropriate and healthy when one suffers a severe loss, RET holds that even mild and moderate, and especially severe, feelings of depression are qualitatively and not quantitatively different from the emotion of extreme sadness. For feelings of sadness stem from the belief, "I really deplore what is happening to me and I strongly wish that it were not occurring," while feelings of depression largely stem from the belief, "Because this loss or frustration is so unfortunate, it should not and must not exist!"

Now RET does not insist that what we normally call feelings of depression can only come when people insist that the unfortunate things in their lives must not or should not exist; for they can sometimes come from other sources (especially physiological sources). But RET hypothesizes that when people think that it is absolutely necessary that they not bring on or be assailed from without by unpleasant events, they almost always tend to depress themselves; while when they rigorously (not rigidly!) stick to thoughts like "No matter how bad this happening is, it should occur because it has occurred. Too damned bad! But I can still enjoy myself in several ways," they very rarely would feel depressed, although they often would feel quite sad, regretful, and frustrated.

I disagree with Lazarus, therefore, when he notes that to be depressed about loss of loved ones, sickness, and the loss of roles and functions in aging which once helped make life attractive "is not disorder unless one wants to argue, ironically, that health requires keeping a stiff upper lip in the face of adversity or engaging in positive thinking (or denial), whereas sickness is giving in to reality." No! "Keeping a stiff upper lip in the face of adversity" often is denial or positive thinking. What RET calls appropriate negative thinking is healthy in the face of adversity, but not absolutistic thinking that insists that this adversity must not exist and that it is therefore horrible when it does. As Lazarus notes, "distressing emotion, per se, should not be thought of as pathological, especially if they have some justification in the actual conditions of life." Right! Distressing emotions are not per se pathological, as RET has said right from its beginnings. But certain kinds of distressing emotions and usually (though not always) extreme ones, are very often self-defeating.

Finally, I agree with Lazarus that "the danger I see in RET is not that it contains anything particularly egregious but that it could come close to being an unquestioned system, a kind of cult, with protagonists and users who may stop thinking about important issues of both science and value." It certainly could, as could any system of psychotherapy. But if RET successfully stays with its commitment to scientific thinking it will, I hope, become a leader in anticultist therapies.

COMMENTS ON MAHONEY, LYDDON, AND ALFORD'S CHAPTER

Mahoney, Lyddon, and Alford have written an excellent, often brilliant, critique of rationalism and the rationalist tradition in psychotherapy; but they have then mistakenly identified RET, which abjures isms of all kinds, including rationalism, with the rationalist position. How ironic! I originally changed the name rational therapy (RT) to rational–emotive therapy (RET) in 1962 largely because it was then being wrongly confused with rationalism. Here, a quarter of a century later, it is still being wrongly accused of and confused with a rationalist position. Let me briefly try to show why it is rational–emotive and not rationalistic, so that (I hope!) other critics will not beat it over the head for what it is not.

1. "Rationalist approaches to psychotherapy have followed a similar path in developing the view that intense negative emotions are symptomatic of disorder and psychopathology." Yes, but not RET! RET specifically differentiates between appropriate feelings (such as sorrow, frustration, displeasure, and annoyance) and inappropriate negative feelings (such as panic, depression, rage, and self-downing). It holds that intense feelings of sadness and frustration, when unfortunate events occur in one's life, are appropriate and good, not bad (since they motivate one to change these events); and that only when these feelings are escalated to disruptive emotions like depression and horror are they pathological. Some of the Stoic philosophers and some present-day "rational" therapists (such as Maultsby, 1984) oppose practically all negative feelings and advocate calmness, serenity, or detachment in the face of misfortune; but I have always said that this is not RET (Ellis, 1969b, 1973, 1985b, 1985d, 1988; Ellis & Becker, 1982; Ellis & Harper, 1975).

Although RET subscribes to some Stoic views, it clearly opposes many of Epictetus's semiascetic philosophies. It espouses long range hedonism, and is in many ways more Epicurean than Stoic.

2. "A causal relationship between iBs [irrational beliefs] and iC's [inappropriate consequences] has also been explicitly advanced." Not for about 15 years! As I mentioned in my comments to the chapter by R. S. Lazarus, RET believes thoughts, feelings, and behavior interact.

Mahoney, Lyddon, and Alford endorse R. M. Schwartz's (1984) statement that "despite the inclusion of a general interactive statement, the lack of specific hypotheses that place affect or behavior in a primary role suggests that RET is in actuality a cognitive primacy theory with a formally undeveloped interactionist stance" (p. 224). This is partly true, since RET has not yet developed its own detailed theory of how emotions and behaviors influence or "cause" thinking but accepts (at least tentatively) others' formulations of such theories—such as Epstein's (1983, 1984). At the same time, RET and other cognitive therapies have not really developed a detailed and empirically tested theory of exactly how thinking influences emotions and actions.

The fact is, however, that RET's theory of therapy clearly says that when clients change their irrational, musturbatory beliefs and make what it calls a profound philosophic change, they not only concomitantly change their disordered feelings and behaviors in a sustained manner but it also states that the best ways of changing self-defeating ideas are often (not always) through modifying—and, especially, forcefully working on—dysfunctional feelings and actions. RET's therapeutic hypotheses, therefore, are never either/or but both/and formulations.

RET has a distinctly interactionist stance; and RET practitioners are trained in being solidly interactional in their use of cognitive, emotive, and behavioral methods of therapy. In doing preferential RET, they use these methods not merely for symptom removal but to hopefully help their clients to make a profound philosophic change, since RET hypothesizes that unless such an attitudinal restructuring is effected, therapeutic results will tend to be moderate and unlasting. I agree with Mahoney, Lyddon, and Alford and with Schwartz, however, that a much more formal development of RET's interactionist therapeutic view is called for and would be highly desirable.

3. "RET's emphasis on cognitive content rather than process and surface structure particulars rather than deep structure personal meanings seems to clearly set it apart from other cognitive approaches of a more structural nature." On the contrary! RET emphasizes "deep structure personal meanings" in several ways: (a) It stresses the meanings or basic philosophies that people irrationally hold, and not merely their sentences or self-statements. (b) It holds that people, on an individual basis, weakly or strongly hold self-defeating attitudes and views. (c) It shows that disturbed individuals repetitively and powerfully practice inappropriate thoughts, feelings, and behaviors, and that therefore there is usually no other way but work and practice to effect basic personality change (Ellis, 1962, 1973, 1985d, 1988). (d) It advocates a wide range of individually tailored methods (Ellis, 1985d). (e) It emphasizes the importance and frequency of metadisturbances or secondary disturbances, such as anxiety about anxiety and depression about depression (Ellis, 1962, 1973, 1985d); Ellis & Becker, 1982; Ellis & Harper, 1975). (f) It holds that people usually have at least two major kinds of absolutistic thinking that produce ego disturbance and discomfort disturbance and that these ideas and disturbances significantly interact and are to be treated in an interactive manner (Ellis, 1979a, 1980a). These are only a few of the major and frequent ways in which RET acknowledges and deals with "deep structure personal meanings" and in which some of the other cognitive–behavioral therapies often fail to do so.

4. Mahoney, Lyddon, and Alford cite Weimer (1982, in press-a) and Hayek (1952, 1964, 1978) against the viability of imposing any form of rational planning and centralized control upon a complex system; and cite Hayek's view that "True rational insight seems indeed to indicate that one of the most important uses is the recognition of the proper limits of

rational control" (Hayek, 1978, p. 93). Correct! But Hayek and Weimer probably go too far when they oppose imposing any form of rational planning and centralized control upon a complex system. In previous writing (Ellis, 1962), I indicate that humans are so complex and in many ways so predisposed to irrational thinking that all psychotherapy, especially a purely rational type of therapy, has its distant dangers and limitations. And RET quite agrees with Weimer's point that "rationality in complex orders is never fully explicitly nor instantly specifiable" (Weimer, 1982, p. 245).

RET, moreover, specifically defines *rational* as self-helping and *irrational* as self-defeating behavior and does not have an absolutistic view of rationality. Mahoney, Lyddon, and Alford note that "the core argument here is for the rationality of helping clients generate for themselves very general and abstract principles that can be applied to an indefinite number of particular problems they may encounter." Right! This is precisely what preferential RET attempts: not to teach clients what is "right" or "wrong" or "good" or "bad" about specific things they do or do not do, but to teach them the scientific method of looking for, discovering, and disputing their own antiscientific, dogmatic thinking. If humans were good scientists, instead of the sloppy scientists that George Kelly (1955) thought them to be, they would have tremendous difficulty making and keeping themselves neurotic. The "profound philosophic change" that RET encourages them to make includes fairly consistently thinking scientifically, realizing when they are not, and fighting (as presumably professional scientists do) to return to scientific attitudes.

5. "Since RET specifies that the true source of resistance lies within the client's beliefs, the therapist can strategically side with the client to actively combat his or her irrationality rather than explore sources of fear that often accompany personal change." If Mahoney, Lyddon, and Alford, who cite my book, *Overcoming Resistance: Rational-Emotive Therapy with Difficult Clients* (Ellis, 1985d) will read it carefully, they will see that I outline many forms of resistance that do not lie within the clients' beliefs; and that the book recommends the exploration of many sources of fear (including fear of change) that often accompany personal change.

6. "RET separates thoughts and emotions into two distinct categories: rational/irrational thoughts and positive/negative emotions." No, RET separates thoughts into (a) rational thoughts (preferences, wishes, desires, wants), (b) irrational thoughts (antiempirical and illogical ideas) that do not necessarily create disturbances (e.g., beliefs in gods and devils), and (c) irrational thoughts (dogmatic, imperative, and musturbatory ideas) that very frequently (though not necessarily) do contribute significantly to disturbances. RET separates emotions into (a) positive emotions that are

self-helpful, (b) positive emotions that are often self-sabotaging, (c) negative feelings that are functional and desirable, (d) negative feelings that are dysfunctional and self-defeating, (e) positive feelings that are self-helping, (f) positive feelings that are self-destructive. The simple dichotomies that Mahoney, Lyddon, and Alford assign to RET are notions that RET actually opposes (Ellis, 1985b).

7. "Even though many of those seeking psychotherapy are experiencing interpersonal problems, the solution presented in RET is intrapersonal in nature." Hardly! RET has from the start been both interpersonal and intrapersonal; and many of its most popular writings emphasize interpersonal problems and their solutions (Ellis, 1957a, 1963a, 1963b, 1976a, 1979b; Ellis & Becker, 1982; Ellis & Harper, 1961a, 1961b, 1975). Instead of employing cognitive restructuring or interpersonal skill training, RET normally employs both. Some writers on psychotherapy have specifically placed RET under the category of interpersonal therapies. RET was one of the pioneering family therapies, and, as I have noted (Ellis, 1982, 1985d; Ellis & Dryden, 1987), it is more systems oriented, in some ways, than is so-called systems family therapy. For it deals with (a) the intrapersonal problems of individuals in a family system, (b) the influence of these individuals on the family, (c) the influence of the family system on the individuals within it, and (d) strategically and actively arranging for the changing of the system as well as helping the individuals in the system change themselves. I have no idea where Mahoney, Lyddon, and Alford got the idea that RET does not actively deal with people's interpersonal and interfamilial problems. It does so through direct advice and suggestion, through problem solving, through skill training, and through other methods of arranging for what they call "complex changes in the dynamic properties of the relationship as a system."

8. Mahoney, Lyddon, and Alford list several reasons why they think RET is popular with therapists and clients, and I feel fairly sure that they are partly correct. But at least two of their reasons seem mistaken: (a) "A formistic thinking style which reduces complex phenomena to simple, dichotomous categories." In some ways, RET practice and theory are indeed simple; but they also have many complexities that Mahoney and his associates ignore. Mahoney, Lyddon, and Alford seem to deliberately avoid considering the complexities of RET while only emphasizing its simplicities. Again, the dichotomous categories they talk about are theirs and not RET's! (b) "An emphasis on intrapersonal sources and solutions to a range of interpersonal difficulties." As noted above, RET emphasizes both intrapersonal and interpersonal problems and deals more thoroughly with both than do most of the other psychotherapies.

9. "The available data suggest that our theoretical orientations

(rationales) and our therapeutic techniques (rituals) are far less important in predicting successful outcome than are the client's psychological characteristics and the quality of the attachment (relationship) between client and counselor." Many authorities have suggested that this is true, but no definitive data exist to substantiate their suggestions. The existing evidence tends to show that the client's psychological characteristics and the quality of the attachment between client and counselor are relevant in predicting successful therapeutic outcome, but so are the theoretical orientations and techniques of the therapist, the competence of the therapist, the personality of the therapist, the successful and unsuccessful events of the client's life while therapy is in progress, and several other factors.

10. "Albert Ellis has been significantly influenced by the Stoic philosopher Epictetus." Yes, but I have some strong differences with Epictetus. He believed in inalterable fate; he did not usually advocate changing obnoxious conditions that can be changed; he was utopian, he downplayed human emotion and pleasure; he advocated calmness, serenity, and detachment; and he had many other ideas which are quite antithetical to RET. The main ideas I took from him (and from some of the early Asian philosophers as well) are, first, that it is not things but largely (not completely!) our view of things that upsets us; and, second, that if we profoundly change our self-upsetting view we can significantly help change our dysfunctional feelings and behaviors. To say, then, as Mahoney, Lyddon, and Alford say, that "Albert Ellis is a modern representative of classical rationalism and Stoicism" is to make an exceptionally false statement, and it is surprising that they have presumably read so many of my writings and still make this allegation. Again, to state that "Ellis invites us to recognize what little control we have over our lives, to renounce any hope of supernatural meaning or salvation, and to accept our lives as they are" is again false. Yes, I think that it is preferable for disturbed people to renounce any hope of supernatural meaning or salvation, though I admit that in some cases this hope helps them (Ellis, 1985d). But I clearly keep saying that we have much control over our lives and that we have only to accept things as they are after we have made concerted efforts to change them and have found these efforts useless. Even then, I keep emphasizing to my clients that they had better only temporarily accept unfortunate events and relationships that they cannot change, and had better virtually never give up the ultimate hope of changing them.

11. Again, Mahoney, Lyddon, and Alford set up a strawperson that they call "rational living" and hold that "with rational living skills, people's expectations are likely to be lowered and their abilities to rationalize their behavior will be improved." Again, they are really citing Epictetus and not Albert Ellis!

With their last sentence, however, I quite agree: "The writings of Albert Ellis and other RET practitioners have helped to clarify the challenging complexities that continue to face the theories and therapies of the future, and that, in itself, is a valuable contribution." Yes! My writings on rational–emotive therapy were at first somewhat simplistic and did not emphasize many of the complexities that were actually included in its practice. They have now, I hope, become more complex and more integrative. Let me summarize and conclude with some of the complexities that are now acknowledged and used by RET. Briefly (and partially) they include the following:

1. People are born with strong tendencies to escalate their rational preferences and desires into absolutistic musts and imperatives. But they also pick up, gullibly accept, and habitually carry on irrational, self-defeating, grandiose beliefs from their parents and their culture.

2. Disturbed feelings and behaviors (e.g., anxiety and depression) largely and importantly stem from (or, better, are contributed to by) dogmatic beliefs. But they also have physiological "causes" or contributions; and they are significantly correlated with environmental activating events that block people's goals and desires.

3. Neurotic feelings and behaviors are almost always concomitants of absolutistic, conscious and/or unconscious, musturbatory beliefs, but not all antiempirical, illogical, false beliefs lead to emotional disturbance.

4. In normal human affairs, practically no pure thoughts, feelings, or behaviors exist. Disturbed people, in particular, have intertwined and interactional ideas, emotions, and actions. Consequently, to significantly change (and maintain the change in) self-defeating thoughts, they usually have to work on their thinking, their feelings, and their behaviors. Often (though not always) the best ways to surrender their crooked thinking is to (forcefully and often uncomfortably) make themselves feel and act differently.

These and many other intricacies of RET (and of psychotherapy in general) are increasingly being discovered. Good! Let us hope that these ongoing discoveries will add to the efficacy of therapeutic theory and practice.

COMMENTS ON A. LAZARUS'S CHAPTER

Arnold Lazarus has nicely explained what multimodal therapy is and how it differs from RET, but he has somewhat missed the boat in understanding what RET is and has therefore mainly criticized what it is not.

He insists that RET is essentially active–directive disputing of irrational beliefs, when that is one of its main features but hardly its essence.

Let me state briefly once again the essence of RET (Ellis, 1962, 1979g, 1979h, 1980b, 1985b, 1985d, 1988; Ellis & Bernard, 1985b; Ellis & Dryden, 1987). People largely (not exclusively) disturb themselves by inventing or adopting irrational beliefs (iBs), particularly absolutistic and dogmatic musts and demands. Their emotional problems and their behavioral dysfunctions mainly stem from their grandiose demands on themselves, on others, and on environmental conditions. But since human thoughts, feelings, and behaviors are not pure but are interactional, people's self-defeating feelings and behaviors also importantly create and affect their irrational beliefs (Ellis, 1962).

RET hypothesizes that there are innumerable ways in which people can change their dysfunctional feelings and behaviors (including some highly irrational ways, e.g., faith healing). But it holds that almost always the best ways include a combination of active–directive cognitive, emotive-evocative, and action-oriented homework methods. Although it can, and often does, employ scores of eclectic methods, it favors techniques most likely to lead clients to make a profound philosophic change in their musturbatory dogmas. These almost always include (1) active–directive teaching clients the ABC RET model of disturbance and of disturbance about disturbance, (2) forcefully disputing their iBs and teaching them the scientific methods of doing so on their own, (3) encouraging them to read RET self-help literature and listen to RET cassettes, (4) reviewing RET Self-Help Report Forms (Sichel & Ellis, 1984), (5) advising clients to vigorously and emotively use rational, coping self-statements, (6) getting them to train themselves to change their inappropriate to appropriate feelings by using rational–emotive imagery and other emotive methods, (7) encouraging the use of *in vivo* (rather than imaginal) desensitization for clients to act against their phobic and avoidant irrational beliefs, (8) encouraging, where feasible, implosive antiphobic and shame-attacking exercises, (9) using meaningful reinforcements as well as stiff penalties to help clients do their RET homework and give up their self-defeating behaviors.

A series of RET sessions normally includes most or all of these techniques. But it includes these cognitive, emotive, and behavioral methods on theoretical, not eclectic, grounds, because they seem to best help people surrender their absolutistic musts. My hypothesis is that methods like forceful disputing, vigorous self-repeated self-statements, dramatic rational–emotive imagery, implosive *in vivo* desensitization, and the enactment of severe penalties for homework infractions are more effective and more efficient in helping clients change their irrational beliefs than are most of the methods used in other forms of cognitive–behavioral therapy (CBT) and multimodal therapy (MMT). So I preferentially use these techniques first. If they do not seem to work too well in individual cases, I add various other therapeutic modalities.

Let me now answer some of Lazarus's specific critiques:

1. "Ellis and perhaps most other RET practitioners have kept pace with the rise of systematic eclecticism." RET was cognitive, emotive, and behavioral from the time I started doing it in 1955 (Ellis, 1962). Systematic eclecticism is mainly a product of the 1970s and 1980s.

2. "The distinctiveness of RET lies in its methods of cognitive restructuring." One distinction of RET is its quick, highly active, forceful methods of cognitive restructuring. But, unlike most of the other cognitive–behavioral schools, it usually emphasizes dramatically changing inappropriate to appropriate feelings, shame-attacking exercises, implosive *in vivo* desensitization, and stiff penalties for homework avoiders.

3. "When using a technique other than rational disputation, shame-attacking exercises, rational–emotive imagery, or some of the other methods developed by Ellis and/or his associates, is one still practicing RET? If the answer is yes, it would seem that RET loses all distinctive meaning or identity and merges totally with the entire field of applied psychology." False! Psychoanalysis often uses suggestion, hypnosis, advice, and didactic teaching, but it is still psychoanalysis as long as it uses these methods within a general analytic framework. RET's theory that humans innately invent and strongly hang on to Jehovian musts and that they easily and naturally habituate themselves to the self-defeating feelings and behaviors that integrally accompany these dogmatic philosophies practically requires that RET favor certain behavioral and emotive–evocative methods. Some of these, such as shame-attacking exercises and rational–emotive imagery, I and my associates specially invented. But other techniques, such as *in vivo* desensitization, implosive homework assignments, and reinforcement and penalizing techniques, were created independently of RET but fit nicely into its theory of disturbance and of therapy. They are therefore routinely used by RETers. Rational–emotive therapy without some of these behavioral and emotive–evocative methods would simply not be RET. To view it simply as cognitive reconstructuring plus a few special exercises is to distort the meaning of RET.

4. "Most RET practitioners seldom use methods outside of actively explaining, interpreting, and disputing clients' irrational beliefs." If so, they are hardly doing good RET. Actually a study by Warren and McLellarn (1987) shows that, in addition to helping clients to do cognitive reconstruction, the majority of associate fellows and fellows of the Institute for

Rational–Emotive Therapy use unconditional acceptance of clients, strong forceful language, social skills training, role playing, behavior rehearsal, rational–emotive imagery, modeling, problem-solving training, contingency contracting, and other nondisputing techniques.

Alvin Mahrer and his associates (Mahrer, Nadler, Gervaize, Sterner, & Talitman, 1988) listened to some of my typical RET sessions and judged them using a general category system of "good moments" derived from and applicable to a broad range of therapeutic approaches as well as a category system explicitly derived from and applicable to RET. They found that in addition to the "good moments" that RET expressly acknowledges (expressing insight-understanding, manifesting a qualitatively altered RET personality state, and manifesting or reporting changes in RET target behaviors), "RET seems to obtain additional categories of client good moments as defined by the general category system of good moments: (a) providing meaningful material about personal self and/or interpersonal relations, (b) communicating expressively, (c) manifesting good working relationship with therapist, and (d) undergoing new behaviors in imminent extratherapy world."

Mahrer and his associates, who are mainly into experiential therapy, also found that

> a careful clinical analysis suggests that the therapist (Albert Ellis) used four methods that were effective in the direct eliciting of new behavior. When the client introduces a possible new behavior yoked with feared consequences, the new behavior change is facilitated by using these methods: (a) the therapist explicates the feared consequences of carrying out the new behavior; (b) the therapist divests the consequences of their fear by even closer constructive analysis of the consequences; (c) the therapist provides the client with a new way of thinking and being congruent with the new behavior; and (d) the therapist energetically encourages the client to carry out the specific and concrete new behavior. These combine into a potentially effective behavior change package of therapeutic procedures.

5. Apart from various extreme psychoanalytic, experiential and mystical ideologies, "everything else in the psychotherapeutic realm would presumably be considered General RET." No. All these techniques, including even some mystical ideologies, can at times be used to help people give up their irrational beliefs. But the "good" cognitive–behavioral methods—such as Wolpe's systematic desensitization and Lazarus's time-tripping imagery—while at times effective, are usually palliative, philosophically shallow, and time-consuming. Therefore, they are mainly used in RET after the more forceful methods mentioned above seem to be failing.

6. The RET goal "appears to achieve a state of veritable undisturbability (rather than merely striving to be less disturbable)." Not so! For many years I have told my professional trainees and public workshop participants that all humans seem to be born with tendencies to be disturbed and that none of them, even when significantly helped by RET, never fall back to disturbance. If they achieve the "elegant" RET cure, they merely are much less disturbed, fall back less frequently, and recover more quickly than they would, I hypothesize, in other forms of therapy.

7. "By including other cognitive distortions within the basic theory, RET would become more flexible and applicable to a wider range of subtle disorders." I doubt it. The kinds of irrational beliefs that Lazarus lists either have hidden musts implied in them or else they stem from and are derivatives of absolutistic demands.

8. "RET practitioners are inclined to dispense cognitive disputation to virtually all comers, whether or not the client is precontemplative." Correct. For it has been my experience that at least 80% of neurotic and borderline clients can fairly quickly benefit from cognitive reconstruction, plus the other important aspects of RET. Most precontemplative clients can be taught to be much more contemplative if therapists do not give up too easily and do not cavalierly assume that they can only be helped by empathic listening, by prolonged abreaction, or by other noncognitive methods.

9. "The literature on rational–emotive therapy has bypassed a host of effective mental-imagery methods." Yes, it has, largely because although there is much anecdotal evidence, such as Lazarus's case history, showing that many mental imagery techniques help people, there are as yet few controlled studies backing their effectiveness. So they are frequently used experimentally in RET, but only rational–emotive imagery is used consistently (Ellis, 1985d; Maultsby & Ellis, 1974).

10. "It is usually advisable for conflict resolution to precede cognitive disputation." Not according to RET! Conflict is the normal human condition, since all of us have different preferences and goals. RET holds that only when people demand that conflicts be resolved their way do they get into emotional trouble. Therefore, RET first looks for their absolutistic musts about conflicts, tries to help them give these up, and then sees whether the conflicts can be resolved.

11. Arnold Lazarus may find that if RET practitioners use the term *had better* instead of *should* and *must*, clients will perceive that it "carries a threatening tone." I very rarely find this to be so. But he is correct about saying that *should* and *must* need not be compulsively challenged by RETers.

12. In his section on the main differences between RET and multimodal therapy (MMT), Lazarus has finally convinced me that MMT, as he

outlines it there, is different from general RET and from general cognitive–behavioral therapy (CBT). For although he clearly states "there is no particular method that is distinctively multimodal," he also gives five distinct procedures that MMT practitioners practically always do. Certainly, RET and CBT practitioners would rarely use any one of these five special MMT methods. General RET, CBT, and MMT, however, significantly overlap because they are all eclectic, comprehensive, and multifaceted. But preferential RET and what might be called preferential MMT significantly differ in several important ways. Personally, I find the major essentials of MMT more of a handicap than an asset in striving for effective and efficient therapy. But they are creative and deserve experimental investigation.

COMMENTS ON GARFIELD'S CHAPTER

Sol Garfield's chapter, "The Client–Therapist Relationship in Rational–Emotive Therapy," has some interesting points to make, most of which I largely agree with. Let me first list some of these agreements:

1. "There is considerable variability among them [clients] and they can be viewed as a common but important variable in psychotherapy." Definitely! I definitely do, as Garfield points out, considerably vary both my style and content in using RET with radically different clients; and I strongly recommend that other therapists do so.

2. "The emphasis on focusing on the client's irrational thoughts and persistently pointing them out exemplifies to many clients the therapist's efforts to help them." Indeed it does! In RET, as Garfield rightly points out, the therapist's showing clients that they definitely upset themselves and can clearly stop doing so indicates strong confidence in their ability to change and thereby usually enhances the therapeutic relationship.

3. "Although the emphasis clearly is on the performance of specified activities, the successful performance of such activities may enhance the therapeutic relationship." Another good point! Merely showing clients that they can effectively do their homework helps them to accept the therapy and the therapist; and when they successfully do this homework their confidence in RET and its practitioner is reinforced.

4. "The therapy is highly focused on matters that are currently meaningful to the client.... I would hypothesize that to most clients this creates a favorable impression and a positive climate for psychotherapeutic work." *Meaningful* is a good word here, since clients give great meaning to their present problems and so does the RET practitioner. Rapport is thus enhanced.

5. "Those who have faith in the basic validity of RET therapy and the necessary personal qualities that seemingly provide maximum results are likely to be successful therapists." Yet, the therapist's absolutistic devotion to RET is dangerous, is, in fact, a disturbance. But his or her confidence in it is most probably therapeutic. I would add, however, that a therapist's great confidence in psychoanalysis, in Rogerian, and in other types of therapy may be productive in the short run but, I hypothesize, be much less therapeutic in the long run than the therapist's confidently using RET.

6. "Ellis combines all this with a positive compliment about the client's brightness and competence and his confidence that the client will do quite well." Yes, this is one of the main relationship techniques of RET and is quite different from the psychoanalyst's adopting a passive stance and abjuring, if he or she is orthodox, any real encouragement and valid complimenting. Instead, RET uses the Adlerian procedure of direct encouragement.

7. "Although the nature of RET contains some features emphasized in well-known forms of brief therapy, RET cannot be considered as strictly a brief form of psychotherapy." Strictly, no. But it is intrinsically more brief than most other forms of therapy because it very quickly and directly tries to get to clients' basic irrational philosophies and to show them how to profoundly change these beliefs. For many people, therefore, it only takes from a few to 15 or 20 sessions; but for severely disturbed and resistant individuals it may take a year or more.

My differences with Garfield's presentation are relatively minor. Let me briefly mention some of them:

1. Garfield implies that I only recently followed Carl Rogers in according clients unconditional acceptance; but actually I did so from the very beginning of RET (Ellis, 1962). Harry Bone (1968), based on my early writing (Ellis, 1962; Ellis & Harper, 1961), concluded,

> It seems to me that Ellis' basic principles of *complete absence of blame*, or 'not blaming *any one* for *anything*, at *any time*' is essentially identical with Rogers' principle of *unconditional positive regard*. The *thoroughness* with which they espouse this principle and its *implications*, together with their respective ways of effectively *implementing* it, distinguishes their systems from other systems. (p. 184, italics in original)

2. "Both general comments in the writings on RET and remarks offered to patients by Ellis frequently refer to the intelligence level and sophistication of clients." Yes, most of my case examples are of intelligent and educated clients; and, like virtually all modes of psychotherapy, RET does

better with these individuals. But it also is one of the few forms of therapy that can be modified so that it is effective with less intelligent and less educated clients, as well as with young children whose mental age is low (Bernard & Joyce, 1984; Ellis & Bernard, 1983b).

3. "In partial support of some of the assertions made earlier of Ellis's style, it can be noted that he is the only one of the three therapists [Rogers, Perls, and Ellis] who emits more words than the client." This is often the case with my first sessions with clients; but as Carl Rogers noted in 1959, when he listened to a series of my sessions with the same client, as therapy progresses, the clients normally talk considerably more than I do.

4. "I know that I, for one, could not perform as does Ellis in therapy. His style fits him, but I would not feel authentic in trying to imitate him precisely." In RET supervision and training at the Institute for Rational–Emotive Therapy, we try to encourage trainees not to imitate my style, but to use much of the basic content of RET in their own style.

5. Garfield, quoting Patterson (1986), implies that my authority and prestige as founder of a school of psychotherapy effectively influence my clients. This is, of course, true in some cases, since some individuals come to see me after they have read my books or listened to my recordings. But the great majority of them are referred by friends or relatives and know little or nothing about me when they start therapy. So I would guess that about 30% of my clients are influenced by my prominence in the field.

As can be seen from the above remarks, my disagreements with Sol Garfield are slight. I think that in his consideration of some of the important factors in the client–therapist relationship in rational–emotive therapy, and particularly in my own use of RET, he has made a significant contribution to the therapeutic literature.

COMMENTS ON SMITH'S CHAPTER[1]

Smith's critical evaluation of empirical tests of the theory of RET is useful, and his critique of existing measures of irrational beliefs is remarkably thorough and incisive. It seems to us, however, that the main focus of Smith's theoretical analysis, "assessing the B in the ABCD model" misses the crux of the theory. As we see RET, its principal focus is therapy; RET is based not on an ABCD, but on an ABCDE model (Ellis & Bernard, 1985b). Smith correctly recognizes that the ABC part of the theory of RET argues that iBs are more important determinants of disturbed Cs than As, and he treats

---

[1]This section was written jointly by Albert Ellis, Russell Leaf, and Roslyn Mass.

the relationship between Bs and Cs as the central core of the theory of RET. In our view, however, RET importantly includes applications of this ABC theory to the treatment of clinical problems, and the D and E of the ABCDE model, where D refers to the process of disputing irrational beliefs and E refers to their consequent replacement with effective rational beliefs, represent the central core of RET (Ellis & Bernard, 1985b, pp. 14–18).

The second part of Smith's chapter, "Defining the Construct to be Assessed," does not seem to focus on therapy. In his discussion of, "evolving definitions of irrationality," he fails to recognize that what mainly has been evolving in rational-emotive therapy are strategies for disputing irrational beliefs, that is, the DE link, rather than the ABC portion of the theory. These concerns over how to develop effective strategies led Ellis to classify iBs so that a relatively small number of rapid and systematic approaches for D and E assessment, in treatment situations, could be developed and taught. For practitioners of RET, the process of disputing irrational beliefs is an assessment process—difficult, variable, partly dependent on experience and training, and clearly involving collaborative effort from a client—as well as the heart of treatment.

As scientist-practitioners, we join Smith in encouraging research to assess the therapy process in RET. However, we argue that the assessment of irrational beliefs is not the central problem when looking at process; it is, rather, the effect of disputing on irrational beliefs. RET does not say, for example, that it is therapeutically useful to challenge negative thinking, but that specific negative beliefs (e.g., "I did poorly at this task, as I absolutely should not have done!") are likely to lead to anxious and depressed feelings. And it says that certain positive beliefs (e.g., "I did well at this task, as I have to do, and therefore I am a noble person who will always succeed at everything!") also are likely to lead to disturbed feelings (e.g., feelings of grandiosity and paranoia). Disputing that emphasizes giving up the demands in such beliefs is time-consuming, repetitive, and difficult but, we argue, the core of RET.

Smith's argument that self-report measures of irrationality are inadequate because they cannot tap unconscious beliefs does not seem relevant when one focuses on the DE link; the issue of awareness is no longer critical because disputing is a conscious process. To set the record straight, Smith partly misquotes Ellis in this connection. What Ellis said in *Humanistic Psychotherapy* was that when we do have unconscious beliefs, our

unconscious, irrational beliefs and value systems are *not*, as the Freudians erroneously contend, so deeply buried in the individual's unconscious mind that it necessarily takes years of psychoanalysis to dig them up and make them conscious. On the contrary, almost all of them are just below the top level of consciousness. (Ellis, 1973, pp. 243-344)

In other words, we have conscious and unconscious beliefs, and even the latter, for the most part, are just below the top level of consciousness and are not (as the Freudians contend) deeply hidden. But our conscious rational and irrational beliefs are, of course, not hidden at all. So when self-report measures of irrational beliefs for clinical use largely include only conscious beliefs (as they obviously do), they still can be fairly good measures of irrationality (even if they also provide partly confounded measures).

Short and Long Lists of Irrational Beliefs

When Smith compares and contrasts Ellis's early lists of rather specific irrational beliefs (e.g., Ellis, 1962; Ellis & Harper, 1961, 1975) with Ellis's more recent and shorter list of three or four more general beliefs (Ellis, 1979g, 1980b, 1984d; Ellis & Bernard, 1983b, 1985b), he correctly points out that the course in the writing of Ellis and other RET theorists is in the direction of the shorter list. We agree that the short, style-oriented list of irrational beliefs is an appropriate focus for research; however, we suggest that the search for "empirical justification" of the shorter list emphasizes assessment of its clinical usefulness. Whether or not a factor analysis, for example, of a long list that focuses on content of irrational beliefs would be of value in evaluating the short, style-oriented list is problematic, given the high probability that the content-oriented list is not exhaustive and given the fact that clients differ on many dimensions of self-expressiveness. When Smith concludes that there is no apparent empirical justification for the shorter grouping (which implies a distillation of higher order, more general beliefs from the earlier, more specific ones), we are not clear what he means by "empirical justification." Ellis's earlier list of irrational beliefs was taken from empirical (i.e., clinical) observations of the beliefs that his clients seemed to hold when they were disturbed; and his later list was taken from additional clarification of even more empirical observations. This classification, into 3 main musts or commands under which the original 12 could be subsumed, was primarily developed as a guide to therapeutic disputing; its most appropriate tests would, presumably, ask whether it provides a superior tool for that purpose. Whenever clients were neurotically disturbed, they seemed to benefit from disputing either one, two, or all three of these iBs, namely (1) "I must do well and/or be approved by significant others or I am an inadequate person," (2) "Other people must treat me kindly and fairly or else they are rotten individuals," and (3) "Conditions under which I live must be safe and comfortable or else the world is a horrible place in which to live and life is hardly worth living."

Both the longer and shorter lists of iBs, therefore, were derived from empirical observation (and abstraction). But even if they were not, why is that important? As Smith notes, "the definition of irrationality in terms of the content of the shorter list of basic beliefs presents an additional approach to the concept, the style of irrational thinking." This means that we now hold that when people change almost any preferential or rational thought into an absolutistic thought, they create an irrational thought that is both antiempirical and illogical and that is very likely to result in emotional and behavioral dysfunction. We hypothesize, in other words, that rigid, inflexible, extreme, unconditional demands on oneself, on other people, and/or on external conditions will usually (not always) make one miserable. Even if Ellis did not get this definition of irrational thinking from empirical observation (and he thinks that he did) and even if it is purely a hypothetical construct (if "pure" constructs actually exist), it seems to us that all that has to be done scientifically is (1) observe when people are emotionally and behaviorally miserable, (2) see if disputing such "definitional" constructs is helpful in alleviating some of their misery, and (3) see if more rational B's are significantly correlated with reduced dysfunction (and perhaps causally correlated). If so, we have empirical justification not only for Ellis's original hypothesis or definition about irrational, absolutistic thoughts but for the "fact" that they are related to dysfunctioning. What else must be done to "empirically justify" RET?

Present Inventories Assess Clinically Significant Dysphoria

Some of Smith's criticism obviously does apply to DE as well as to iB assessment. Actually, as Smith notes, RET does not greatly emphasize self-report inventories at any stage, including tests of rationality, but largely assesses how disturbed people are by how they respond to efficient therapy, such as RET. This is one of the notions Smith criticizes as tautological, since if the efficient therapy does not work, we tend to define the client as being more disturbed than if, in a similar length of time with similar effort, the therapy does work. This kind of tautology, however, seems inevitable when we try to fix almost anything. If a piece of wood is broken in several places or it has one large hole and normal glue will not fix it, we define it as "badly" instead of "a little" broken. In RET, if people have several irrational ideas and they hold on to some of them rigidly and if they also get poor emotional and behavioral results until they give up these ideas, we define them as "disturbed" (and may refer to them as "difficult customers"), and when they surrender their irrational beliefs and act more functionally we define them as improved by RET. All therapies (and repair procedures) seem to do this; and we are not clear as to how they can completely do otherwise. Research that focuses on changes in B's (the DE process) could help make such judgments of disturbance less tautological.

From our perspective, the low discriminant validity that troubles Smith (i.e., that correlations between putative measures of beliefs and putative measures of distress are so high as to make the measures almost indistinguishable) actually supports the theory of rational–emotive therapy, which predicts moderately high correlations (as Smith acknowledges, in part).

In his emphasis on the assessment of iBs, Smith focuses on cognitive activities which reflect the full diversity of human experience and which maximize the significance of group and individual differences. The irrational beliefs of clients are incredibly diverse, and purely cognitive self-report inventories probably would provide quite limited guides for clinical intervention (Ellis, 1946; Gynther & Green, 1982). Smith is correct when he states, "A close examination of the item content of the irrational belief scales reveals a probable cause of the poor discriminant validity. Many items contain references to dysfunctional behaviors and affects. On some, irrational beliefs are only implied by the described maladaptive affective responses to a potentially upsetting situation." It is possible, of course, that these references help clients to judge their irrational beliefs more accurately, for example, by prompting conscious reflection about previously unconscious attitudes. It is an empirical question, not an a priori one, whether such contents increase or decrease the validity of a measure of iBs. Empirically, even if all items on an inventory referred to feelings and behaviors, it is still possible to validate the degree to which the various items reflect musturbatory thinking and to distinguish better from worse inventories. Practically all the existing irrational belief scales were really designed to see whether disturbed individuals subscribe to more irrationalities than do nondisturbed individuals. Smith argues that all of the irrational belief inventories, including the IBT and RBI, perhaps also assess a more general dimension, previously labeled general dysphoria (Gotlib, 1984) or negative affectivity (D. Watson & Clark, 1984). If this is true—and many studies using the Irrational Belief Test and the Rational Behavior Inventory have shown that their scores correlate significantly with scores on both general dysphoria and specific dysphoria (e.g., anxiety and depression) tests—it is hardly surprising, but it may explain why the present inventories have some clinical value; assessment of dysphoria is usually clinically useful.

Smith's criticism that RET may slide into "wholism" if it cannot separately assess iBs and clinically relevant Cs may constructively lead to the caveat that RET, and other forms of cognitive therapy, had better be more precise than they sometimes are in specifying exactly which beliefs are most often likely to lead to which affects and behaviors. Smith is correct that belief and affect are not intended to be synonymous concepts in RET, since it holds that certain kinds of belief (notably, rigid and musturbatory ones) are significantly correlated with, and in all probability contribute to, certain kinds of affect (notably, disturbed feelings). If unconfounded empirical definitions of measures to assess thoughts, feelings, and behaviors cannot be developed, as we think is actually feasible, then we may have to stop using these terms in theoretical discussions and instead use more complex terms, as Ellis implied in his earliest writings on RET (Ellis, 1958a, 1962). Thus, instead of saying, "I believe I must succeed at every important task I perform," we might say, "I believe-feel-and-find-myself-compelled-to-succeed at every important task I perform." And instead of saying, "I feel like an inadequate person when I fail at an important task," we might say, "I feel-like-think-I-am-and-act-like an inadequate person when I fail at an important task." This more complex way of stating our thoughts, feelings, and behaviors might be more accurate than our present conventional shorthand ways of doing so. What is more useful for theory may also (or may not) be more useful in therapy.

Smith's chapter is a valuable contribution in that it clearly shows some of the present limitations of research into the kinds of irrationalities that RET hypothesizes are significantly correlated with dysfunctional emotions and behaviors and points the way toward the improvement of clinically oriented research into RET. If heeded, many of the points in his chapter may well benefit the theory and practice of RET and of other schools of therapy. Indeed, the ongoing process of evaluative research on therapy at the Institute for Rational–Emotive Therapy has already been influenced in a positive way by considering how many of his points relate to issues about the DE process, and, in addition, our different perspectives have been clarified during discussions fueled by his remarks.

COMMENTS ON HAAGA AND DAVISON'S CHAPTER

Haaga and Davison have done a very careful and incisive review of most of the published outcome studies of RET; and, although they have deliberately omitted scores of dissertations and studies published in out-of-the-way publications, theirs is probably the most comprehensive review of this area that has yet been done. They are to be congratulated on their thoroughness and their unusual objectivity.

In summarizing and commenting upon Haaga and Davison's main findings, let me make the following observations. First, although about 200 outcome studies (including many that Haaga and Davison omit) have now been done, it seems quite clear that these RET experiments have almost always unclearly defined what RET really is and have only very partially included the main RET methods that I have outlined in many of my publications (Ellis, 1962, 1969b, 1971c, 1973, 1985b, 1985d; Ellis & Dryden, 1987; Ellis & Grieger, 1986; Ellis & Whiteley, 1979). They have largely utilized only one of RET's main aspects, cognitive restructuring (CR) or systematic rational restructuring (SSR). While SSR is a major component of RET, as well as intrinsic to several other cognitive–behavioral therapies (Bandura, 1977b; Beck, 1976a; Goldfried & Davison, 1976; Mahoney, 1974; Meichenbaum, 1977a), its singular use is definitely not RET.

When used clinically, both general or nonpreferential as well as specialized or preferential RET are complex and multimodal modes of therapy that almost invariably include several cognitive, several emotive, and several behavioral methods. General RET is synonymous with general cognitive–behavioral therapy; and specialized or preferential RET includes, as I point out in my other comments in this book, several multifaceted philosophic and behavioral components. Thus, I would characterize "real" or "pronounced" RET along the following lines:

1. It actively–directively shows clients that they have distinct (explicit and/or implicit) iBs and that these involve absolutistic, dogmatic, rigid shoulds, oughts, musts, demands, commands, insistences, and necessities (Ellis, 1985b, 1987a, 1988).

2. It often (not always) firmly and forcefully disputes clients' basic absolutistic ideas until they change them to distinct, though still often strong, preferences. It helps them to differentiate clearly between passionately wanting success, approval, justice, and comfort and insistently needing these desiderata.

3. RET helps clients to unconditionally and nondemandingly accept themselves while, at the same time, to acknowledge and work against their self-sabotaging and socially damaging acts, deeds, and performances.

4. RET tries to help clients to actualize themselves, to live longer and more enjoyably, but in the process to become long-range instead of short-range hedonists: to more fully enjoy themselves both today and tomorrow. Consequently, it encourages clients to become more disciplined and to ameliorate their low frustration tolerance.

5. RET uses a number of forceful, vigorous, evocative–emotive methods of helping people make a profound philosophic change, and it consequently teaches them to use several emotive–dramatic methods as homework assignments to effect and maintain deep attitudinal changes.

To this end, it favors techniques like rational–emotive imagery, shame-attacking exercises, powerful self-statements, forceful self-dialogues, and humor.

6. RET almost invariably employs consistent and persistent behavioral homework, especially *in vivo* desensitization. It often encourages clients to stay in undesirable situations until they first work on some of their emotional problems about these situations and then see whether they want to change the activating events or external conditions of their lives.

7. When clients are cognitively, emotively, and behaviorally working to keep their values, standards, and preferences but to surrender their commands and demands on themselves, on others, and on the world, RET also encourages and teaches them how to change the obnoxious conditions of their lives for better conditions. It consequently employs a ''systems'' approach to therapy that includes problem solving, strategies planning, skill training, information giving, and other techniques of changing (and sometimes revolutionizing) the activating events of people's lives.

8. RET almost always uses psychoeducational techniques in addition to regular individual or group therapy. It encourages clients to read RET books and pamphlets, to listen to audiocassettes, and to attend suitable talks and workshops lead by trained RETers.

9. RET shows clients how they can use its self-help forms (Sichel & Ellis, 1984) and has its therapists go over these forms with clients to see that they are correctly filled out and worked at.

10. RET regularly employs principles of behavioral reinforcement, as well as behavioral penalties, when clients fail to do their agreed-upon therapy assignments.

11. RET, when it is preferential, includes a humanistic philosophy and teaches clients that they will continue to be fallible humans, never perfect, never godlike; and that they can fully accept themselves while still rating their traits and performances, just because they are alive, just because they are human (Ellis, 1962, 1972a, 1973; Ellis & Becker, 1982; Ellis & Harper, 1975).

In sum, preferential or specialized RET (as distinct from general cognitive–behavioral therapy) is almost always comprehensive, multimodal, systematic, and humanistic; and in virtually no instance do the studies that Haaga and Davison incisively analyze in this chapter utilize this kind of ''real'' RET. Haaga and Davison's review convincingly proves that the ''old'' RET, or systematic rational restructuring, is fairly effective. For considering the limited RET hypotheses investigated, and considering the omission from their review of scores of masters and doctoral dissertations (most of which proved to be favorable outcome studies), cognitive restructuring came off reasonably well.

As Haaga and Davison point out, their critique shows that cognitive restructuring often helps people in controlled studies. For it seems to significantly help, in many instances, individuals who have general, social, and test anxiety; who seek stress reduction; and who suffer from work problems, moderate obsessions, tension headaches, Type A behavior pattern, stuttering, anger problems, antisocial behavior, unassertiveness, and depression. Not a bad record! So Haaga and Davison's review largely indicates that one major component of RET, systematic rational restructuring, even when used without RET's other main components, often helps troubled people significantly.

The Haaga and Davison chapter, however, points up several important deficiencies in contemporary RET outcome studies and makes a number of notable suggestions for future research. It particularly shows that, in comparison to some more incisive studies of Beck's cognitive therapy, RET research has been distinctly lacking.

This is good to know. Although the Haaga and Davison review indicates many serious problems of all psychotherapy research—few of which have been as yet nicely resolved—I think that it indicates that RET outcome research has been particularly cavalier and lax and that if RET is to produce better outcome results in adequately controlled studies, it had better be much more on its toes.

These studies, as the authors rightly indicate, are almost exclusively investigations of the outcome of using cognitive restructuring or systematic rational restructuring with experimental and control groups. They therefore test one of the main hypotheses of RET—that when people change their irrational beliefs they also tend to change their feelings and behaviors. But even in this respect, they virtually never test the primary RET cognitive hypotheses of the last 15 years, namely, that dogmatic shoulds, oughts, and musts are central to neurotic disturbances and that musturbatory thinking is mainly to be targeted and disputed in preferential rational–emotive therapy (Ellis, 1979f, 1985b, 1985d, 1987a, 1988; Ellis & Dryden, 1987).

Virtually none of the outcome studies cited by Haaga and Davison deal with this preferential and "real" kind of RET. Aside from a few studies (such as Forsterling, 1985), it has not yet been tested; and the Haaga and Davison review convincingly shows that it had soon better be.

CONCLUDING COMMENTS

The chapters in this book have given me considerable food for thought and made me realize that I had better update and revise some of the fundamental aspects and theories of RET. Tentatively, I would reformulate several of them along the following lines:

1. People largely become (or make themselves) emotionally disturbed mainly through their rigid, inflexible, absolutistic, dogmatic philosophies (or irrational beliefs). They have many attributions, inferences, and other false or exaggerated cognitions that are involved with their disturbances; but most of these are derivatives of their absolutistic, unconditional thoughts and would exist more rarely than they do if the dogmas that impel and sustain them were eliminated.

2. What we call our "emotions" have a huge cognitive component (though are not identical with our thoughts). But our cognitions also have a strong emotional component; and cognitions, emotions, and behaviors are rarely, if ever, pure but are interactional, reciprocal, and transactional. They all importantly influence each other.

3. When people become significantly less disturbed they have usually, consciously or unconsciously, made a significant cognitive change, have given up some of their dogmatic musts, have become more flexible in their thinking about achieving their goals and values, and have begun to accept alternate solutions to their practical and emotional problems instead of rigidly sticking to the "solutions" that they previously held.

4. In terms of therapeutic methods, the most pervasive, far-reaching, and lasting one probably consists of people's making a profound philosophic change, especially their keeping their major preferences and values (their goal orientation to happiness) but surrendering their dogmatic irrational beliefs (notably, their imperatives) that get them into emotional trouble.

5. Probably the best way to help many people make a profound, healthy philosophic change is to show them, with persuasive and educational methods, the precise details of their musturbatory thinking and to teach them the scientific method of thinking skeptically, nonabsolutistically, and flexibly. If people can be helped to change these insistences to strong preferences, they will tend to make themselves significantly less emotionally disturbed.

6. Because musturbatory demands are partially created and importantly reinforced by certain kinds of actions and avoidances (e.g., fear of encountering others is reinforced by continual avoidance of encountering them), many kinds of performance anxiety require counterconditioning actions as well as disputational arguments to overcome performance and social anxiety. Thus, forcing oneself to behave more socially will often help one overcome one's irrational belief that one cannot effectively socialize and that social rejection is terrible.

7. Sometimes actions speak louder than words, especially in psychotherapy. So forcing ourselves to counterattack our fearful actions may be the best way to overcome our irrational fears; and *in vivo*

desensitization of a phobia may be more effective than cognitive or imaginal desensitization. Thus, if we keep playing tennis in spite of our horror of failing at it, we may show ourselves that we can improve our game and that we do survive when we fail. By this kind of *in vivo* desensitization we can sometimes actually turn a horrible act into a pleasurable one.

8. Action, even when done in spite of our fears, often leads to skill training. If we are afraid to dance poorly, our terror of doing so will often keep us away from practicing dancing. But if we force ourselves to engage in dancing, we will often improve at this activity, thereby lose our rational belief that we are likely to fail, and perhaps also undercut our irrational belief that it is horrible to fail and that we are worthless people if we fail.

References

Abramowitz, C. V., Abramowitz, S. I., Roback, H. B., & Jackson, C. (1974). Differential effectiveness of directive and nondirective group therapies as a function of client internal-external control. *Journal of Consulting and Clinical Psychology, 42*, 849–853.

Adler, A. (1927). *Understanding human nature.* New York: Greenberg.

Adler, A. (1929). *The science of living.* New York: Greenberg.

Alden, L., Safran, J., & Weideman, R. (1978). A comparison of cognitive and skills training strategies in the treatment of unassertive clients. *Behavior Therapy, 9*, 843–846.

Alexander, F. G., & Selesnick, S. T. (1966). *The history of psychiatry.* New York: Harper & Row.

Allport, F. H. (1955). *Theories of perception and the concept of structure.* New York: Wiley.

Allport, G. W. (1966). Traits revisited. *American Psychologist, 21*, 1–10.

Alpert, R., & Haber, R. (1960). Anxiety in academic achievement situations. *Journal of Abnormal and Social Psychology, 61*, 207–215.

American Psychiatric Association. (1980). *Diagnostic and statistical manual of mental disorders* (3rd ed.). Washington, DC: Author.

American Psychological Association. (1986). Awards for distinguished professional contributions: Albert Ellis. *American Psychologist, 4*, 380–397.

Antonovsky, A. (1979). *Health, stress and coping.* San Francisco, CA: Jossey-Bass.

Arnkoff, D. B. (1980). Psychotherapy from the perspective of cognitive theory. In M. J. Mahoney (Ed.), *Psychotherapy process.* New York: Plenum.

Arnkoff, D. B. (1981). Flexibility in practicing cognitive therapy. In G. Emery, S. D. Hollon, & R. C. Bedrosian (Eds.), *New directions in cognitive therapy* (pp. 203–223). New York: Guilford.

Arnkoff, D. B. (1986). A comparison of the coping and restructuring components of cognitive restructuring. *Cognitive Therapy and Research, 10*, 147–158.

Arnkoff, D. B., & Glass, C. R. (1982). Clinical cognitive constructs: Examination, evaluation, and elaboration. In P. C. Kendall (Ed.), *Advances in cognitive-behavioral research and therapy* (Vol. 1, pp. 1–34). New York: Academic Press.

Arnold, M. B. (Ed.). (1960). *Emotion and personality* (2 vols). New York: Columbia University Press.

Arnold, M. B. (Ed.). (1970). *Feelings and emotions: The Loyola Symposium.* New York: Academic Press.

Atkinson, L. (1983). Rational-emotive therapy versus systematic desensitization: A comment on Moleski and Tosi. *Journal of Consulting and Clinical Psychology*, 51, 776–778.

Averill, J. R. (1982). *Anger and aggression: An essay on emotion*. New York: Springer-Verlag.

Ayer, A. J. (1936). *Language, truth, and logic*. New York: Dover.

Baars, B. J. (1986). *The cognitive revolution in psychology*. New York: Guilford.

Bain, J. A. (1928). *Thought control in everyday life*. New York: Funk & Wagnalls.

Baisden, H. (1980). *Irrational beliefs: A constant validity study*. Unpublished doctoral dissertation, University of Minnesota, Minneapolis.

Bandler, R. (1985). *Using your brain—for a change*. Moab, UT: Real People Press.

Bandura, A. (1969). *Principles of behavior modification*. New York: Holt, Rinehart & Winston.

Bandura, A. (1977a). Self-efficacy: Toward a unifying theory of behavioral change. *Psychological Review*, 84, 191–215.

Bandura, A. (1977b). *Social learning theory*. Englewood Cliffs, NJ: Prentice-Hall.

Bandura, A. (1978). The self system in reciprocal determinism. *American Psychologist*, 33, 344–358.

Bandura, A. (1982). Self-efficacy mechanisms in human agency. *American Psychologist*, 37, 122–147.

Bandura, A. (1986). *Social foundations of thought and action: A social cognitive theory*. Englewood Cliffs, NJ: Prentice-Hall.

Bandura, A., & Adams, N. E. (1977). Analysis of self-efficacy theory of behavioral change. *Cognitive Therapy and Research*, 1, 287–310.

Barabasz, A. F., & Barabasz, M. (1981). Effects of rational-emotive therapy on psychophysiological and reported measures of test anxiety arousal. *Journal of Clinical Psychology*, 37, 511–514.

Barnes, G. E., & Vulcano, B. A. (1982). Measuring rationality independent of social desirability. *Personality and Individual Differences*, 3, 303–309.

Bartley, W. W., III. (1962). *The retreat to commitment*. New York: Knopf.

Beck, A. T. (1967). *Depression*. New York: Harper (Hoeber).

Beck, A. T. (1976a). *Cognitive therapy and the emotional disorders*. New York: International Universities Press.

Beck, A. T. (1976b). *Depression: Clinical, experimental, and theoretical aspects*. New York: Hoeber.

Beck, A. T. (1985). Cognitive therapy, behavior therapy, psychoanalysis, and pharmacotherapy: A cognitive continuum. In M. J. Mahoney & A. Freeman (Eds.), *Cognition and psychotherapy* (pp. 325–347). New York: Plenum.

Beck, A. T., Hollon, S. D., Young, J., Bedrosian, R. C., & Budenz, D. (1985). Combined cognitive-pharmacotherapy versus cognitive therapy in the treatment of depressed outpatients. *Archives of General Psychiatry*, 42, 142–148.

Beck, A. T., Rush, A. J., Shaw, B. F., & Emery, G. (1979). *Cognitive therapy of depression: A treatment manual*. New York: Guilford.

Beck, A. T., Ward, C. H., Mendelson, M., Mock, J. E., & Erbaugh, J. K. (1961). An inventory for measuring depression. *Archives of General Psychiatry*, 4, 561–571.

Becker, I. M., & Rosenfeld, J. G. (1976). Rational-Emotive Therapy—A study of initial therapy sessions of Albert Ellis. *Journal of Clinical Psychology*, 32, 872–876.

Bellack, A. S., & Hersen, M. (Eds.). (1985). *Dictionary of behavior therapy techniques*. New York: Pergamon Press.

Benson, H. (1975). *The relaxation response*. New York: Morrow.

Berger, P. L. (1977). *Facing up to modernity*. New York: Basic Books.

Berger, P. L., Berger, B., & Kellner, H. (1973). *The homeless mind*. New York: Random House.

Bergin, A. E. (1980a). Psychotherapy and religious values. *Journal of Consulting and Clinical Psychology*, 48, 95–105.

Bergin, A. E. (1980b). Religious and humanistic values: A reply to Ellis and Walls. *Journal of Consulting and Clinical Psychology, 48,* 643–645.

Bergin, A. E., & Lambert, M. J. (1978). The evaluation of psychotherapeutic outcome. In S. L. Garfield & A. E. Bergin (Eds.), *Handbook of psychotherapy and behavior change* (2nd ed., pp. 139–189). New York: Wiley.

Bernard, M. E. (1981). Private thought in rational emotive psychotherapy. *Cognitive Therapy and Research, 5,* 125–142.

Bernard, M. E. (1986). *Staying rational in an irrational world.* Melbourne, Australia: McCulloch-Macmillan.

Bernard, M. E., & Joyce, M. R. (1984). *Rational-emotive therapy with children and adolescents: Theory, treatment strategies, preventative methods.* New York: Wiley.

Bernard, M. E., & Laws, W. (1985). *The child and adolescent scale of irrationality.* Unpublished manuscript, University of Melbourne.

Bernstein, D. A., & Borkovec, T. D. (1973). *Progressive relaxation training: A manual for the helping professions.* Champaign, IL: Research Press.

Bernstein, D. A., Borkovec, T. D., & Coles, M. G. H. (1986). Assessment of anxiety. In A. R. Ciminero, K. S. Calhoun & H. E. Adams (Eds.), *Handbook of behavioral assessment* (2nd ed., pp. 353–403). New York: Wiley.

Biran, M., Augusto, F., & Wilson, G. T. (1981). *In vivo* exposure vs. cognitive restructuring in the treatment of scriptophobia. *Behaviour Research and Therapy, 19,* 525–532.

Biran, M., & Wilson, G. T. (1981). Treatment of phobic disorders using cognitive and exposure methods: A self-efficacy analysis. *Journal of Consulting and Clinical Psychology, 49,* 886–899.

Blackburn, I. M., Bishop, S., Glen, A. I. M., Whalley, L. J., & Christie, J. E. (1981). The efficacy of cognitive therapy in depression: A treatment trial using cognitive therapy and pharmacotherapy, each alone and in combination. *British Journal of Psychiatry, 139,* 181–189.

Blackburn, I. M., Eunson, K. M., & Bishop, S. (1986). A two-year naturalistic follow-up of depressed patients treated with cognitive therapy, pharmacotherapy, and a combination of both. *Journal of Affective Disorders, 10,* 67–75.

Block, J. (1978). Effects of a rational-emotive mental health program on poorly achieving, disruptive high school students. *Journal of Counseling Psychology, 25,* 61–65.

Block, J. (1980). Effects of rational emotive therapy on overweight adults. *Psychotherapy: Theory, Research and Practice, 17,* 277–280.

Bone, H. (1968). Two proposed alternatives to psychoanalytic interpretation. In E. F. Hammer (Ed.), *Use of interpretation in treatment* (pp. 169–196). New York: Grune & Stratton.

Bortner, R. W. (1969). A short rating scale as a potential measure of pattern A behavior. *Journal of Chronic Diseases, 22,* 87–91.

Bower, G. H. (1981). Mood and memory. *American Psychologist, 36,* 129–148.

Briddell, D. W., & Leiblum, S. R. (1976). The multimodal treatment of spastic colitis and incapacitating anxiety: A case study. In A. A. Lazarus (Ed.), *Multimodal behavior therapy* (pp. 160–169). New York: Springer.

Buck, R. (1985). Prime theory: An integrated view of motivation and emotion. *Psychological Review, 92,* 389–413.

Budman, S. H. (Ed.). (1981). *Forms of brief therapy.* New York: Guilford.

Burgess, P. M. (1986). *Belief systems and emotional disturbance: An evaluation of the rational-emotive model.* Doctoral dissertation, University of Melbourne.

Burns, D. (1980). *Feeling good.* New York: Morrow.

Burrell, M. J. (1987). Cognitive psychology, epistemology, and psychotherapy: A motor-evolutionary perspective. *Psychotherapy, 24,* 225–232.

Cacioppo, J. T., & Petty, R. E. (1981). Social psychological procedures for cognitive response assessment: The thought-listing technique. In T. V. Merluzzi, C. R. Glass, & M. Genest (Eds.), *Cognitive assessment* (pp. 309–342). New York: Guilford.

Campbell, D., & Fiske, D. (1959). Convergent and discriminant validation by the multitrait-multimethod matrix. *Psychological Bulletin*, 56, 81–105.

Camus, A. (1960). *The myth of Sisyphys and other essays*. New York: Vintage Books.

Candland, D. K., Fell, J. P., Keen, E., Leshner, A. I., Plutchik, R., & Tarpey, R. M. (Eds.). (1977). *Emotion*. Belmont, CA: Brooks/Cole.

Cangelosi, A., Gressard, C. G., & Mines, R. A. (1980). The effects of a rational thinking group on self-concepts in adolescents. *School Counselor*, 27, 357–361.

Cannon, W. B. (1932). *The wisdom of the body*. New York: Norton.

Cannon, W. B. (1939). *The wisdom of the body* (2nd ed.). New York: Norton.

Capra, F. (1983). *The turning point*. New York: Bantam.

Carmody, T. P. (1978). Rational-emotive, self-instructional, and behavioral assertion training: Facilitating maintenance. *Cognitive Therapy and Research*, 2, 241–253.

Carnegie, D. (1948). *How to stop worrying and start living*. New York: Simon & Schuster.

Carson, T. P. (1986). Assessment of depression. In A. R. Ciminero, K. S. Calhoun, & H. E. Adams (Eds.), *Handbook of behavioral assessment* (2nd ed., pp. 404–445). New York: Wiley.

Cash, T. F. (1984). The irrational beliefs test: Its relationship with cognitive-behavioral traits and depression. *Journal of Clinical Psychology*, 40, 1399–1405.

Cash, T. F., Rimm, D. C., & MacKinnon, R. (1986). Rational-irrational beliefs and the effects of the Velten mood induction procedure. *Cognitive Therapy and Research*, 10, 461–467.

Collins, A. W. (1985). *Thought and nature: Studies in rationalist philosophy*. Notre Dame, IN: University of Notre Dame Press.

Comte, A. (1893). *Cours de philosophie positive*. University of Paris, III.

Conoley, C. W., Conoley, J. C., McConnell, J. A., & Kimzey, C. E. (1983). The effect of the ABCs of rational emotive therapy and the empty-chair technique of gestalt therapy on anger reduction. *Psychotherapy: Theory, Research and Practice*, 20, 112–117.

Cormier, W. H., & Cormier, S. L. (Eds.). (1985). *Interviewing strategies for helpers: Fundamental skills and cognitive behavioral interventions*. Monterey, CA: Brooks/Cole.

Costello, C. G. (1976). *Anxiety and depression: The adaptive emotions*. Montreal, Canada: McGill-Queens University Press.

Coué, E. (1922). *The practice of autosuggestion*. New York: Doubleday.

Coulter, H. L. (1977). *Divided legacy: A history of the schism in medical thought* (Vols. 1, 2, & 3). Washington: Wehawkin Book Company.

Coyne, J. C., & Gotlib, I. H. (1983). The role of cognition in depression: A critical review. *Psychological Bulletin*, 94, 472–505.

Craighead, W. E., Kimball, W., & Rehak, P. (1979). Mood changes, physiological responses, and self-statements during social rejection imagery. *Journal of Consulting and Clinical Psychology*, 47, 385–396.

Daly, M. J., & Burton, R. L. (1983). Self-esteem and irrational beliefs: An explanatory investigation with implications for counseling. *Journal of Counseling Psychology*, 30, 361–366.

Danysh, J. (1974). *Stop without quitting*. San Francisco, CA: International Society of General Semantics.

Darwin, C. (1873). *The expression of the emotions in man and animals*. New York: Appleton.

Davison, G. C., Feldman, P. M., & Osborn, C. E. (1984). Articulated thoughts, irrational beliefs, fear of negative evaluation. *Cognitive Therapy and Research*, 8, 349–362.

Davison, G. C., Robins, C., & Johnson, M. K. (1983). Articulated thoughts during simulated situations: A paradigm for studying cognition in emotion and behavior. *Cognitive Therapy and Research*, 7, 17–40.

Deardorff, W. W., & Funabiki, D. (1985). A diagnostic caution in screening for depressed college students. *Cognitive Therapy and Research*, 9, 277–284.

Deffenbacher, J. L., Zwemer, W. A., Whisman, M. A., Hill, R. A., & Sloan, R. D. (1986). Irrational beliefs and anxiety. *Cognitive Therapy and Research, 10*, 281–292.

Dekker, J., Dronkers, J., & Staffeleu, J. (1985). Treatment of sexual dysfunctions in male-only groups: Predicting outcome. *Journal of Sex and Marital Therapy, 11*, 80–90.

Dempsey, P. (1964). An unidimensional depression scale for the MMPI. *Journal of Consulting Psychology, 28*, 364–370.

Depue, R. A., & Monroe, S. M. (1986). Conceptualization and measurement of human disorder in life stress research: The problem of chronic disturbance. *Psychological Bulletin, 99*, 36–51.

De Rivera, J. H. (1977). A structural theory of the emotions. *Psychological Issues, 4* (Monograph 40).

De Rivera, J. H. (1984). The structure of emotional relationships. In P. Shaver (Ed.), *Review of personality and social psychology: Vol. 5. Emotions, relationships, and health* (pp. 116–145). Beverly Hills, CA: Sage.

DiGiuseppe, R. (1986). The implication of the philosophy of science for rational-emotive theory and therapy. *Psychotherapy, 23*, 634–639.

DiGiuseppe, R., & Kassinove, H. (1976). Effects of a rational-emotive school mental health program on children's emotional adjustment. *Journal of Community Psychology, 4*, 382–387.

DiGiuseppe, R., & Miller, N. J. (1977). A review of outcome studies on rational-emotive therapy. In A. Ellis & R. Grieger (Eds.), *Handbook of rational-emotive therapy* (pp. 72–95). New York: Springer.

DiGiuseppe, R., Sutton-Simon, K., McGowen, L., & Gardner, F. (in press). A comparative outcome study of four cognitive therapies in the treatment of social anxiety. *Journal of Rational–Emotive and Cognitive Behavior Therapies.*

DiLoreto, A. O. (Ed.). (1971). *Comparative psychotherapy: An experimental analysis.* Chicago, IL: Aldine-Atherton.

Dollard, J., & Miller, N. E. (1950). *Personality and Psychotherapy.* New York: McGraw-Hill.

Doppelt, L. H. (1984). *Level of rationality and the effectiveness of rational restructuring and self-control desensitization with socially anxious adults.* Unpublished doctoral dissertation, University of Oregon, Eugene.

Dowd, E. T., & Milne, C. R. (1986). Paradoxical interventions in counseling psychology. *Counseling Psychologist, 14*, 237–282.

Dryden, W. (1984a). Rational-emotive therapy and cognitive therapy: A critical comparison. In M. A. Reda & M. J. Mahoney (Eds.), *Cognitive psychotherapies: Recent developments in theory, research, and practice* (pp. 81–99). Cambridge, MA: Ballinger.

Dryden, W. (1984b). *Rational-emotive therapy: Fundamentals and innovations.* London: Croom Helm.

Dryden, W. (1986a). A case of theoretically consistent eclecticism: Humanizing a computer "addict." *International Journal of Eclectic Psychotherapy, 5*, 309–327.

Dryden, W. (1986b). Language and meaning in rational-emotive therapy. In W. Dryden & P. Trower (Eds.). *Rational-emotive therapy: Recent developments in theory and practice* (pp. 34–46). Bristol, UK: Institute for RET.

Dryden, W., & Ellis, A. (1988). Rational-emotive therapy. In K. Dobson (Ed.), *Handbook of cognitive-behavioral therapies.* New York: Guilford Press.

Dubois, P. (1906). *The influence of the mind on the body.* New York: Funk & Wagnalls.

Dubois, P. (1908). *The psychic treatment of nervous disorders.* New York: Funk & Wagnalls.

Dubois, P. (1911). *The education of self.* New York: Funk & Wagnalls.

Dyer, W. (1977). *Your erroneous zones.* New York: Funk & Wagnalls.

D'Zurilla, T. (1988). Problem solving therapies. In K. S. Dabem (Ed.), *Handbook of Cognitive-Behavioral Therapies.* New York: Guilford.

D'Zurilla, T. J., & Goldfried, M. R. (1971). Problem solving and behavior modification. *Journal of Abnormal Psychology, 78*, 107–126.

Ehrenwald, J. (1976). *History of psychotherapy: From healing magic to encounter.* New York: Aronson.

Eidelson, R. J., & Epstein, N. (1982). Cognition and relationship maladjustment: Development of a measure of dysfunctional relationship beliefs. *Journal of Consulting and Clinical Psychology, 50,* 715–720.

Eliade, M. (1967). *Myths, dreams, and mysteries: The encounter between contemporary faiths and archaic realities.* New York: Harper & Row.

Ellenberger, H. F. (1970). *The discovery of the unconscious.* New York: Basic Books.

Ellis, A. (1946). The validity of personality questionnaires. *Psychological Bulletin, 43,* 385–440.

Ellis, A. (1950). *An introduction to the principles of scientific psychoanalysis* (Genetic Psychology Monographs). Provincetown, MA: Journal Press.

Ellis, A. (1956). An operational reformulation of some of the basic principles of psychoanalysis. *Psychoanalytical Review, 43,* 163–180.

Ellis, A. (1957a). *How to live with a neurotic: At home and at work.* New York: Crown. (Rev. ed. published 1975, Hollywood, CA: Wilshire Books).

Ellis, A. (1957b). Outcome of employing three techniques of psychotherapy. *Journal of Clinical Psychology, 13,* 334–350.

Ellis, A. (1957c). Rational psychotherapy and individual psychology. *Journal of Individual Psychology, 13,* 38–44.

Ellis, A. (1958a). Rational psychotherapy. *Journal of General Psychology, 59,* 35–49. (Reprinted 1959, New York: Institute for Rational-Emotive Therapy)

Ellis, A. (1958b). *Sex without guilt.* New York: Lyle Stuart. (Ref. ed. published 1965, New York: Lyle Stuart)

Ellis, A. (1962). *Reason and emotion in psychotherapy.* Secaucus, NJ: Lyle Stuart.

Ellis, A. (1963a). *The intelligent woman's guide to manhunting.* New York: Lyle Stuart & Dell.

Ellis, A. (1963b). *Sex and the single man.* Secaucus, NJ: Lyle Stuart.

Ellis, A. (1969a, September/October). Rationality in sexual morality. *Humanist.* pp. 4–5.

Ellis, A. (1969b). A weekend of rational encounter. *Rational Living, 4*(2), 1–8.

Ellis, A. (1971a). A critique by Albert Ellis. In A. O. DeLoreto (Ed.), *Comparative psychotherapy: An experimental analysis* (pp. 213–221). Chicago, IL: Aldine-Atherton.

Ellis, A. (1971b). *Growth through reason.* Palo Alto, CA: Science & Behavior Books; Hollywood, CA: Wilshire Books.

Ellis, A. (Speaker). (1971c). *How to stubbornly refuse to be ashamed of anything* [Cassette recording]. New York: Institute for Rational-Emotive Therapy.

Ellis, A. (1972a). *Psychotherapy and the value of a human being.* New York: Institute for Rational-Emotive Therapy.

Ellis, A. (1972b). *The sensuous person: Critique and corrections.* Secaucus, NJ: Lyle Stuart and New American Library.

Ellis, A. (1972c). Sexual adventuring and personality growth. In H. A. Otto (Ed.), *The new sexuality* (pp. 94–109). Palo Alto, CA: Science and Behavior Books. (Reprinted 1972, New York: Institute for Rational-Emotive Therapy)

Ellis, A. (1973). *Humanistic psychotherapy: The rational-emotive approach.* New York: McGraw-Hill.

Ellis, A. (1974). Rational-emotive theory: Albert Ellis. In A. Burton (Ed.), *Operational theories of personality* (pp. 308–344). New York: Brunner/Mazel.

Ellis, A. (1975). *RET abolishes most of the human ego.* Paper presented at the American Psychological Association convention, Chicago, IL.

Ellis, A. (1976a). The biological basis of human irrationality. *Journal of Individual Psychology, 32,* 145–168. (Reprinted 1976, New York: Institute for Rational-Emotive Therapy)

Ellis, A. (1976b). *Sex and the liberated man.* Secaucus, NJ: Lyle Stuart.

Ellis, A. (1977a). Psychotherapy and the value of a human being. In A. Ellis & R. Grieger (Eds.), *Handbook of rational-emotive therapy* (pp. 99–112). New York: Springer.

Ellis, A. (1977b). Rational-emotive therapy: Research data that supports the clinical and personality hypotheses of RET and other modes of cognitive-behavior therapy. *Counseling Psychologist, 7*, 2–42.

Ellis, A. (1977c). Rejoinder: Elegant and inelegant RET. *Counseling Psychologist, 7*, 73–82.

Ellis, A. (1977d). Intimacy in psychotherapy. *Rational Living, 12*, 13–19.

Ellis, A. (Speaker). (1978a). *How to be happy though mated* [Cassette recording]. New York: Institute for Rational-Emotive Therapy.

Ellis, A. (1978b). Toward a theory of personality. In R. J. Corsini (Ed.), *Readings in current personality theories* (pp. 298–311). Itasca, IL: Peacock.

Ellis, A. (1979a). Discomfort anxiety: A new cognitive behavioral construct. *Rational Living, 14*(2), 3–8.

Ellis, A. (1979b). *The intelligent woman's guide to dating and mating.* Secaucus, NJ: Lyle Stuart.

Ellis, A. (1979c). The issue of force and energy in behavior change. *Journal of Contemporary Psychotherapy, 10*, 83–97.

Ellis, A. (1979d). A note on the treatment of agoraphobics with cognitive modification or prolonged exposure *in vivo. Behaviour Research and Therapy, 17*, 162–164.

Ellis, A. (1979e). Toward a new theory of personality. In A. Ellis & J. M. Whiteley (Eds.), *Theoretical and empirical foundations of rational-emotive therapy* (pp. 7–32). Monterey, CA: Brooks/Cole.

Ellis, A. (1979f). The practice of rational-emotive therapy. In A. Ellis & J. M. Whiteley (Eds.), *Theoretical and empirical foundations of rational-emotive therapy* (pp. 61–100). Monterey, CA: Brooks/Cole.

Ellis, A. (1979g). The theory of rational-emotive therapy. In A. Ellis & J. M. Whiteley (Eds.), *Theoretical and empirical foundations of rational-emotive therapy* (pp. 33–60). Monterey, CA: Brooks/Cole.

Ellis, A. (1979h). Rational-emotive therapy: Research data that support the clinical and personality hypotheses of RET and other modes of cognitive–behavior therapy. In A. Ellis & J. M. Whiteley (Eds.), *Theoretical and empirical foundations of rational-emotive therapy* (pp. 101–173). Monterey, CA: Brooks/Cole.

Ellis, A. (1979i). Rejoinder: Elegant and inelegant RET. In A. Ellis & J. M. Whiteley (Eds.), *Theoretical and empirical foundations of rational-emotive therapy* (pp. 240–267). Monterey, CA: Brooks/Cole.

Ellis, A. (1980a). Discomfort anxiety: A new cognitive behavioral construct. *Rational Living, 15*(1), 25–30.

Ellis, A. (1980b). An overview of the clinical theory of rational-emotive therapy. In R. Grieger & J. Boyd (Eds.), *Rational-emotive therapy: A skills based approach* (pp. 1–31). New York: Van Nostrand-Reinhold.

Ellis, A. (1980c). Psychotherapy and atheistic values: A response to A. E. Bergin's "Psychotherapy and religious values." *Journal of Consulting and Clinical Psychology, 48*, 635–639.

Ellis, A. (1980d). Rational-emotive therapy and cognitive behavior therapy: Similarities and differences. *Cognitive Therapy and Research, 4*, 325–340.

Ellis, A. (Speaker). (1980e). *Twenty-two ways to brighten up your love life* [Cassette recording]. New York: Institute for Rational-Emotive Therapy.

Ellis, A. (1981). Dr. Albert Ellis's list of 21 irrational beliefs that lead to sex problems and disturbances. In A. B. Gerber (Ed.), *The book of sex lists* (pp. 46–48). Secaucus, NJ: Lyle Stuart.

Ellis, A. (1982a). Rational-emotive family therapy. In A. M. Horne & M. M. Ohlsen (Eds.), *Family counseling and therapy* (pp. 302–328). Itasca, IL: Peacock.

Ellis, A. (1982b). A reappraisal of Rational-Emotive Therapy's theoretical foundations and therapeutic methods: A reply to Eschenreoder. *Cognitive Therapy and Research, 6,* 393–398.

Ellis, A. (1983). *The case against religiosity.* New York: Institute for Rational-Emotive Therapy.

Ellis, A. (1984a). The essence of RET-1984. *Journal of Rational-Emotive Therapy, 2,* 19–25.

Ellis, A. (1984b). Foreword: Cognitive, affective, and behavioral aspects of rational-emotive therapy. In W. Dryden, *Rational-emotive therapy: Fundamentals and innovations* (pp. vii–xxvi). London: Croon Helm.

Ellis, A. (1984c). Is the unified-interaction approach to cognitive-behavior modification a reinvention of the wheel? *Clinical Psychology Review, 4,* 215–218.

Ellis, A. (1984d). Rational-emotive therapy. In R. J. Corsini (Ed.), *Current psychotherapies* (pp. 196–238). Itasca, IL: Peacock.

Ellis, A. (1984e). Sex therapies. In R. J. Corsini (Ed.), *Encyclopedia of psychology* (p. 308). New York: Wiley.

Ellis, A. (1984f). *Intellectual fascism.* New York: Institute for Rational-Emotive Therapy.

Ellis, A. (1985a). Cognition and affect in emotional disturbance. *American Psychologist, 40,* 471–472.

Ellis, A. (1985b). Expanding the ABCs of rational-emotive therapy. In M. Mahoney & A. Freeman (Eds.), *Cognition and psychotherapy* (pp. 313–323). New York: Plenum.

Ellis, A. (1985c). Free will and determinism: A second story. *Journal of Counseling and Development, 64,* 286.

Ellis, A. (1985d). *Overcoming resistance: Rational-emotive therapy with difficult clients.* New York: Springer.

Ellis, A. (1985e). Rational-emotive therapy. In A. S. Bellack & M. Hersen (Eds.), *Dictionary of behavior therapy techniques* (pp. 177–181). New York: Pergamon Press.

Ellis, A. (1987a). The evolution of rational-emotive therapy (RET) and cognitive behavior therapy (CBT). In J. K. Zeig (Ed.), *The evolution of psychotherapy* (pp. 107–132). New York: Brunner/Mazel.

Ellis, A. (1987b). The impossibility of achieving consistently good mental health. *American Psychologist, 42,* 364–375.

Ellis, A. (1987c). A sadly neglected cognitive element in depression. *Cognitive Therapy and Research, 11,* 121–146.

Ellis, A. (1988). *How to stubbornly refuse to make yourself miserable about anything—yes, anything!* New York: Lyle Stuart.

Ellis, A., & Abrahms, E. (1978). *Brief psychotherapy in medical and health practice.* New York: Springer.

Ellis, A., & Becker, I. (1982). *A guide to personal happiness.* North Hollywood, CA: Wilshire.

Ellis, A., & Bernard, M. E. (Eds.). (1983a). *Rational-emotive approaches to the problems of childhood.* New York: Plenum.

Ellis, A., & Bernard, M. E. (1983b). An overview of rational-emotive approaches to the problems of childhood. In A. Ellis & M. E. Bernard (Eds.), *Rational-emotive approaches to the problems of childhood* (pp. 3–43). New York: Plenum.

Ellis, A., & Bernard, M. E. (Eds.). (1985a). *Clinical applications of rational-emotive therapy.* New York: Plenum.

Ellis, A., & Bernard, M. E. (1985b). What is rational-emotive therapy (RET)? In A. Ellis & M. E. Bernard (Eds.), *Clinical applications of rational-emotive therapy* (pp. 1–30). New York: Plenum.

Ellis, A., & Bernard, M. E. (1986). What is rational-emotive therapy (RET)? In A. Ellis & R. M. Grieger (Eds.), *Handbook of rational-emotive therapy* (Vol. 2, pp. 3–30). New York: Springer.

Ellis, A., & Dryden, W. (1987). *The practice of rational-emotive therapy.* New York: Springer.

Ellis, A., & Grieger, R. (Eds.). (1977). *Handbook of rational-emotive therapy.* New York: Springer.

Ellis, A., & Grieger, R. (Eds.). (1986). *Handbook of rational-emotive therapy* (2 vols.). New York: Springer.

Ellis, A., & Harper, R. A. (1961). *A guide to rational living.* Englewood Cliffs, NJ: Prentice-Hall; North Hollywood, CA: Wilshire.

Ellis, A., & Harper, R. A. (1975). *A new guide to rational living.* North Hollywood, CA: Wilshire.

Ellis, A., & Whiteley, J. M. (Eds.). (1979). *Theoretical and empirical foundations of rational-emotive therapy.* Monterey, CA: Brooks/Cole.

Ellis, T. E., & Ratliff, K. G. (1986). Cognitive characteristics of suicidal and non-suicidal psychiatric inpatients. *Cognitive Therapy and Research, 10,* 625–634.

Emde, R. N. (1984). Levels of meaning for infant emotions: A biosocial view. In K. E. Scherer & P. Ekman (Eds.), *Approaches to emotion* (pp. 77–107). Hillsdale, NJ: Erlbaum.

Emmelkamp, P. M. G. (1986). Behavior therapy with adults. In S. L. Garfield & A. E. Bergin (Eds.), *Handbook of psychotherapy and behavior change* (3rd ed., pp. 385–442). New York: Wiley.

Emmelkamp, P. M. G., Brilman, E., Kuiper, H., & Mersch, P. (1986). The treatment of agoraphobia: A comparison of self-instructional training, rational-emotive therapy, and exposure *in vivo. Behavior Modification, 10,* 37–53.

Emmelkamp, P. M. G., Kuipers, A. C. M., & Eggeraat, J. B. (1978). Cognitive modification versus prolonged exposure *in vivo:* A comparison with agoraphobics as subjects. *Behaviour Research and Therapy, 16,* 33–41.

Emmelkamp, P. M. G., & Mersch, P. P. (1982). Cognition and exposure *in vivo* in the treatment of agoraphobia: Short-term and delayed effects. *Cognitive Therapy and Research, 6,* 77–90.

Emmelkamp, P. M. G., Mersch, P., & Vissia, E. (1985). The external validity of analogue outcome research: Evaluation of cognitive and behavioral interventions. *Behaviour Research and Therapy, 23,* 83–86.

Emmelkamp, P. M. G., Mersch, P., Vissia, E., & Van der Helm, M. (1985). Social phobia: A comparative evaluation of cognitive and behavioral interventions. *Behaviour Research and Therapy, 23,* 365–369.

Endler, N. S., Hunt, J. McV., & Rosenstein, A. J. (1962). An S-R inventory of anxiousness. *Psychological Monographs, 76*(17, Whole No. 536).

Epictetus. (1956). *Enchiridion* (G. Long, Trans.). South Bend, IN: Regenery-Gateway. (Original work undated.)

Epstein, S. (1983). A research paradigm for the study of personality and emotions. In M. M. Page (Ed.), *Personality: Current theory and research* (pp. 92–153). Lincoln: University of Nebraska Press.

Epstein, S. (1984). Emotions from the perspective of cognitive self theory. In P. Shaver (Ed.), *Review of personality and social psychology* (pp. 1–59). Beverly Hills, CA: Sage.

Erdelyi, M. H. (1974). A new look at the new look: Perceptual defence and vigilance. *Psychological Review, 81,* 1–25.

Erickson, M. H. (1965). The use of symptoms as an integral part of psychotherapy. *American Journal of Clinical Hypnosis, 8,* 57–65.

Eschenroeder, C. (1982). How rational is rational-emotive therapy? A critical appraisal of its theoretical foundations and therapeutic methods. *Cognitive Therapy and Research, 6,* 381–392.

Everaerd, W., & Dekker, J. (1985). Treatment of male sexual dysfunction: Sex therapy compared with systematic desensitization and rational emotive therapy. *Behaviour Research and Therapy, 23,* 13–25.

Everaerd, W., Dekker, J., Dronkers, J., Van der Rhee, K., Staffeleu, J., & Wiselius, G. (1982). Treatment of homosexual and heterosexual dysfunction in male-only groups of mixed sexual orientation. *Archives of Sexual Behavior, 11,* 1–10.

Ewart, C., & Thoresen, C. (1977). The rational-emotive manifesto. *Counseling Psychologist*, 7(1), 52–56.

Eysenck, H. J. (1986). Consensus and controversy: Two types of science. In S. Modgil & C. Modgil (Eds.), *Hans Eysenck: Consensus and controversy* (pp. 375–398). Philadelphia, PA: Falmer.

Fay, A. (1978). *Making things better by making them worse*. New York: Hawthorn.

Fennell, M. J. V., & Teasdale, J. D. (1987). Cognitive therapy for depression: Individual differences and the process of change. *Cognitive Therapy and Research*, 11, 253–271.

Festinger, L. (1964). Behavioural support for opinion change. *Public Opinion Quarterly*, 28, 404–410.

Feyerabend, P. (1975). *Against method*. London: NLB.

Finn, T., & DiGiuseppe, R. & Culver (in press). The effectiveness of rational-emotive therapy in the reduction of muscle contraction headache. *Journal of Cognitive Psychotherapies: An International Quarterly*.

Fishbein, M., & Ajzen, J. (1975). *Belief, attitude, intention, and behavior: An introduction to theory and research*. Reading, MA: Addison-Wesley.

Fiske, S. T., & Taylor, S. T. (1984). *Social cognition*. New York: Random House.

Fodor, J. A. (1983). *The modularity of mind*. Cambridge, MA: MIT Press.

Fodor, J. A. (1985). Precis of the modularity of mind. An Open Peer Commentary. *Behavioral and Brain Sciences*, 8, 1–42.

Folkman, S. (1984). Personal control stress and coping processes: A theoretical analysis. *Journal of Personality and Social Psychology*, 46, 839–852.

Forsterling, F. (1985). Rational-emotive therapy and attribution theory: An investigation of the cognitive determinants of emotions. *British Journal of Cognitive Psychotherapy*, 3(1), 15–25.

Fox, N. A., & Davidson, R. J. (1984). EEG asymmetry and the development of affect. In N. A. Fox & R. J. Davidson (Eds.), *The psychology of affective development*. Hillsdale, NJ: Erlbaum.

Frances, A., Clarkin, J., & Perry, S. (1984). *Differential therapeutics in psychiatry: The art and science of treatment selection*. New York: Brunner/Mazel.

Frank, J. D. (1973). *Persuasion and healing* (2nd ed.). Baltimore, MD: Johns Hopkins University Press.

Frank, J. D. (1979). The present status of outcome studies. *Journal of Consulting and Clinical Psychology*, 47, 310–316.

Frank, J. D. (1985). Therapeutic components shared by all psychotherapies. In M. J. Mahoney & A. Freeman (Eds.), *Cognition and psychotherapy* (pp. 49–79). New York: Plenum.

Frankl, V. E. (1960). Paradoxical intention: A logotherapeutic technique. *American Journal of Psychotherapy*, 14, 520–535.

Frankl, V. (1963). *Man's search for meaning*. New York: Washington Square Press.

Frankl, V. E. (1975). Paradoxical intention and dereflection. *Psychotherapy: Theory, Research & Practice*, 12, 226–237.

French-Belgian Collaborative Group. (1982). Ischemic heart disease and psychological patterns. *Advances in Cardiology*, 29, 25–31.

Freud, S. (1915-1917). *A general introduction to psychoanalysis*. New York: Doubleday, 1943.

Friedman, M. (1974). *The hidden human image*. New York: Dell.

Friedman, M., & Rosenman, R. H. (1974). *Type A behavior and your heart*. New York: Knopf.

Gardner, H. (1985). *The mind's new science: A history of the cognitive revolution*. New York: Basic Books.

Gardner, P., & Oei, T. P. S. (1981). Depression and self esteem: An investigation that used behavioral and cognitive approaches to the treatment of clinically depressed clients. *Journal of Clinical Psychology*, 37, 128–135.

Garfield, S. L. (1973). Basic ingredients or common factors in psychotherapy? *Journal of Consulting and Clinical Psychology, 41*, 9–12.

Garfield, S. L. (1977). Research on the training of professional psychotherapists. In A. S. Gurman & A. M. Razin (Eds.), *Effective psychotherapy: A handbook of research*. Oxford: Pergamon.

Garfield, S. L. (1980). *Psychotherapy: An eclectic approach*. New York: Wiley.

Garfield, S. L. (1982). Electicism and integration in psychotherapy. *Behavior Therapy, 13*, 610–623.

Garfield, S. L. (1986). Research on client variables in psychotherapy. In S. L. Garfield & A. E. Bergin (Eds.), *Handbook of psychotherapy and behavior change* (3rd ed.; pp. 213–256). New York: Wiley.

Gazzaniga, M. S. (1985). *The social brain*. New York: Basic Books.

Goldfried, M. R. (1971). Systematic desensitization as training in self-control. *Journal of Consulting and Clinical Psychology, 37*, 228–234.

Goldfried, M. R. (1980a). Psychotherapy as coping skills training. In M. J. Mahoney (Ed.), *Psychotherapy process: Current issues and future directions* (pp. 89–119). New York: Plenum.

Goldfried, M. R. (1980b). Toward the delineation of therapeutic change principles. *American Psychologist, 35*, 991–999.

Goldfried, M. R. (Ed.). (1982). *Converging themes in psychotherapy*. New York: Springer.

Goldfried, M. R., & Davison, G. C. (1976). *Clinical behavior therapy*. New York: Holt, Rinehart & Winston.

Goldfried, M. R., Decenteceo, E. T., & Weinberg, L. (1974). Systematic rational restructuring as a self-control technique. *Behavior Therapy, 5*, 247–254.

Goldfried, M. R., Linehan, M. M., & Smith, J. L. (1978). Reduction of test anxiety through cognitive restructuring. *Journal of Consulting and Clinical Psychology, 46*, 32–39.

Goldfried, M. R., Padawer, W., & Robins, C. (1984). Social anxiety and the semantic structure of heterosexual interactions. *Journal of Abnormal Psychology, 27*, 86–97.

Goldfried, M. R., & Sobocinski, D. (1975). Effect of irrational beliefs on emotional arousal. *Journal of Consulting and Clinical Psychology, 43*, 504–510.

Goldstein, A., & Wolpe, J. (1971). A critique by Alan Goldstein and Joseph Wolpe. In A. DiLoreto, Ed., *Comparative psychotherapy: An experimental analysis* (pp. 222–232). Chicago, IL: Aldine-Atherton.

Gombatz, M. W. (1983). *The effectiveness on problem resolution of three different treatment modalities: Client-centered, rational-emotive therapy and paradoxical directives*. Unpublished doctoral dissertation, College of William and Mary, Williamsburg, VA.

Gomes-Schwartz, B. (1978). Effective ingredients in psychotherapy: Predictions of outcome from process variables. *Journal of Consulting and Clinical Psychology, 46*, 1023–1035.

Gotlib, I. H. (1984). Depression and general psychopathology in university students. *Journal of Abnormal Psychology, 93*, 19–30.

Gould, S. J. (1977). *Ever since Darwin: Reflections in natural history*. New York: Norton.

Grieger, R. M. (1986). From a linear to a contextual model of the ABC's of RET. In A. Ellis & R. M. Grieger (Eds.), *Handbook of rational-emotive therapy* (Vol. 2, pp. 59–80). New York: Springer.

Grieger, R. M., & Boyd, I. (1980). *Rational-emotive therapy: A skills-based approach*. New York: Van Nostrand-Reinhold.

Guidano, V. F. (1984). A constructivist outline of cognitive processes. In M. A. Reda & M. J. Mahoney (Eds.), *Cognitive psychotherapies: Recent developments in theory, research, and practice* (pp. 31–45). Cambridge, MA: Ballinger.

Guidano, V. F. (1987). *Complexities of the self: A developmental approach to psychopathology and therapy*. New York: Guilford Press.

Guidano, V. F., & Liotti, G. A. (1983). *Cognitive processes and emotional disorders*. New York: Guilford.

Guidano, V. F., & Liotti, G. A. (1985). A constructivist foundation for cognitive therapy. In M. J. Mahoney & A. Freeman (Eds.), *Cognition and psychotherapy* (pp. 101–142). New York: Plenum.

Gynther, M. D., & Green, S. B. (1982). Methodological problems in research with self-report inventories. In P. C. Kendall & J. N. Butcher (Eds.), *Handbook of research methods in clinical psychology* (pp. 355–386). New York: Wiley.

Haaga, D. A. (1987). Treatment of the Type A behavior pattern. *Clinical Psychology Review, 7*, 557–574.

Hammen, C. L., Jacobs, M., Mayol, A., & Cochran, S. D. (1980). Dysfunctional cognitions and the effectiveness of skills and cognitive-behavioral assertion training. *Journal of Consulting and Clinical Psychology, 48*, 685–695.

Harlow, H. F. (1953). Mice, monkeys, men and motives. *Psychological Review, 60*, 23–32.

Harper, R. A. (1959). *Psychoanalysis and psychotherapy: Thirty Six Systems*. Englewood Cliffs, NJ: Prentice-Hall.

Harrell, T. H., Chambless, D. L., & Calhoun, J. F. (1981). Correlational relationships between self-statements and affective states. *Cognitive Therapy and Research, 5*, 159–173.

Hauck, P. A. (1980). *Brief counseling with RET*. Philadelphia, PA: Westminster Press.

Hayek, F. A. (1952). *The sensory order*. Chicago, IL: University of Chicago Press.

Hayek, F. A. (1964). The theory of complex phenomena. In M. Bunge (Ed.), *The critical approach to science and philosophy: Essays in honor of K. R. Popper* (pp. 332–349). New York: Free Press.

Hayek, F. A. (1967). *Studies in philosophy, politics, and economics*. Chicago, IL: University of Chicago Press.

Hayek, F. A. (1978). *New studies in philosophy, politics, economics and the history of ideas*. Chicago, IL: University of Chicago Press.

Hayek, F. A. (1982). The sensory order after 25 years. In W. B. Weimer & D. S. Palermo (Eds.), *Cognition and the symbolic processes* (Vol. 2, pp. 287–293). Hillsdale, NJ: Erlbaum.

Heesacker, M., Heppner, P. P., & Rogers, M. E. (1982). Classics and emerging classics in counseling psychology. *Journal of Counseling Psychology, 29*, 400–405.

Heidegger, M. (1962). *Being and time*. New York: Harper & Row.

Heider, F. (1958). *The psychology of interpersonal relations*. New York: Wiley.

Heller, E. (1959). *The disinherited mind*. New York: Meridian.

Hempel, C. G. (1966). *Philosophy of natural science*. Englewood-Cliffs, NJ: Prentice-Hall.

Herink, R. (Ed.). (1980). *The psychotherapy handbook: The A to Z guide to more than 250 different therapies in use today*. New York: New American Library.

Hilgard, E. R. (1980). The trilogy of mind: Cognition, affection, and conation. *Journal of the History of the Behavioral Sciences, 16*, 107–117.

Himle, D. P., Thyer, B. A., & Papsdorf, J. D. (1982). Relationships between rational beliefs and anxiety. *Cognitive Therapy and Research, 6*, 219–223.

Hjelle, L. A., & Ziegler, D. J. (1981). *Personality theories: Basic assumptions, research, and applications* (2nd ed.). New York: McGraw-Hill.

Hoffman, M. L. (1985). Affect, motivation, and cognition. In E. T. Higgins & R. Sorrentino (Eds.), *Handbook of motivation and cognition: Foundations of social behavior*. New York: Guilford.

Hogg, J. A., & Deffenbacher, J. L. (1986). Irrational beliefs, depression, and anger among college students. *Journal of College Student Personnel, 27*, 349–353.

Hollon, S. D., & Beck, A. T. (1986). Research on cognitive therapies. In S. L. Garfield & A. E. Bergin (Eds.), *Handbook of psychotherapy and behavior change* (3rd ed., pp. 443–482). New York: Wiley.

Hollon, S. D., & Kriss, M. R. (1984). Cognitive factors in clinical research and practice. *Clinical Psychology Review, 4*, 35–76.

Holt, R. R. (Ed.). (1971). *New horizon for psychotherapy*. New York: International Universities Press.

Holt, R. R., & Luborsky, L. (1958). *Personality patterns of psychiatrists: A study in selection techniques* (Vol. 1). New York: Basic Books.

Horney, K. (1937). *The neurotic personality of our time.* New York: Norton.

Howard, G. S., Nance, D. W., & Myers, P. (1986). Adaptive counseling and therapy: An integrative, eclectic model. *Counseling Psychologist, 14,* 363–442.

Hymen, S. P., & Warren, R. (1978). An evaluation of rational-emotive imagery as a component of rational-emotive therapy in the treatment of test anxiety. *Perceptual and Motor Skills, 46,* 847–853.

Ingram, R. E. (Ed.). (1986). *Information processing approaches to clinical psychology.* New York: Academic Press.

Isen, A. M., Shalker, T. E., Clark, M., & Karp, E. (1978). Affect, accessibility of material in memory, and behavior: A cognitive loop? *Journal of Personality and Social Psychology, 36,* 1–12.

Izard, C. E. (1978). On the ontogenesis of emotions and emotion-cognition relationships in infancy. In M. Lewis & L. Rosenblum (Eds.), *The development of affect* (pp. 389–413). New York: Plenum.

James, W. (1890). *Principles of psychology.* New York: Holt.

James, W. (1958). *The varieties of religious experience.* New York: New American Library. (Original work published 1902)

Jasnow, M. (1982). *Effects of relaxation training and rational emotive therapy on anxiety reduction in sixth grade children.* Unpublished doctoral dissertation, Hofstra University, Hempstead, NY.

Jenkins, C. D., Zyzanski, S. J., & Rosenman, R. H. (1971). Progress toward validation of a computer-scored test for the Type A coronary-prone behavior pattern. *Psychosomatic Medicine, 33,* 193–202.

Jenni, M. A., & Wollersheim, J. P. (1979). Cognitive therapy, stress management training, and the Type A behavior pattern. *Cognitive Therapy and Research, 3,* 61–73.

Jones, R. (1968). *A factored measure of Ellis' irrational belief system with personality and maladjustment correlates.* Unpublished doctoral dissertation, Texas Technical College, Lubbock.

Joubert, C. E. (1984). Irrational beliefs and response sets. *Psychological Reports, 54,* 42–65.

Kanner, A. D., Coyne, J. C., Schaefer, C., & Lazarus, R. S. (1981). Comparisons of two modes of stress measurement: Daily hassles and uplifts versus major life events. *Journal of Behavioral Medicine, 4,* 1–39.

Kanter, N. J., & Goldfried, M. R. (1979). Relative effectiveness of rational restructuring and self-control desensitization in the reduction of interpersonal anxiety. *Behavior Therapy, 10,* 472–490.

Karasu, T. B. (1986). The specificity versus nonspecificity dilemma: Toward identifying therapeutic change agents. *American Journal of Psychiatry, 143,* 687–695.

Karst, T. O., & Trexler, L. D. (1970). Initial study using fixed-role and rational-emotive therapy in treating public-speaking anxiety. *Journal of Consulting and Clinical Psychology, 34,* 360–366.

Kassinove, H. (1986). Self-reported affect and core irrational thinking: A preliminary analysis. *Journal of Rational-Emotive Therapy 4*(2), 119–130.

Kassinove, H., Crisci, R., & Tiegerman, S. (1977). Developmental trends in rational thinking: Implications for rational-emotive school mental health programs. *Journal of Community Psychology, 5,* 226–274.

Kassinove, H., Miller, N., & Kalin, M. (1980). Effects of pretreatment with rational-emotive bibliotherapy and rational-emotive audiotherapy on clients waiting at community health center. *Psychological Reports, 46,* 851–857.

Kazdin, A. E. (1982). Single-case experimental designs. In P. C. Kendall & J. N. Butcher (Eds.), *Handbook of research methods in clinical psychology* (pp. 461–490). New York: Wiley.

Kazdin, A. E. (1986a). Comparative outcome studies of psychotherapy: Methodological issues and strategies. *Journal of Consulting and Clinical Psychology, 54,* 95–105.

Kazdin, A. E. (1986b). The evaluation of psychotherapy: Research design and methodology. In S. L. Garfield & A. E. Bergin (Eds.), *Handbook of psychotherapy and behavior change* (3rd ed., pp. 23–68). New York: Wiley.

Keller, J. F., Croake, J. W., & Brooking, J. Y. (1975). Effects of a program in rational thinking on anxieties in older persons. *Journal of Counseling Psychology, 22,* 54–57.

Kelly, G. A. (1955). *The psychology of personal constructs.* New York: Norton.

Kelly, L. M. (1982). *Rational-emotive therapy versus Lewinsohnian based approaches to the treatment of depression.* Unpublished doctoral dissertation, University of Georgia, Athens.

Kendall, P. C. (1982). Behavioral assessment and methodology. In C. M. Franks, G. T. Wilson, P. C. Kendall, & K. D. Brownell (Eds.), *Annual review of behavior therapy: Theory and practice* (Vol. 8, pp. 39–81). New York: Guilford.

Kendall, P. C. (Ed.). (1983). *Advances in cognitive-behavioral research and therapy* (Vol. 2). New York: Academic Press.

Kendall, P. C. (1984). Cognitive processes and procedures in behavior therapy. In C. M. Franks, G. T. Wilson, P. C. Kendall & K. D. Brownell, *Annual review of behavior therapy: Theory and practice* (Vol. 10, pp. 123–163). New York: Guilford.

Kendall, P. C., & Hollon, S. D. (1980). Assessing self-referent speech: Methods in the measurements of self-statements. In P. C. Kendall & S. D. Hollon (Eds.), *Assessment strategies for cognitive-behavioral interventions* (pp. 85–118). New York: Academic Press.

Kendall, P. C., & Korgeski, G. P. (1979). Assessment and cognitive-behavioral interventions. *Cognitive Therapy and Research, 3,* 1–21.

Kendall, P. C., & Norton-Ford, J. D. (1982). Therapy outcome research methods. In P. G. Kendall & J. N. Butcher (Eds.), *Handbook of research methods in clinical psychology* (pp. 429–460). New York: Wiley.

Kiesler, D. J. (1966). Some myths of psychotherapy research and the search for a paradigm. *Psychological Bulletin, 65,* 110–136.

Kiesler, D. J. (1971). Experimental designs in psychotherapy research. In A. E. Bergin & S. L. Garfield (Eds.), *Handbook of psychotherapy and behavior change: An empirical analysis* (pp. 36–74). New York: Wiley.

Kihlstrom, J. F., & Nasby, V. (1980). Cognitive tasks in clinical assessment: An exercise in applied psychology. In P. C. Kendall & S. D. Hollon (Eds.), *Assessment strategies for cognitive-behavioral interventions* (pp. 287–317). New York: Academic Press.

Klarriech, S., DiGiuseppe, R., & DiMattia, D. (1987). Dispelling the "uniformity myth" in EAP's. *Professional Psychology, 18,* 140–144.

Klein, G. S. (1958). Cognitive control and motivation. In G. Lindzey (Ed.), *Assessment of human motives.* New York: Holt, Rinehart & Winston.

Klinger, E. (1975). Consequences of commitment to and disengagement from incentives. *Psychological Review, 82,* 1–25.

Knaus, W. (1974). *Rational-emotive education: A manual for elementary school teachers.* New York: Institute for Rational Living.

Knaus, W., & Bokor, S. (1975). The effects of rational-emotive education lessons on anxiety and self-concept in sixth grade students. *Rational Living, 10,* 7–10.

Kobasa, S. C. (1979). Stressful life events, personality and health: An inquiry into hardiness. *Journal of Personality and Social Psychology, 37,* 1–11.

Kobasa, S. C., Maddi, S. R., & Courington, S. (1981). Personality and constitution as mediators in the stress-illness relationship. *Journal of Behavioral Medicine, 5,* 391–404.

Korzybski, A. (1933). *Science and sanity.* San Francisco, CA: International Society for General Semantics.

Koss, M. P., & Butcher, J. N. (1986). Research on brief psychotherapy. In S. L. Garfield & A. E. Bergin (Eds.), *Handbook of psychotherapy and behavior change* (3rd ed.; pp. 627–670). New York: Wiley.

Kreitler, H., & Kreitler, S. (1976). *Cognitive orientation and behavior*. New York: Springer.
Krug, S. E., Scheier, I. H., & Cattell, R. B. (1976). *Handbook for the IPAT anxiety scale* (rev. ed.). Champaign, IL: Institute of Personality and Ability Testing.
Kuhn, T. S. (1970). *The structure of scientific revolutions* (2nd ed.). Chicago, IL: University of Chicago Press.
Kuhn, T. S. (1977). *The essential tension*. Chicago, IL: University of Chicago Press.
Kuiper, N. A., & MacDonald, M. R. (1983). Reason, emotion, and cognitive therapy. *Clinical Psychology Review, 3*, 297–316.
Kwee, M. G. T. (1984). *Klinische multimodale gedrags-therapie*. Lisse, Switzerland: Swets & Zeitlinger.
Kwee, M. G. T., & Duivenvoorden, H. J. (1985). Multimodal residential therapy in two cases of anorexia nervosa (adult body weight phobia). In A. A. Lazarus (Ed.), *Casebook of multimodal therapy* (pp. 116–138). New York: Guilford Press.
Kwee, M. G. T., & Lazarus, A. A. (1986). Multimodal therapy: The cognitive-behavioural tradition and beyond. In W. Dryden & W. Golden (Eds.), *Cognitive-behavioural approaches to psychotherapy* (pp. 320–355). London: Harper & Row.
Lakatos, I. (1970). Falsification and the methodology of scientific research programmes. In I. Lakatos & A. Musgraves (Eds.), *Criticism and the growth of knowledge* (pp. 91–196). London: Cambridge University Press.
Lake, A., Rainey, J., & Papsdorf, J. D. (1979). Biofeedback and rational-emotive therapy in the management of migraine headache. *Journal of Applied Behavior Analysis, 12*, 127–140.
Lange, A. J., & Jakubowski, P. (1976). *Responsible assertive behavior*. Champaign, IL: Research Press.
Lasch, C. (1978). *The culture of narcissism: American life in an age of diminishing expectations*. New York: Norton.
Lashley, K. S. (1926). Studies of cerebral function in learning. VII. The relation between cerebral mass, learning and recreation. *Journal of Comparative Neurology, 41*, 1–58.
Lazarus, A. A. (1967). In support of technical eclecticism. *Psychological Reports, 21*, 415–416.
Lazarus, A. A. (1971). *Behavior therapy and beyond*. New York: McGraw-Hill.
Lazarus, A. A. (1976). *Multimodal behavior therapy*. New York: Springer.
Lazarus, A. A. (1977). Toward an egoless state of being. In A. Ellis & R. Grieger (Eds.), *Handbook of rational-emotive therapy* (pp. 113–118). New York: Springer.
Lazarus, A. A. (1979). Can RET become a cult? In A. Ellis & J. M. Whiteley (Eds.), *Theoretical and empirical foundations of rational-emotive therapy* (pp. 236–239). Monterey, CA: Brooks/Cole.
Lazarus, A. A. (1981). *The practice of multimodal therapy*. New York: McGraw-Hill.
Lazarus, A. A. (1984a). *In the mind's eye*. New York: Guilford Press.
Lazarus, A. A. (1984b). Multimodal therapy. In R. J. Corsini (Ed.), *Current Psychotherapies* (3rd ed., pp. 491–530). Itasca, IL: Peacock.
Lazarus, A. A. (1984c). The specificity factor in psychotherapy. *Psychotherapy in Private Practice, 2*, 43–48.
Lazarus, A. A. (1986a). Multimodal psychotherapy: Overview and update. *International Journal of Eclectic Psychotherapy, 5*, 95–103.
Lazarus, A. A. (1986b). Multimodal therapy. In J. C. Norcross (Ed.), *Handbook of eclectic psychotherapy* (pp. 65–93). New York: Brunner/Mazel.
Lazarus, A. A., & Fay, A. (1975). *I can if I want to*. New York: Warner.
Lazarus, R. S. (1966). *Psychological stress and the coping process*. New York: McGraw-Hill.
Lazarus, R. S. (1982). Thoughts on the relations between emotion and cognition. *American Psychologist, 37*, 1019–1024.
Lazarus, R. S. (1983). The costs and benefits of denial. In S. Breznitz (Ed.), *The denial of stress* (pp. 1–30). New York: International Universities Press.
Lazarus, R. S. (1984). On the primacy of cognition. *American Psychologist, 39*, 124–129.
Lazarus, R. S. (1985). The trivialization of distress. In J. C. Rosen & L. J. Solomon (Eds.),

Preventing health risk behaviors and promoting coping with illness: Vol. 8. Vermont Conference on the Primary Prevention of Psychopathology (pp. 279–298). Hanover, NH: University Press of New England.

Lazarus, R. S. (1986). Comment on LeDoux's sensory systems and emotion: A model of affective processing. *Integrative Psychiatry, 4,* 245–247.

Lazarus, R. S., Averill, J. R., & Opton, E. M. (1973). Emotion and cognition: With special reference to anxiety. In C. K. D. Spielberger (Ed.), *Anxiety: Current trends in theory and research* (Vol. 2). New York: Academic Press.

Lazarus, R. S., Coyne, J. C., & Folkman, S. (1982). Cognition, emotion, and motivation: The doctoring of Humpty-Dumpty. In R. W. J. Neufeld (Ed.), *Psychological stress and psychopathology* (pp. 218–239). New York: McGraw-Hill.

Lazarus, R. S., DeLongis, A., Folkman, S., & Gruen, R. (1985). Stress and adaptional outcomes: The problem of confounded measures. *American Psychologist, 40,* 770–779.

Lazarus, R. S., & Folkman, S. (1984). *Stress, appraisal and coping.* New York: Springer.

Lazarus, R. S., Kanner, A. D., & Folkman, S. (1980). Emotions: A cognitive-phenomenological analysis. In R. Plutchik & H. Kellerman (Eds.), *Emotion: Theory, research, and experience: Vol. 1. Theories of emotion* (pp. 189–217). New York: Academic Press.

Lazarus, R. S., & Smith (in press). Knowledge and appraisal in the cognition–emotion relationship. *Cognition and Emotion.*

LeDoux, J. E. (1986). Sensory systems and emotion: A model of affective processing. *Integrative Psychiatry, 4,* 237–248.

Lent, R. W., Russell, R. K., & Zamostny, K. P. (1981). Comparison of cue-controlled desensitization, rational restructuring, and a credible placebo in the treatment of speech anxiety. *Journal of Consulting and Clinical Psychology, 49,* 608–610.

Leventhal, H. (1984). A perceptual motor theory of emotion. In K. R. Scherer & P. Ekman (Eds.), *Approaches to emotion* (pp. 271–291). Hillsdale, NJ: Erlbaum.

Leventhal, H., & Tomarken, A. J. (1986). Emotion: Today's problems. In M. B. Rosenzweig & L. W. Porter (Eds.), *Annual Review of Psychology* (pp. 565–610). Palo Alto, CA: Annual Reviews.

LeVine-Welsh, P. C. (1982). *The effects of three treatments which incorporate rational-emotive techniques and assertion behavior in adult women.* Unpublished doctoral dissertation, Virginia Polytechnic Institute, Blacksburg.

Lewin, K. A. (1931). Environmental forces in child behavior and development. In C. Murchison (Ed.), *A handbook of child psychology* (pp. 342–359). Worcester, MA: Clark University Press.

Lewin, K. A. (1935). *A dynamic theory of personality* (K. E. Zener & D. K. Adams, Trans.). New York: McGraw-Hill.

Lewinsohn, P. M. (1975). The behavioral study and treatment of depression. In M. Hersen, R. M. Eisler, & P. M. Miller (Eds.), *Progress in behavior modification* (Vol. 1, pp. 19–64). New York: Academic Press.

Linehan, M. M., Goldfried, M. R., & Goldfried, A. P. (1979). Assertion therapy: Skill training or cognitive restructuring. *Behavior Therapy, 10,* 372–388.

Lipsky, M. J., Kassinove, H., & Miller, N. J. (1980). Effects of rational-emotive therapy, rational role reversal, and rational-emotive imagery on the emotional adjustment of community mental health center patients. *Journal of Consulting and Clinical Psychology, 48,* 366–374.

Lohr, J. M., & Bonge, D. (1981). On the distinction between illogical and irrational beliefs and their relationship to anxiety. *Psychological Reports, 48,* 191–194.

Lohr, J. M., & Bonge, D. (1982a). The factorial validity of the Irrational Beliefs Test: A psychometric investigation. *Cognitive Therapy and Research, 6,* 225–230.

Lohr, J. M., & Bonge, D. (1982b). Relationships between assertiveness and factorially validated measures of irrational beliefs. *Cognitive Therapy and Research, 6,* 353–356.

Lohr, J. M., Bonge, D., & Jones, C. (1983). Social desirability and endorsement of irrational beliefs. *Psychological Reports, 53,* 395–397.

London, P. (1964). *The modes and morals of psychotherapy*. New York: Holt, Rinehart & Winston.

Lowen, A. (1975). *Bioenergetics*. New York: Coward.

Lubin, B. (1967). *Depression adjective check lists: Manual*. Princeton, NJ: Educational and Industrial Testing Service.

Luborsky, L., Crits-Christoph, P., Alexander, L., Margolis, M., & Cohen, M. (1983). Two helping alliance methods of predicting outcomes of psychotherapy. *Journal of Nervous and Mental Disease, 171*, 480–491.

Lukes, S. (1970). Some problems about rationality. In B. R. Wilson (Ed.), *Rationality* (pp. 194–213). Worcester, UK: Basil Blackwell.

Lyotard, J. F. (1984). *The postmodern condition: A report on knowledge*. Minneapolis: University of Minnesota Press.

Madigan, R. J., & Bollenbach, A. K. (1986). The effects of induced mood on irrational thoughts and views of the world. *Cognitive Therapy and Research, 10*, 547–562.

Mahoney, M. J. (1974). *Cognition and behavior modification*. Cambridge, MA: Ballinger.

Mahoney, M. J. (1976). *The scientist*. Cambridge, MA: Ballinger.

Mahoney, M. J. (1977a). A critical analysis of rational-emotive theory and therapy. *Counseling Psychologist, 7*(1), 44–46.

Mahoney, M. J. (1977b). Personal science: A cognitive learning theory. In A. Ellis & R. Grieger (Eds.), *Handbook of rational-emotive therapy* (pp. 352–366). New York: Springer.

Mahoney, M. J. (1977c). Reflections on the cognitive-learning trend in psychotherapy. *American Psychologist, 32*, 5–13.

Mahoney, M. J. (1978). Experimental methods and outcome evaluation. *Journal of Consulting and Clinical Psychology, 46*, 660–672.

Mahoney, M. J. (1979). A critical analysis of rational-emotive therapy. In A. Ellis & J. M. Whiteley (Eds.), *Theoretical and empirical foundations of rational-emotive therapy* (pp. 177–180). Monterey, CA: Brooks/Cole.

Mahoney, M. J. (Ed.). (1980a). *Psychotherapy process: Current issues and future directions*. New York: Plenum.

Mahoney, M. J. (1980b). Psychotherapy and the structure of personal revolutions. In M. J. Mahoney (Ed.), *Psychotherapy process: Current issues and future directions* (pp. 157–180). New York: Plenum.

Mahoney, M. J. (1986). The tyranny of technique. *Counseling and Values, 30*, 169–174.

Mahoney, M. J. (1988a). The cognitive sciences and psychotherapy. In K. S. Dobson (Ed.), *Handbook of cognitive-behavioral therapies*. New York: Guilford.

Mahoney, M. J. (1988b). *Human change processes: Notes on the facilitation of personal development*. New York: Basic Books.

Mahoney, M. J., & Freeman, A. (Eds.). (1985). *Cognition and psychotherapy*. New York: Plenum.

Mahoney, M. J., & Nezworski, T. (1985). Cognitive-behavioral approaches to children's problems. *Journal of Abnormal Child Pychology, 13*, 467–476.

Mahrer, A. R., Nadler, W. P., Gervaize, P. A., Sterner, I., & Talitman, E. A. (in press). Good moments in rational-emotive therapy: Some unique features of this approach. *Journal of Rational-Emotive Therapy*.

Malan, D. H. (1963). *A study of brief psychotherapy*. New York: Plenum.

Malan, D. H. (1976). *Toward the validation of dynamic psychotherapy*. New York: Plenum.

Malkiewich, L. E., & Merluzzi, T. V. (1980). Rational restructuring versus desensitization with clients of diverse conceptual levels: A test of a client-treatment matching model. *Journal of Counseling Psychology, 27*, 453–461.

Malouff, J. M. (1984). *A study of brief, cognitive treatment for depressed persons who have recently experienced a marital separation*. Unpublished doctoral dissertation, Arizona State University, Tempe.

Malouff, J. M., & Schutte, N. S. (1986). Development and validation of a measure of irrational belief. *Journal of Consulting and Clinical Psychology, 54*, 860–862.

Malouff, J. M., Valdenegro, J., & Schutte, N. S. (1988). Further validation of a measure of irrational belief. *Journal of Rational Emotive Therapy*, 189–193.

Maltz, M. (1960). *Psycho-cybernetics*. Englewood Cliffs, NJ: Prentice-Hall.

Mandler, G. (1984). *Mind and body: Psychology of emotion and stress*. New York: Morton.

Marlatt, G. A., & Gordon, J. B. (Eds.). (1985). *Relapse prevention: Maintenance strategies in the treatment of addictive behaviors*. New York: Guilford.

Maslow, A. (1962). *Towards a Psychology of Being*. Princeton, New Jersey: Van Nostrand.

Maultsby, M. C., Jr. (1971). *Handbook for rational self-counseling*. Madison, WI: Association for Rational Thinking.

Maultsby, M. C., Jr. (1977). Rational-emotive imagery. In A. Ellis & R. Grieger (Eds.), *Handbook of rational-emotive therapy* (vol. 1, pp. 225–230). New York: Springer.

Maultsby, M. C., Jr. (1984). *Rational behavior therapy*. Englewood Cliffs, NJ: Prentice-Hall.

Maultsby, M. C., Jr., & Ellis, A. (1974). *Technique for using rational-emotive imagery*. New York: Institute for Rational-Emotive Therapy.

McClelland, D. C. (1951). *Personality*. New York: Sloane.

McGee, P. D. (1984). *Cognitive-behavioral intervention in stress management*. Unpublished doctoral dissertation, Texas Woman's University, Denton.

McKnight, D. L., Nelson, R. O., Hayes, S. C., & Jarrett, R. B. (1984). Importance of treating individually assessed response classes in the amelioration of depression. *Behavior Therapy*, **15**, 315–335.

McLellarn, R. W., Bornstein, P. H., & Carmody, T. P. (1986). A methodological critique of the structured-interview assessment of Type A behavior. *Journal of Cardiopulmonary Rehabilitation*, **6**, 21–25.

Meehl, P. E. (1978). Theoretical risks and tabular asterisks: Sir Karl, Sir Ronald, and the slow progress of soft psychology. *Journal of Consulting and Clinical Psychology*, **46**, 806–834.

Meichenbaum, D. H. (1972). *Therapist manual for cognitive behavior modification*. Unpublished manuscript. University of Waterloo, Ontario, Canada.

Meichenbaum, D. H. (1977a). *Cognitive-behavior modification*. New York: Plenum.

Meichenbaum, D. H. (1977b). Dr. Ellis, please stand up. *Counseling Psychologist*, **7**, 43–44b.

Meichenbaum, D. H. (1985). *Stress innoculation training*. New York: Pergamon.

Meichenbaum, D. H., & Butler, L. (1980). Cognitive ethology: Assessing the streams of cognition and emotion. In K. Blankstein, P. Pliner, & J. Polivy (Eds.), *Advances in the study of communication and affect: Assessment and modification of emotional behavior* (Vol. 6). New York: Plenum.

Melzack, R., & Casey, K. L. (1970). The affective dimension of pain. In M. B. Arnold (Ed.), *Feelings and emotions: The Loyola Symposium*. New York: Academic Press.

Merluzzi, T. V., Rudy, T. E., & Glass, C. R. (1981). The information-processing paradigm: Implications for clinical science. In T. V. Merluzzi, C. G. Glass, & M. Genest (Eds.), *Cognitive assessment* (pp. 77–124). New York: Guilford.

Messer, S. B., & Meinster, M. O. (1980). Interaction effects of internal vs. external locus of control and directive vs. non-directive therapy: Fact or fiction? *Journal of Psychology*, **36**, 283–288.

Miller, N., & Kassinove, H. (1978). Effects of lecture, rehearsal, written homework, and IQ on the efficacy of a rational emotive school mental health program. *Journal of Community Psychology*, **6**, 366–373.

Moleski, R., & Tosi, D. J. (1976). Comparative psychotherapy: Rational-emotive therapy versus systematic desensitization in the treatment of stuttering. *Journal of Consulting and Clinical Psychology*, **44**, 309–311.

Moore, G. E. (1948). *Principia ethica*. London: Cambridge University Press.

Moustakas, C. (1985). Humanistic or humanism? *Journal of Humanistic Psychology*, **25**, 5–12.

Munjack, D. J., Schlaks, A., Sanchez, V. C., Usigli, R., Zulueta, A., & Leonard, M. (1984). Rational-emotive therapy in the treatment of erectile failure: An initial study. *Journal of Sex and Marital Therapy*, **10**, 170–175.

Murphy, G. E., Simons, A. D., Wetzel, R. D., & Lustman, P. J. (1984). Cognitive therapy and pharmacotherapy, singly and together, in the treatment of depression. *Archives of General Psychiatry*, **41**, 33–41.

Murray, H. A. (1938). *Explorations in personality: A clinical and experimental study of fifty men of college age*. New York: Oxford University Press.

Myers, I. B. (1962). *The Myers-Briggs type indicator* (2nd ed.). Princeton, NJ: Educational Testing Service.

Neisser, U. (1967). *Cognitive psychology*. New York: Appleton-Century-Crofts.

Nelson, R. (1977). Irrational beliefs and depression. *Journal of Consulting and Clinical Psychology*, **15**, 1190-1191.

Neuman, J. (1985). *Exposure in imagery, thought stopping and rational-emotive therapy in the treatment of obsessions*. Unpublished doctoral dissertation, Hofstra University, Hempstead, NY.

Newmark, C. S., & Whitt, J. K. (1983). Endorsement of Ellis' irrational beliefs as a function of DSM-III psychotic diagnoses. *Journal of Clinical Psychology*, **39**, 820–823.

Nicholls, J. G., Licht, B. G., & Pearl, R. A. (1982). Some dangers of using personality questionnaires to study personality. *Psychological Bulletin*, **92**, 572–580.

Nisbett, R. E., & Wilson, T. D. (1977). Telling more than we can know: Verbal reports on mental processes. *Psychological Reviews*, **84**, 231–259.

Norcross, J. C. (Ed.). (1986). *Handbook of eclectic psychotherapy*. New York: Brunner/Mazel.

Norcross, J. C. (Ed.). (1987). *Casebook of eclectic psychotherapy*. New York: Brunner/Mazel.

Novaco, R. M. (1975). *Anger control: The development and evaluation of an experimental treatment*. Lexington, MA: Lexington Books.

Novaco, R. W. (1979). The cognitive regulation of anger and stress. In P. C. Kendall & S. D. Hollon (Eds.), *Cognitive behavioral interventions: Theory, research and procedures* (pp. 241–285). New York: Academic Press.

O'Keefe, E. J., & Castaldo, C. J. (1985). Multimodal therapy for anorexia nervosa: An holistic approach to treatment. *Psychotherapy in Private Practice*, **3**, 19–29.

O'Malley, S. S., Suh, C. S., & Strupp, H. H. (1983). The Vanderbilt Psychotherapy Process Scale: A report on the scale development and a process-outcome study. *Journal of Consulting and Clinical Psychology*, **52**, 581–586.

Omizo, M. M., Cubberly, W. E., & Omizo, S. A. (1985). The effects of rational-emotive education groups on self-concept and locus of control among learning disabled children. *Exceptional Child*, **32**, 13–19.

Parloff, M. B. (1984). Psychotherapy research and its incredible credibility crisis. *Clinical Psychology Review*, **4**, 95–109.

Patterson, C. H. (1986). *Theories of counseling and psychotherapy* (4th ed.). New York: Harper & Row.

Paul, G. L. (1966). *Insight versus desensitization in psychotherapy*. Stanford, CA: Stanford University Press.

Peale, N. V. (1960). *The power of positive thinking*. Englewood Cliffs, NJ: Prentice-Hall.

Pepper, S. C. (1942). *World Hypotheses*. Berkeley: University of California Press.

Piers, E., & Harris, D. (1969). *Manual for the Piers-Harris Children's Self Concept Scale*. Nashville, TN: Counselor Recordings and Tests.

Plutchik, R. (1966). Emotions as adaptive reactions: Implications for therapy. *Psychoanalytic Review*, **53**, 105–110.

Plutchik, R. (1970). Emotions, evolution and adaptive processes. In M. B. Arnold (Ed.), *Feelings and emotions: The Loyola Symposium* (pp. 3–24). New York, London: Academic Press.

Plutchik, R. (1977). Cognitions in the service of emotions: An evolutionary perspective. In D. K. Candland, J. P. Fell, E. Keen, A. I. Leshner, R. Plutchik, & R. M. Tarpey (Eds.), *Emotion.* Belmont, CA: Brooks/Cole.

Plutchik, R. (1980). *Emotion: A psychoevolutionary synthesis.* New York: Harper & Row.

Plutchik, R. (1984). Emotions: A general psychorevolutionary theory. In K. B. Scherer & P. Ekman (Eds.), *Approaches to emotion* (pp. 197–220). Hillsdale, NJ: Erlbaum.

Plutchik, R., & Kellerman, H. (Eds.). (1980). *Emotion: Theory, research, and experience* (Vol. 1). New York: Academic Press.

Polanyi, M. (1958). *Personal knowledge: Towards a post-critical philosophy.* Chicago, IL: University of Chicago Press.

Polanyi, M. (1966). *The tacit dimension.* New York: Doubleday.

Popper, K. R. (1962). *Objective knowledge.* London: Oxford.

Pribram, K. H. (1970). Feelings as monitors. In M. B. Arnold (Ed.), *Feelings and emotions: The Loyola Symposium.* New York: Academic Press.

Primakoff, L., Epstein, N., & Covi, L. (1986). Homework compliance: An uncontrolled variable in cognitive therapy outcome research. *Behavior Therapy, 17,* 433–446.

Prochaska, J. O. (1984). *Systems of psychotherapy: A transtheoretical analysis.* Homewood, IL: Dorsey Press.

Prochaska, J. O., & DiClemente, C. C. (1986). The transtheoretical approach. In J. C. Norcross (Ed.), *Handbook of eclectic psychotherapy* (pp. 163–200). New York: Brunner/Mazel.

Rachman, S. J., & Wilson, G. T. (1980). *The effects of psychological therapy* (2nd ed.). Oxford: Pergamon.

Raimy, V. (1975). *Misunderstandings of the self.* San Francisco, CA: Jossey-Bass.

Randall, J. H., Jr., & Buchler, J. (1960). *Philosophy: An introduction.* New York: Barnes & Noble.

Ray, J. B., & Bak, J. S. (1980). Comparison and cross-validation of the Irrational Beliefs Test and the Rational Behavior Inventory. *Psychological Reports, 46,* 541–542.

Reda, M. A., & Mahoney, M. J. (Eds.). (1984). *Cognitive psychotherapies: Recent developments in theory, research, and practice.* Cambridge, MA: Ballinger.

Review Panel on Coronary-Prone Behavior and Coronary Heart Disease (1981). Coronary-prone behavior and coronary heart disease: A critical review. *Circulation, 63,* 1199–1215.

Ricketts, M. S., & Galloway, R. E. (1984). Effects of three different one-hour single-session treatments for test anxiety. *Psychological Reports, 54,* 115–120.

Rieff, P. (1966). *The triumph of the therapeutic.* New York: Harper & Row.

Robbins, A. (1986). *Unlimited power.* New York: Simon & Schuster.

Roehling, P. V., & Robin, A. L. (1986). Development and validation of the Family Beliefs Inventory: A measure of unrealistic beliefs among parents and adolescents. *Journal of Consulting and Clinical Psychology, 54,* 693–697.

Rogers, C. R. (1959). A theory of therapy, personality, and interpersonal relationships, as developed in the client-centered framework. In S. Koch (Ed.), *Psychology: A study of a science* (Vol. 3, pp. 184–256). New York: McGraw-Hill.

Rohsenow, D. J., & Smith, R. E. (1982). Irrational beliefs as predictors of negative affective states. *Motivation and Emotion, 6,* 299–314.

Rorer, L. G. (1987). *Rational-emotive theory. 1. An integrated psychological and philosophical basis.* Unpublished manuscript, Miami University, Oxford, OH.

Rose, N. (1982). *Effects of rational emotive education and rational emotive imagery on the adjustment of disturbed and normal elementary school children.* Unpublished doctoral dissertation, Hofstra University, Hempstead, NY.

Roseman, I. (1984). Cognitive determinants of emotion: A structural theory. In P. Shaver (Ed.), *Review of personality and social psychology: Vol. 5. Emotions, relationships, and health* (pp. 11–36). Beverly Hills, CA: Sage Publications.

Rosenman, R. H., Brand, E. J., Jenkins, C. D., Friedman, M., Straus, R., & Vurm, M. (1975). Coronary heart disease in the Western Collatorative Group Study: Final follow-up experience of 8-1/2 years. *JAMA, Journal of the American Medical Association, 233*, 872–877.

Roskies, E., Seraganian, P., Oseasohn, R., Hanley, J. A., Collu, R., Martin, N., & Smilga, C. (1986). The Montreal Type A Intervention Project: Major findings. *Health Psychology, 5*, 45–69.

Rotter, J. B. (1954). *Social learning and clinical psychology*. Englewood Cliffs, NJ: Prentice-Hall.

Rotter, J. B. (1966). Generalized expectancies for internal versus external control of reinforcement. *Psychological Monographs: General and Applied, 80* (Whole No. 609).

Rotter, J. B. (1975). Some problems and misconceptions related to the construct of internal versus external control of reinforcement. *Journal of Consulting and Clinical Psychology, 43*, 56–67.

Ruderman, A. J. (1986). Bulimia and irrational beliefs. *Behaviour Research and Therapy, 24*, 193–197.

Rush, A. J., Beck, A. T., Kovacs, M., & Hollon, S. D. (1977). Comparative efficacy of cognitive therapy and pharmacotherapy in the treatment of depressed outpatients. *Cognitive Therapy and Research, 1*, 17–38.

Russell, B. (1945). *A history of western philosophy*. New York: Simon & Schuster.

Russell, P. L., & Brandsma, J. M. (1974). A theoretical and empirical integration of the rational-emotive and classical conditioning theories. *Journal of Consulting and Clinical Psychology, 42*, 389–397.

Sachs, J. C. (1983). Negative factors in brief psychotherapy: An empirical assessment. *Journal of Consulting and Clinical Psychology, 51*, 557–564.

Sarason, I. G., Johnson, J. H., & Seigel, J. M. (1978). Assessing the impact of life changes: Development of the Life Experience Survey. *Journal of Consulting and Clinical Psychology, 46*, 932–946.

Sarason, S., Davidson, K., Lighthall, F., Waite, R., & Ruebush, B. (1960). *Anxiety in elementary school children*. New York: Wiley.

Sarbin, T. R. (1985). *Emotion as situated actions*. Paper presented at a conference entitled, "The Role of Emotions in Ideal Human Development," Clark University, Heinz Werner Institute of Developmental Psychology, Worcester, MA, June 21-22.

Sartre, J. P. (1948). A sketch of a phenomenological theory. *The emotions: Outline of a theory*. New York: Philosophical Library.

Scherer, K. R., & Ekman, P. (Eds.). (1984). *Approaches to emotion*. Hillsdale, NJ: Erlbaum.

Schwartz, G. E., Davison, R. J., & Coleman, D. J. (1978). Patterning of cognitive and somatic processes in the self-regulation of anxiety: Effects of meditation versus exercise. *Psychosomatic Medicine, 40*, 321–328.

Schwartz, R. M. (1982). Cognitive-behavior modification: A conceptual review. *Clinical Psychology Review, 2*, 267–293.

Schwartz, R. M. (1984). Is rational-emotive therapy a truly unified interactive approach?: A reply to Ellis. *Clinical Psychology Review, 4*, 219–226.

Seeman, J. (1976). Comments on DiGiuseppe and Kassinove. *Journal of Community Psychology, 4*, 388.

Shahar, A., & Merbaum, M. (1981). The interaction between subject characteristics and self-control procedures in the treatment of interpersonal anxiety. *Cognitive Therapy and Research, 5*, 221–224.

Sherman, A. R. (1969). *Behavioral approaches to the treatment of phobic anxiety*. Unpublished doctoral dissertation, Yale University, New Haven, CT.

Shorkey, C. T., & Sutton-Simon, K. (1983). Reliability and validity of the Rational Behavior Inventory with a clinical population. *Journal of Clinical Psychology, 39*, 34–38.

Shorkey, C. T., & Whiteman, V. L. (1977). Development of the Rational Behavior Inventory: Initial validity and reliability. *Education and Psychological Measurement, 37*, 527–534.

Sichel, J., & Ellis, A. (1984). *RET self-help form*. New York: Institute for Rational-Emotive Therapy.

Sifneos, P. E. (1981). Short-term anxiety provoking psychotherapy: Its history, technique, outcome and instruction. In S. H. Budman (Ed.), *Forms of brief therapy* (pp. 45–81). New York: Guilford.

Silberschatz, G., & Curtis, J. T. (1986). Clinical implications of research on brief dynamic psychotherapy. II. How the therapist helps or hinders therapeutic progress. *Psychoanalytic Psychology, 3*, 27–37.

Simons, A. D., Garfield, S. L., & Murphy, G. E. (1984). The process of change in cognitive therapy and pharmacotherapy for depression. *Archives of General Psychiatry, 41*, 45–51.

Simons, A. D., Lustman, P. J., Wetzel, R. D., & Murphy, G. E. (1985). Predicting response to cognitive therapy of depression: The role of learned resourcefulness. *Cognitive Therapy and Research, 9*, 79–89.

Simons, A. D., Murphy, G. E., Levine, J. E., & Wetzel, R. D. (1986). Cognitive therapy and pharmacotherapy for depression. *Archives of General Psychiatry, 43*, 43–48.

Smith, C. A., & Ellsworth, P. C. (1985). Patterns of cognitive appraisal in emotion. *Journal of Personality and Social Psychology, 48*, 813–838.

Smith, D. (1982). Trends in counseling and psychotherapy. *American Psychologist, 37*, 802–809.

Smith, T. W. (1982). Irrational beliefs in the cause and treatment of emotional distress: A critical review of the rational-emotive model. *Clinical Psychology Review, 2*, 505–522.

Smith, T. W. (1983). Change in irrational beliefs and the outcome of rational-emotive psychotherapy. *Journal of Consulting and Clinical Psychology, 51*, 156–157.

Smith, T. W. (1986). On resisting the ABC's of rational-emotive therapy. *Contemporary Psychology, 31*, 847–848.

Smith, T. W., & Allred, K. D. (1986). Rationality revisited: A reassessment of the empirical support for the rational-emotive model. In P. C. Kendall (Ed.), *Advances in cognitive-behavioral research and therapy* (Vol. 5, pp. 63–87). New York: Academic Press.

Smith, T. W., Boaz, T. L., & Denney, D. R. (1984). Endorsement of irrational beliefs as a moderator of the effects of stressful life events. *Cognitive Therapy and Research, 8*, 363–370.

Smith, T. W., & Brehm, S. S. (1981). Cognitive correlates of the Type A coronary-prone behavior pattern. *Motivation and Emotion, 5*, 215–223.

Smith, T. W., Houston, B. K. & Zurawski, R. M. (1984). Irrational beliefs and the arousal of emotional distress. *Journal of Counseling Psychology, 31*, 190–201.

Smith, T. W., Ingram, R. E., & Brehm, S. S. (1983). Social anxiety, anxious self-preoccupation, and recall of self-relevant information. *Journal of Personality and Social Psychology, 44*, 1287–1288.

Smith, T. W., & Zurawski, R. M. (1983). Assessment of irrational beliefs: The question of discriminant validity. *Journal of Clinical Psychology, 39*, 976–979.

Solomon, G. S. & Ray, J. B. (1984). Irrational beliefs of shoplifters. *Journal of Clinical Psychology, 40*, 1075–1077.

Solomon, R. C. (1980). Emotions and choice. In A. O. Rorty (Ed.), *Explaining emotions* (pp. 251–281). Berkeley: University of California Press.

Spencer, H. (1901). *The principles of psychology*. New York: Westminster.

Sperry, R. (1982). Some effects of disconnecting the cerebral hemispheres. *Science, 217*, 1223–1226.

Spielberger, C. D. (1980). *The Test Anxiety Inventory*. Palo Alto, CA: Consulting Psychologists Press.

Spielberger, C. D., Gorsuch, R., & Lushene, R. (1970). *Manual for the State-Trait Anxiety Inventory*. Palo Alto, CA: Consulting Psychologists Press.

Spielberger, C. D., Jacobs, G. A., Russell, S., & Crane, R. S. (1983). Assessment of anger: The State-Trait Anger Scale. In J. N. Butcher & C. D. Spielberger (Eds.), *Advances in personality assessment* (Vol. 2). Hillsdale, NJ: Erlbaum.

Spitzer, R. L., Endicott, J., & Robins, E. (1978). Research diagnostic criteria: Rationale and reliability. *Archives of General Psychiatry, 35*, 773–782.

Sprenkle, D. H., Keeney, B. P., & Sutton, P. M. (1982). Theorists who influence clinical members of AAMFT: A research note. *Journal of Counseling Psychology, 29*, 400–405.

Staats, A. W. (1981). Paradigmatic behaviorism, unified theory construction methods, and the zeitgeist of separatism. *American Psychologist, 36*, 239–256.

Stanley-Jones, D. (1970). The biological origins of love and hate. In M. B. Arnold (Ed.), *Feelings and emotions: The Loyola Symposium*. New York: Academic Press.

Stevenson, C. L. (1944). *Ethics and language*. New Haven, CT: Yale University Press.

Stewart, J. R. (1983). *The effects of two therapeutic approaches on anxiety reduction and client satisfaction with consideration of client hemisphericity.* Unpublished doctoral dissertation, University of Toledo, Toledo, OH.

Stone, G. (1982). *A cognitive-behavioral approach to counseling psychology: Implications for practice, research, and training.* New York: Praeger.

Strupp, E. (1973). On the basic ingredients of psychotherapy. *Journal of Consulting and Clinical Psychology, 41*, 1–8.

Suinn, R. M. (1969). The STABS, a measure of test anxiety for behavior therapy: Normative data. *Behaviour Research and Therapy, 7*, 335–339.

Suinn, R. M. (1974). Behavior therapy for cardiac patients. *Behavior Therapy, 5*, 569–571.

Sutton-Simon, K. (1980). Assessing belief systems: Concepts and strategies. In P. C. Kendall & S. D. Hollon (Eds.), *Assessment strategies for cognitive-behavioral interventions* (pp. 59–84). New York: Academic Press.

Taylor, J. A. (1953). A personality scale of manifest anxiety. *Journal of Abnormal and Social Psychology, 18*, 285–290.

Teasdale, J. D. (1985). Psychological treatments for depression: How do they work? *Behaviour Research and Therapy, 23*, 157–165.

Teasdale, J. D., & Fennell, M. J. V. (1982). Immediate effects on depression of cognitive therapy interventions. *Cognitive Therapy and Research, 6*, 343–352.

Teasdale, J. D. Fennell, M. J. V., Hibbert, G. A., & Amies, P. L. (1984). Cognitive therapy for major depressive disorder in primary care. *British Journal of Psychiatry, 144*, 400–406.

Thorpe, G. L., Amatu, H. I., Blakey, R. S., & Burns, L. E. (1976). Contributions of overt instructional rehearsal and "specific insight" to the effectiveness of self-instructional training: A preliminary study. *Behavior Therapy, 7*, 504–511.

Thurman, C. W. (1983). Effects of a rational-emotive treatment program on Type A behavior among college students. *Journal of College Student Personnel, 24*, 417–423.

Thurman, C. W. (1984). Cognitive-behavioral interventions with Type A faculty. *Personnel and Guidance Journal, 62*, 358–362.

Thurman, C. W. (1985a). Effectiveness of cognitive-behavioral treatments in reducing Type A behavior among university faculty. *Journal of Counseling Psychology, 32*, 74–83.

Thurman, C. W. (1985b). Effectiveness of cognitive-behavioral treatments in reducing Type A behavior among university faculty—One year later. *Journal of Counseling Psychology, 32*, 445–448.

Tiegerman, S., & Kassinove, H. (1977). Effects of assertive training and cognitive components of rational therapy on assertive behaviors and interpersonal anxiety. *Psychological Reports, 40*, 535–542.

Tobacyk, J., & Milford, G. (1982). Criterion validity for Ellis' irrational beliefs: Dogmatism and uncritical inferences. *Journal of Clinical Psychology, 38*, 605–607.

Tomkins, S. S. (1962). *Affect, imagery, consciousness: Vol. 1. The positive affects.* New York: Springer.

Tomkins, S. S. (1963). *Affect, imagery, consciousness: Vol. 2. The negative affects.* New York: Springer.

Tomkins, S. S. (1981). The quest for primary motives: Biography and autobiography of an idea. *Journal of Personality and Social Psychology, 41,* 306–329.

Tosi, D. J., Forman, M. A., Rudy, D. R., & Murphy, M. A. (1986). Factor analysis of the Common Beliefs Survey III: A replication study. *Journal of Consulting and Clinical Psychology, 54,* 404–405.

Trexler, L. D., & Karst, T. O. (1972). Rational-emotive therapy, placebo, and no-treatment effects on public-speaking anxiety. *Journal of Abnormal Psychology, 79,* 60–67.

Turner, S. M., & Michelson, L. (1984). Conceptual, methodological, and clinical issues in the assessment of anxiety disorders. *Journal of Behavioral Assessment, 6,* 265–279.

Vallis, T. M., Shaw, B. F., & Dobson, K. S. (1986). The cognitive therapy scale: Psychometric properties. *Journal of Consulting and Clinical Psychology, 54,* 381–385.

Velten, E. A. (1968). A laboratory task for induction of mood states. *Behaviour Research and Therapy, 6,* 473–482.

Vestre, N. D. (1984a). Irrational beliefs and self-reported depressed mood. *Journal of Abnormal Psychology, 93,* 239–241.

Vestre, N. D. (1984b). Test-retest reliability of the Idea Inventory. *Psychological Reports, 54,* 873.

Vestre, N. D., & Burnis, J. J. (1988). Irrational beliefs and the impact of stressful life events. *Journal of Rational-Emotive Therapy, 6,* 58–64.

von Pohl, R. (1982). *A study to assess the effects of rational-emotive therapy with a selected group of emotionally disturbed children in day and residential treatment.* Unpublished doctoral dissertation, University of Alabama, Birmingham.

Wachtel, P. L. (1977). *Psychoanalysis and behavior therapy: Toward an integration.* New York: Basic Books.

Wakefield, S. (1982). *Reducing stressful impact of life events by modifying irrational beliefs.* Unpublished doctoral dissertation, Arizona State University, Tempe.

Walen, S. R., DiGiuseppe, R., & Wessler, R. L. (1980). *A practitioner's guide to rational-emotive therapy.* New York: Oxford University Press.

Walsh, T. A. (1982). *Rational-emotive therapy and progressive relaxation in the reduction of trait anxiety of college undergraduate students who enroll in anxiety reduction workshops.* Unpublished doctoral dissertation, University of the Pacific, Stockton, CA.

Warren, R., Deffenbacher, J. L., & Brading, P. (1976). Rational-emotive therapy and the reduction of test anxiety in elementary school students. *Rational Living, 11,* 26–29.

Warren, R., & McLellarn, R. W. (1987). What do RET therapists think they are doing: An international survey. *Journal of Rational-Emotive Therapy, 5,* 71–91.

Warren, R., Smith, G., & Velten, E. (1984). Rational-emotive therapy and the reduction of interpersonal anxiety in junior high school students. *Adolescence, 19,* 893–902.

Watson, D., & Clark, L. A. (1984). Negative affectivity: The disposition to experience aversive emotional states. *Psychological Bulletin, 96,* 465–490.

Watson, D., & Friend, R. (1969). Measurement of social-evaluative anxiety. *Journal of Consulting and Clinical Psychology, 33,* 448–457.

Watson, J. B. (1930). *Behaviorism.* Chicago, IL: University of Chicago Press.

Weil, A. (1983). *Health and healing.* Boston, MA: Houghton Mifflin.

Weimer, W. B. (1977). A conceptual framework for cognitive psychology: Motor theories of the mind. In R. Shaw & J. Bransford (Eds.), *Perceiving, acting, and knowing* (pp. 267–311). Hillsdale, NJ: Erlbaum.

Weimer, W. B. (1980). Psychotherapy and philosophy of science. In M. J. Mahoney (Ed.), *Psychotherapy process: Current issues and future directions.* New York: Plenum.

Weimer, W. B. (1982). Hayek's approach to the problems of complex phenomena: An introduction to the theoretical psychology of the sensory order. In W. B. Weimer & D. S. Palermo (Eds.), *Cognition and the symbolic processes* (Vol. 2, pp. 267-311). Hillsdale, NJ: Erlbaum.

Weimer, W. B. (in press-a). *Rationalist constructivism, scientism and the study of man and society*. Hillsdale, NJ: Erlbaum.

Weimer, W. B. (in press-b). Rationality in complex orders is never fully explicit nor instantly specificable. In G. Radnitzky & W. W. Bartley (Eds.), *Evolutionary epistemology and theories of rationality*. New York: Paragon House.

Weiner, B. (1985). An attributional theory of achievement motivation and emotion. *Psychological Review, 92*, 548–573.

Weinrach, S. G. (1980). Unconventional therapist: Albert Ellis. *Personnel and Guidance Journal, 59*, 152–160.

Weissman, A. N. (1978). *Development and validation of the Dysfunctional Attitudes Scale (DAS)*. Paper presented at the 12th annual convention of the Association for the Advancement of Behavior Therapy, Chicago, IL.

Werner, H. (1984). *Cognitive therapy: A humanistic approach*. New York: Free Press.

Wessler, R. A., & Wessler, R. L. (1980). *The principles and practice of rational-emotive therapy*. San Francisco, CA: Jossey-Bass.

Wessler, R. L. (1984). Alternative conceptions of rational-emotive therapy: Toward a philosophically neutral psychotherapy. In M. A. Reda & M. J. Mahoney (Eds.), *Cognitive psychotherapies: Recent developments in theory, research, and practice* (pp. 65–79). Cambridge, MA: Ballinger.

Wessler, R. L. (1986a). A critical appraisal of therapeutic efficacy studies. In W. Dryden & P. Trower (Eds.), *Rational-emotive therapy: Recent developments in theory and practice* (pp. 73–84). Bristol, UK: Institute for RET.

Wessler, R. L. (1986b). Varieties of cognitions in the cognitively oriented psychotherapies. In A. Ellis & R. M. Grieger (Eds.), *Handbook of rational-emotive therapy* (Vol. 2, pp. 46–58). New York: Springer.

White, R. W. (1959). Motivation reconsidered: The concept of competence. *Psychological Review, 66*, 297–333.

Wilcox, R. R. (1985). *Advances in basic statistics: Vol. 2. Basic hypothesis testing procedures*. Los Angeles, CA: UCLA Center for the Study of Evaluation.

Wilkins, W. (1986). Therapy-therapist confounds in psychotherapy research. *Cognitive Therapy and Research, 10*, 3–11.

Wilson, G. T. (1978). Methodological considerations in treatment outcome research on obesity. *Journal of Consulting and Clinical Psychology, 46*, 687–702.

Wilson, G. T., & Evans, I. M. (1977). The therapist-client relationship in behavior therapy. In A. S. Gurman & A. M. Razin (Eds.), *Effective psychotherapy: A handbook of research* (pp. 544–565). New York: Pergamon.

Winch, P. (1958). *The idea of a social science*. London: Routledge & Kegan-Paul.

Wise, E. H., & Haynes, S. N. (1983). Cognitive treatment of test anxiety: Rational restructuring versus attentional training. *Cognitive Therapy and Research, 7*, 69–77.

Wolfe, J. L., & Fodor, I. G. (1977). Modifying assertive behavior in women: A comparison of three approaches. *Behavior Therapy, 8*, 567–574.

Wolpe, J. (1958). *Psychotherapy by reciprocal inhibition*. Stanford, CA: Stanford University Press.

Woolfolk, R. L., & Richardson, F. C. (1984). Behavior therapy and the ideology of modernity. *American Psychologist, 39*, 777–786.

Yu, A., & Schill, T. (1976). Rational-emotive therapy as a treatment in reducing vulnerability to criticism. *Rational Living, 11*, 12–14.

Zajonc, R. B. (1980). Feeling and thinking: Preferences need no inferences. *American Psychologist, 35*, 151–175.

Zajonc, R. B. (1984). On the primacy of affect. *American Psychologist, 39*, 117–123.

Zettle, R. D., & Hayes, S. C. (1980). Conceptual and empirical status of rational-emotive therapy. In M. Hersen, R. M. Eisler, & P. M. Miller (Eds.), *Progress in behavior modification* (Vol. 9, pp. 126–166). New York: Academic Press.

Zilbergeld, B., & Lazarus, A. A. (1987). *Mind power: Getting what you want through mental training.* Boston, MA: Little, Brown.

Zimmer, J. M., & Cowles, K. H. (1972). Content analysis using Fortran: Applied to interviews conducted by C. Rogers, F. Perls and A. Ellis. *Journal of Counseling Psychology, 19,* 161–166.

Zimmer, J. M., & Pepyne, E. W. (1971). A descriptive and comparative study of dimensions of counselor response. *Journal of Counseling Psychology, 18,* 441–447.

Zuckerman, M., Lubin, B., & Robins, S. (1965). Validation of the Multiple Affect Adjective Check List in clinical situations. *Journal of Consulting Psychology, 29,* 594.

Zurawski, R. M., & Smith, T. W. (1987). Assessing irrational beliefs and emotional distress: Evidence and implications of limited discriminant validity. *Journal of Counseling Psychology, 34.*

Zwemer, W. A., & Deffenbacher, J. L. (1984). Irrational beliefs and anxiety. *Journal of Counseling Psychology, 31,* 391–393.

List of Previous Volumes

PERSONALITY, PSYCHOPATHOLOGY, AND PSYCHOTHERAPY
A Series of Monographs, Texts, and Treatises
David T. Lykken and Philip C. Kendall, Editors

INDEX